THE CIVIL WAR IN SPAIN

1936-1939

GATHERED AND ANNOTATED BY

Robert Payne

FOUNDED 1838

GPPS

G. P. Putnam's Sons   New York

© *1962 BY ROBERT PAYNE*

Library of Congress Catalog
Card Number: 62-7352

MANUFACTURED IN THE UNITED STATES OF AMERICA

FOR ANTONIO

Contents

Maps showing the progress of the war
will be found following page 14

Some Spanish Political Parties

CNT   (Confederación Nacional del Trabajo)—National Labor Federation, the trade union of the Anarchist Party.

FAI   (Federación Anarquista Ibérica)—Spanish Anarchist Federation, the Anarchist Party.

POUM   (Partido Obrero de Unificación Marxista)—United Marxist Labor Party, a Communist Party with Trotskyist leanings.

PSUC   (Partido Socialista Unificado de Cataluña)—United Socialist Party of Catalonia, Catalan Socialist Party later under Communist domination.

UGT   (Unión General del Trabajadores)—General Union of Workers, Spanish Socialist Party later under Communist domination.

CHRONOLOGICAL TABLE

1936	February 16	General elections. Victory of the Left.
	July 12	Murder of José Castillo.
	July 13	Murder of Calvo Sotelo.
	July 17-18	Garrisons at Melilla, Larache and Tetuán in Spanish Morocco rise against the civil government.
	July 20	Storming of Montaña barracks in Madrid. Death of General Sanjurjo.
	July 23	Inauguration of Committee of National Defense in Burgos.
	August 9	Fall of Mérida.
	August 15	Fall of Badajoz.
	August 19	Murder of Federico García Lorca.
	September 4	Francisco Largo Caballero becomes Prime Minister. Fall of Irún.
	September 27	Relief of Alcázar.
	October 1	Franco declared "Chief of the Spanish State."
	October 4	Italians occupy Ibiza.
	November 6	Caballero government flees to Valencia.
	November 7-8	International Brigade reaches Madrid.
	November 20	Execution of José Antonio Primo de Rivera in Alicante.
	November 30	Buenaventura Durruti killed.
1937	February 8	Fall of Málaga.
	February 11	Battle of Jarama.
	March 8-13	Rout of Italians at Guadalajara.
	April 26	Germans destroy Guernica.
	May 4-7	Anarchist revolt in Barcelona.
	May 17	Caballero government falls. Dr. Juan Negrín becomes Prime Minister

	May 29	Almería bombarded by German fleet.
	June 1	General Mola killed flying from Pamplona to Burgos.
	June 19	Fall of Bilbao.
	July 6-26	Battle of Brunete.
	August 25	Santander falls.
	September 3	Government troops capture Belchite.
	October 21	Gijón falls; virtual end of northern campaign.
	December 15	Government troops attack Teruel.
1938	January 11	Heavy bombardment of Barcelona.
	January 30	Franco sets up government.
	February 21	Rebels retake Teruel.
	March 6	*Baleares,* Franco cruiser, sunk.
	March 9	Rebels open Aragón offensive.
	March 16-17	Barcelona bombed eight times.
	April 15	Rebels reach Vinaroz on Mediterranean coast.
	June 17	Rebels take Castellón.
	July 24-25	Colonel Modesto leads Fifth Army across the Ebro.
	September 21	Dr. Negrín announces at Geneva the Spanish government decision to withdraw all volunteers.
	September 22	International Brigade withdrawn from front.
	December 23	Franco opens offensive on Catalonia.
1939	January 26	Barcelona falls.
	February 1	Last meeting of Cortes at Figueras.
	March 28	Madrid falls.
	March 29	Active hostilities cease.
	April 1	United States recognizes Franco.
	May 19	Victory parade.

Preface

HISTORY is a voice, a face, a bomb fragment, a child crying in the night. It is the sum of all our loves, disasters and triumphs arranged in intelligible order and lit by the light of the human imagination, for there is no history unless men patiently and imaginatively record it. And every age must record it anew.

History is the light of dying fires and new flames coming to birth. It is the wind which sweeps through centuries. It is a young girl singing in a meadow and a child carried on its father's shoulders for the first time. Always history is "for the first time," and that is why it is so difficult to write. That is why ideally all history should be written by poets.

Until recently history was a scholarly game played among fading documents in musty libraries. We know better now. The modern historian has greater resources than ever before. Through films and tape recordings he can reach back into the living past, bringing the dead face and the dead voice into the present. He can see the battle as the front-line cameramen saw it, not as the commanding general wished to see it, and where the camera fails to reveal the thoughts and emotions of the men fighting, there are always letters, diaries, battle signals, and the accounts of trained and informed reporters to fill the gaps. Sometimes a sheet of paper or a pocketbook dropped on a battlefield may tell us more about the real nature of the battle than all the historians' commentaries.

Even though we read the words of the men who fought in the war, and see the battles on film, and listen to the authentic voices of the protagonists, the historian's task remains inhumanly difficult. It is not only that he is confronted with questions of selection, evaluation and taste, and the increasingly arduous task of sorting the truly important

11

from the ephemeral, but he must make the prodigious leap of the imagination into the past. Times change. Thought patterns change. Ordinary human behavior changes continually. We do not know—we can only barely guess at—the mental processes of the ancient Greeks as they fought their interminable wars. Even in classical times the meanings of words changed, and since we have only their words to go by, we are always in danger of misinterpreting their simplest statements and their simplest emotions.

What is true of the ancient Greeks is also true of the Spanish Civil War fought little more than twenty years ago. Already that war seems to belong to ancient history. The emotions it aroused are already foreign to us. The idealism of the young who rushed to the defense of the Republic seems suspect now; it was not at the time. The Requetés who went into battle singing "Death the Bride" seem to belong to medieval history. Ghosts walked over Spain, and some became palpable, and some died, and still others changed their shape and assumed new disguises. And sometimes the historian may wonder how to disentangle the ghosts from the living presences of the men who suffered through that long and improbable agony.

We are accustomed to think of the Civil War in Spain as a conflict between liberals and reactionaries, or between Fascists and Communists, or between the right and the left. But history rarely provides such simple confrontations. The confusions and complications of the war were unending. Neither the Republicans nor the insurgents possessed a clear-cut policy, and their aims shifted as often as their battle lines. Monarchists, Falangists, German and Italian fascists, Anarchists, Communists, Socialists, Trotskyists, Moors, Carlists, Basque and Catalan nationalists each fought for their own deviating purposes. Ultimately it was a war of ideas, so many ideas that they curiously and disastrously negated each other. Some thirty armed sects quarreled over the dying body of Spain. When the war ended, nothing had been solved, no idea predominated, no social peace was established, and a feudal dictatorship, ruling by force of arms, provided an outward show of stability which only emphasized the dangerous turmoil within. The Spaniards were perhaps grateful for a rest from the compelling power of ideas, but the body of Spain continued to die.

We shall not understand the Spanish Civil War unless we go back to history, even to ancient history. Caesar's Commentaries on Spain tell us more than many newspaper reports. The Spaniards fought with a violence which terrified Caesar, who on one famous occasion panicked in their midst. Throughout history the Spanish have fought with a relentless passion to annihilate, not subdue, their enemies. *"Viva la Muerte!"* cried the Spanish Anarchist, and the same cry was uttered by Fascist generals. The Falangists flew the red-black flag symbolizing blood and death in proud imitation of the Anarchists, who had flown the flag long before the Falange movement was invented. Anarchists and Falangists were brothers under the skin, and death was always the landscape they understood best. In that landscape they walked with their heads held high.

While Caesar throws light upon the relentless fury with which the Spaniards hurled themselves into the fight, El Greco helps to explain the complete dedication of a Spaniard at the service of an idea. The Anarchists were moved by religious devotions, sang their hymns with religious fire, were deeply and helplessly committed to lives of sacrifice. They spoke of brotherhood as the saints speak of Heaven. They represented a very real segment of traditional Spanish belief, and their faces shone with the joy of their own reckless certainties. The Carlists, too, fought battles which could have little meaning for our modern mechanical age, and seem to have stepped out of El Greco's portraits.

There is a sense in which the Spanish Civil War was a long-drawn despairing protest on behalf of *dignidad,* and no history of the war will be complete unless it places the typical Spanish concept of honor in the forefront of the battle. For the Spaniard life without *dignidad* was a vain thing, and every social class had its own conception of honor to be defended at all costs, even at the cost of annihilation and massacre. Honor was greater than life. It was for the sake of honor that men lived, and every diminution of honor was paid for in blood. The savagery of the war can only be explained by an unquenchable desire to satisfy spiritual needs.

So intensely personal was the conflict that the Spanish themselves have been at a loss to understand their own motives, and no satisfactory history of the war has been written by a Spaniard. Nor is it likely that foreigners will fare better, but at least the foreigners were able to observe the visible events of the war with clarity and detachment, and with a compassion denied to the men fighting in the ranks. The best writing about the war came from foreign correspondents, who continually risked their lives to cover the battles. Henry Buckley, Jay Allen, and Herbert Matthews were ideal reporters, and I have leaned on them heavily in the documentary mosaic which follows. I found only one Spaniard who rivaled them in the power to present the colors and atmosphere of a scene. This was Arturo Barea, whose auto-biography *The Forging of a Rebel* deserves to rank with André Malraux's *Man's Hope* as one of the major documents of the war.

Those of us who were there sometimes feel that the Civil War in Spain has already entered into legend. We see the olive groves and the parched plains and the faces of those proud and dark-eyed people, and an incandescent light seems to fall on them. They are larger than life, and very bright against the skyline, and there is something about them which reminds us of the Homeric heroes as they strode across the plains of Troy. Sometimes, too, we find ourselves wondering why men fought so bitterly for a bitter land.

We shall never know the full story of the Civil War in Spain, nor exactly what brought it about, nor how many died. The theories are endless and will not help us. It is best to see the faces of the men who took part, and watch them as they steel themselves to fight. Here you will see the war through the eyes of those who fought it, and the reporters who were close to it, and with luck you will catch the authentic timbre of their voices.

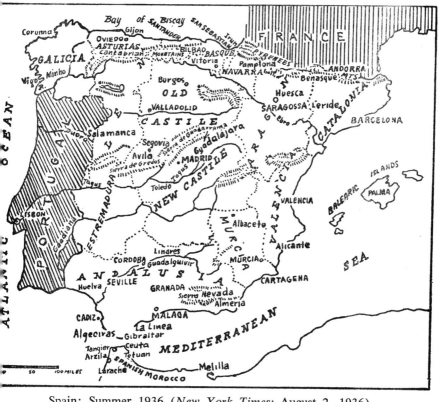

Spain: Summer 1936 (*New York Times:* August 2, 1936)

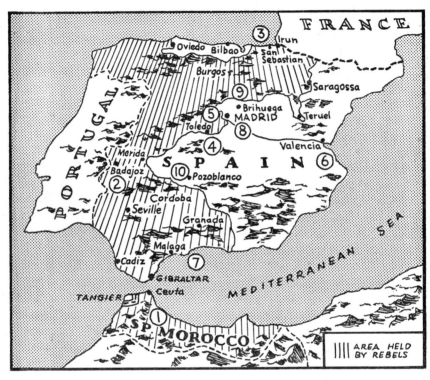

1. July 17, 1936—The revolt began in Morocco.
2. Aug. 16—Rebels seized Badajoz.
3. Sept. 12—San Sebastian fell to Rebels.
4. Sept. 28—Rebels took Toledo.
5. Oct. 21—The siege began at Madrid.
6. Nov. 6—Government moved to Valencia.
7. Feb. 8, 1937—Malaga fell to Rebels.
8. Feb. 18—Loyalists held Valencia road.
9. Mar. 18—Italian Legion defeated at Brihuega.
10. Mar. 30—Loyalists won at Pozoblanco.

The first nine months of war (*New York Times:* April 11, 1937)

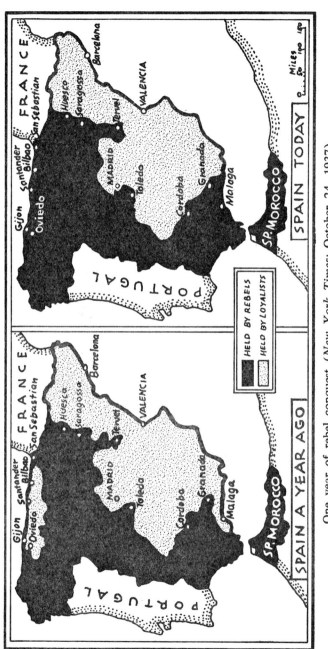

One year of rebel conquest (*New York Times*: October 24, 1937)

HELD BY INSURGENTS

HELD BY LOYALISTS

REGAINED LAST
WEEK BY LOYALISTS

0   50   100   150 MILES

Summer 1938 (*New York Times:* July 31, 1938)

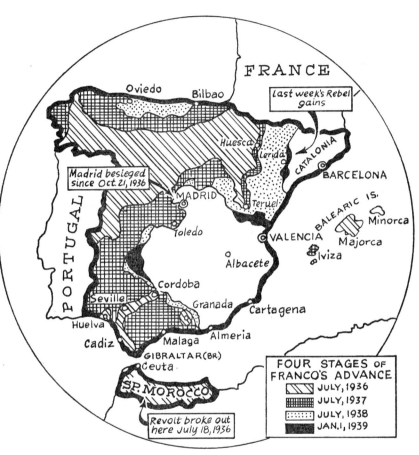

Franco's Advance (*New York Times:* January 1, 1939)

THE CIVIL WAR IN SPAIN
1936-1939

Eyewitness accounts of the
Spanish Civil War taken from
letters, reporters' dispatches,
diaries, official records, and
other material by a reporter who
was in Spain in 1938.

The Generals Launch the Uprising

*A*T the beginning of July 1936 nearly all the preparations for the uprising were complete. During interminable conferences going back to 1932 they had planned every detail of the conspiracy. Hitler and Mussolini had given their blessing. Vast sums of money were at the disposal of the conspirators. Most of the army commanders had been approached, and had sworn an oath of loyalty to the small group of generals who proposed to assume power. The chief of the conspirators was General José Sanjurjo, a sixty-four-year-old veteran of the Spanish-American war, known as "the Lion of the Riff" for his victories in Spanish Morocco.

There remained only the task of coordinating the various components of the uprising and choosing a precise date. The coordination of the conspiracy proved to be astonishingly difficult, largely because the Monarchists acted with extreme caution. Communists and Anarchists had wind of the plot. In Madrid political assassinations were becoming the commonplaces of daily life. A young socialist Assault Guard, José Castillo, was murdered by Falangists on July 12th. A few hours later Calvo Sotelo, a former minister and leader of the opposition in the Cortes, was murdered in revenge. All the evidence suggests that this murder triggered the uprising.

This is a police report of the murder of Calvo Sotelo:

In the early hours of the morning of July 13 a service truck bearing the number 17 drove out of the Pontejos Barracks, went down Diego de León Street and finally turned into Velázquez Street where it pulled up on the right hand side opposite 89 Velázquez Street. Here was the apartment of Señor Calvo Sotelo.

Captains Condés, José del Rey and Victoriano Cuenca thereupon descended, together with a number of Assault Guards. The outer gate was opened by the night watchman, and they then climbed the stairs to the apartment and rang the bell. A servant answered, but did not open the door. They were asked what they wanted. They replied that they had orders to search the apartment. Still without opening the door, the servant withdrew and spoke with Señor Sotelo, who had retired for the night. He rose, went out into the hall, opened the door, and asked them what they wanted. Captain Condés, who was wearing civilian clothes, showed a military pass and explained that he had orders to search the apartment. Then with the others he made a show of searching the apartment, taking care to cut the telephone wires.

At this point Señor Calvo Sotelo was told that police headquarters had ordered his arrest. He replied that as a member of the Cortes he was immune from arrest except in the case of flagrant crime, and he had committed no such crime. When he tried to telephone police headquarters, he realized that the line had been cut. Members of his household were trying to leave the apartment to obtain help, but they were prevented. Señor Sotelo continually protested against the actions of the Assault Guards. Finally, on receiving the word of honor of Captain Condés that in five minutes he would be at police headquarters and allowed to make any declaration he thought fit, he agreed to accompany them.

He went back to his bedroom to finish dressing, followed by Captains Condés and del Rey. Meanwhile his wife succeeded in packing a handbag with toilet utensils, notepaper and a pen. She kept imploring him not to go.

Señor Sotelo then went into the children's room, kissing each of them in turn as they slept. The eldest child Conchita woke up and asked where he was going. He reassured her, and took leave of his wife in the hallway, promising to call her from the police station, "unless," he added, "these gentlemen have come to blow out my brains." Then he climbed down the stairs and at the street door told the gatekeeper to inform his brothers, but on no account to tell his parents. He climbed into the service car, and then turned to Captain Condés and asked him whether he was coming into the car. "Yes, I am coming," the captain said. "Well, we shall soon find out what it is all about," Señor Sotelo said, and he waved a last good-bye to his family, who were standing at the window and waving.

Señor Sotelo got into the third compartment of the truck (the first being occupied by the driver), and he took the fourth seat. An Assault Guard and a cavalry trooper sat beside him. Immediately behind him sat Victoriano Cuenca. Captains Condés and del Rey occupied seats next to the driver, and the rest of the men filled the remaining seats.

The truck reached the point where Ayala and Velázquez Streets cross, and here Victoriano Cuenca drew out a pistol and fired two shots at the back of Señor Sotelo's head so quickly that the other men in the truck had the impression that only one shot had been fired. The victim slipped down on the floor between the seats. Without slowing down, the truck proceeded to the East Cemetery, and stopped outside the gates. Captains Condés and del Rey presented themselves to the administrator of the cemetery. They explained that they were police officers and they ordered the gates opened. Then they drove into the cemetery and the body was dumped near the mortuary, and was later carried into the mortuary by workmen. The truck drove off.

They had driven only a few yards when the driver said: "Someone will surely denounce us." Condés replied: "Don't worry. Nothing will happen," and José del Rey said: "Whoever whispers a word about this is a dead man. We'll kill him in the same way that we killed that swine."

The murder of Calvo Sotelo precipitated the uprising. Secret orders went out to the army commanders to strike on the night of July 17, and it was hoped that all over Spain and in the Spanish possessions in Africa the army would be in full command by the middle of the morning. There would be no civil war. Instead there would be a sudden and dramatic seizure of power.

Such a seizure took place in Spanish Morocco, where General Francisco Franco, then a comparatively minor actor in the conspiracy, issued a manifesto calling upon all Spaniards to revolt:

Spaniards! Whoever feels a holy love of Spain, whoever among the Army and the Navy has made profession of faith in the service of his country, whoever has sworn to defend her from her enemies, the Nation calls you to her defense. With each day the situation in Spain becomes more critical; in most of her fields and villages anarchy reigns; the authority of the government is employed to foment revolution. The pistol and the machine gun render all people equal. Revolutionary strikes paralyze the life of the Nation. The Constitution, suspended and weakened, suffers total eclipse. . . .

Similar manifestoes were published wherever the uprising was successful. In Burgos, quickly captured by the army, preparations were made for welcoming General Sanjurjo, who would assume supreme command. He was staying in Estoril in Portugal, waiting for a plane to fly him to Burgos. The weather was unusually foggy, and the Monarchist pilot, Juan Antonio Ansaldo, had to postpone the flight. Here he describes the death of General Sanjurjo:

I telephoned several times to Estoril to explain what had happened, and I was told that the general accompanied by a few friends was still waiting for me. I found myself pacing up and down like a caged lion, in a state of mind bordering on insanity, as I wondered what on earth was going to happen in Burgos where the generals and high officials and great crowds were gathered about the aerodrome, impatient to acclaim Sanjurjo as the head of Nationalist Spain.

At half past one the atmospheric conditions became even worse, and I decided to postpone the flight. However, while I was having lunch an hour later, the mist lifted. I rushed out to the airplane, completed the necessary formalities, and flew off to La Marinha, where I landed without any trouble. As I taxied up to the landing area, I could hear people shouting enthusiastically.

Now at last there were clear skies and the memory of the accursed mist vanished from my mind.

The general climbed into the airplane with heavy suitcases. I suggested discreetly that it might be better to travel light, for we were undertaking a long and dangerous journey and we carried a heavy load of gasoline. I was told: "They are the general's uniforms. He cannot arrive in Burgos without his uniforms, and on the eve of his triumphal entry into Madrid."

I did not dare to discuss the matter with the general, trusting to my luck which had so often accompanied me in the past. I was told that at lunch Sanjurjo had listened to the radios from cities where the uprising had been successful. Hearing himself acclaimed, and listening to the news all pitched in a tone of optimism, and the playing of the "Royal March," he said: "To know that my flag is waving over Spain while I am listening to the music of that hymn makes me content to die."

I reached the end of the landing field and turned the nose of the plane toward the trees on the opposite side. I told the general it would be wiser for him to lean forward as we rose off the ground. With the motor revving up, the brakes on, I threw the stick forward toward the dashboard, and then I let her race across the field. The trees were coming closer, but I deliberately held the plane to the ground, waiting till the speed indicator registered 15 kilometers more than the basic speed necessary to lift the plane, as one always does in difficult flights. In this way one can always get a sudden necessary lift with a reasonable margin of safety.

A moment before the plane was to take off into the air, I heard a violent knocking sound, and this was followed by a sudden shaking of the whole plane. I thought perhaps a wheel had smashed, but pulled the stick back. I had the feeling that even with a broken wheel it would still be possible to make a landing in Burgos.

However, as we flew over the trees, I realized that our speed, instead of increasing, was becoming progressively less, so that there was the danger that the airplane might break up while in flight. The shaking was also growing worse. It occurred to me that the propeller might have broken. We were no longer at the speed necessary for maintaining lift, and so I decided to come down. I cut off the motor and aimed for a plowed field directly in front of me.

Between the ground and the airplane there was a wall about three feet high. Somehow I had to get the plane over the wall. The heat, and the weight of the heavily loaded plane, prevented it, and we crashed on top of the wall. If there had been only two or three inches of leeway, we would have got over it safely and somehow brought the plane to the ground, without much harm done.

At this moment sensations and memories were all mixed up, as always happens in an accident of this kind. It is difficult for me to provide a clear and coherent account of what happened during the next few minutes.

I seemed to be half-unconscious, like someone awaking from a deep and pleasant sleep. I knew I was covered with blood, but felt no pain. The general was still sitting there, but his face seemed oddly sprinkled with powder. For the moment I was aware of an immense feeling of hopelessness at the failure of our enterprise: it was the hopelessness of a child who sees his toys broken. This was followed by an extraordinary feeling of serenity and resignation, and the knowledge that death would not be unpleasant. I had indeed made my confession and taken communion some thirty hours before at Saint-Jean-de-Luz: I was not afraid to enter the next world. On the contrary the thought of dying delighted and captivated me.

I do not know how much time passed, perhaps no more than a quarter of a minute altogether.

The airplane was in flames. A reserve tank of gasoline, amounting to twenty-four liters, was behind the cockpit, burning furiously, but I felt no pain from it, though I realized I would have to do something. I realized too that it was necessary to renounce the delights of death. I tried to open the cockpit door, but it was locked. My wrist was broken, and I could do nothing with the door. I shouted: "General, General, open the door, we are on fire!" He made no reply, but his lips were half open and smiling. My uniform was on fire. Mechanically, without knowing what I was doing, I somehow succeeded in opening the door and throwing myself down on the ground. I stood up and reached up for the general, who was still sitting in the plane, and the plane was still straddling the wall. I pulled, but he would not come. I was being choked by black smoke, and soon I lost consciousness.

A few minutes later a peasant came running across the fields, and he too tried to pull the general from the burning plane. But he was no more successful than I had been. The flames were leaping high.

When the flames died down, there was only the twisted wreckage and the poor white bones of the general.

The strange death of General Sanjurjo in Portugal left the officers' revolt without a leader. The next most important general was Manuel Goded, Captain-General of the Balearic Islands, who was to command the revolt in Catalonia. He flew to Barcelona, and was immediately arrested and made the private prisoner of President Luis Companys. It seemed likely that there would be a struggle for power among the remaining high officers in the conspiracy.

Among those who sought power avidly was the phenomenally

audacious General Gonzalo Queipo de Llano, Inspector General of the Carabineros, a tall, thin, angular man with heavy eyebrows and a mouth like a trap. In the past he had supported the Republic; now he turned against it with unbridled fury and a startling courage. Almost single-handed, he captured the entire garrison in Seville, and then went on to destroy all opposition within the city.

He arrived in Seville on the afternoon of July 17 with only his aide-de-camp López Guerrero and a staff captain called Escribano, their only weapons being the revolvers at their belts. He had been on an official tour of customs posts, and congratulated himself on having accomplished "20,000 miles of conspiracy." During the evening he laid his plans. The next morning he found an empty office in the garrison headquarters—it was very hot and the officers were taking a long weekend—and there installed himself. Prowling along a corridor, he met the garrison commander, General Villa-Abraille. According to General Queipo de Llano, the following conversation took place:

"What are you doing here?" asked General Villa-Abraille.

"I have come to tell you the time has come to make a decision. Either you are with your comrades in arms, or you are with the Government which is leading Spain to ruin."

"I shall always remain faithful to the Government."

"Very well! I have the orders of the military committee to blow out your brains, but since I am your friend and I hope to avoid violence, let us hope you will see the error of your ways."

"I repeat that I shall obey the orders of the Government."

"In that case I shall have to have you shot or put under arrest. It will be enough to put you under arrest. Go back to your office."

"I understand perfectly," the general said, and then he turned to the other officers. "Gentlemen, I wish you to notice that I am submitting only to force."

"Quite right," I said. "You are submitting to force, and you are going back into your office."

I gave him a slight push in the direction of the door. On the way he kept turning to the officers, explaining that he was in fact submitting only to force. We all followed him into his office. There I begged him for the last time to think deeply about the course he intended to pursue, reminding him of conversations between us during the previous weeks, and explaining that I was putting him under arrest. Then General López Vieta, his chief of staff, said: "Then I, too, must be put under arrest."

"Of course. If that's what you want," I said.

Then Colonel Hidalgo, who was also on the staff, said: "I, too, should be arrested."

"I have no objection," I said.

So it was with the other officers. They were all placed in the room under arrest. I tore out the telephone wires, and was about to lock the door with a key when I discovered there was no key. So I called a corporal and told him to shoot anyone who attempted to escape. "If anyone leaves this office, I shall have you shot," I told him. And no one escaped.

I then went to the infantry barracks, under the command of General Allanegui, a man who had conducted brilliant campaigns in Morocco. I was amazed to see the troops drawn up under arms on the square. I found the officers of the regiment standing around a colonel. I went up to him.

"I have come to shake your hand, my dear colonel," I said, "and to congratulate you for putting yourself on the side of your brothers-in-arms in these hours when the fate of the country is being decided."

I had never met him before.

"I have decided to support the Government," the colonel said. "I shall obey only the orders coming from my superior officer."

I did my best to conceal my surprise and indignation, and said calmly: "Shall we pursue the interview in your office?"

So we entered the very small office: a colonel, a lieutenant colonel, a major or two, and some captains. I was accompanied only by my aide-de-camp, López Guerrero. There was no room for any more. Some captains and lieutenants were gathered on the two or three steps just outside the office.

Once inside the office, I addressed myself to the colonel.

"Is it possible," I said, "that you who have seen the course pursued by the wretched Government as it guides the destiny of our country, and the shabby treatment inflicted on the army—is it possible that you will have anything to do with the Government?" .

"Yes, it is possible," he said.

"Then I am obliged to withdraw from you the command of the regiment."

I turned to the lieutenant colonel.

"Lieutenant colonel," I said, "will you take command of the regiment?"

"No, I follow my colonel," he said, and he stepped forward and stood beside the colonel.

I turned to a major and asked him whether he would take the command.

He answered in the same way as the lieutenant colonel.

"Well, which of you will take command of the regiment?" I said to the captains.

From them I received the same reply. So I turned to my aide-de-camp and ordered him to go to division headquarters and fetch Colonel Cuesta, one of those who had accompanied me on my journey.

He left me alone with these officers, all of them bitterly hostile to me. There followed an embarrassing moment of silence, which was broken by Major Pérez, one of their officers, who explained with tears in his eyes that they were on our side, but remembered vividly what happened after the Sanjurjo rising in 1931 and they feared there would be the same consequences.

"It is not at all the same thing today," I replied. "It cannot happen as it happened then, because this time it is a question of death or victory at a decisive moment. It is better to die than to live in dishonor."

Then Colonel Cuesta entered, and he too asked them on which side they would fight. I decided to take extraordinary risks. Leaving the room, I went out among the captains gathered on the steps.

"Is there among you," I asked, "one who would be able to take command of the regiment?"

At first there was no reply. Finally a certain Captain Fernández, from Cordova, permitted himself a gentle smile.

"Well, do you think you could take over the command?" I said.

"Yes, sir."

"Very well, take over the command."

At that moment General Allanegui attempted to leave the room. I held him by the arms, and said with great force: "Where do you think you are going?"

"I am going to talk with my men."

"No, you are not! You are going to stay in that room!"

Saying this, I put my hand to my revolver, as though I had made up my mind to shoot him, and I said: "Don't make me use violence!"

I was holding him firmly by the wrist, and all the time my other hand was in my pocket and my finger round the trigger of the revolver. In a voice which must have sounded like thunder, I shouted: "Please understand we shall stop at nothing!"

Then I took my revolver from the pocket and roared at the top of my lungs: "You are my prisoners! Follow me!"

So they followed me, and we passed the soldiers on guard, and followed the road from the barracks to the division headquarters and I bundled them into the office where I kept my first prisoners.

General Queipo de Llano was a little puzzled by the ease with which he was able to bluff the garrison into surrender. "From time to time," *he related, "I had to rub my eyes to make sure I was not dreaming."*

His victory was complete: there remained only the mopping-up *campaign, which he proceeded to embark on with his accustomed* *vigor. One of his associates, Don Antonio Bahamonde y Sánchez* *de Castro, who was one of those brought in to maintain the civil* *government in Seville, and who later defected, describes the scene* *after Queipo de Llano took power.*

Days before the insurrection broke out in Seville, one lived in an atmosphere of unrest owing to events that occurred at different points in Spain, principally in Madrid, among which were the assassination of the Lieutenant of the Assault Guards, Señor Castillo, followed by that of Calvo Sotelo.

Rumours were in circulation regarding a Fascist uprising. The Fascists, not numerous in Andalusia, could not count upon a sufficient number of adherents to constitute a danger by themselves.

Military men, monarchists for the most part, in spite of having accepted the Republic, see in the triumph of the Popular Front a menace to their privileges of caste.

The desire of some, and the fear of the rest, was a military revolt. It was in this that one perceived the danger.

On the city walls, at every corner, labor organizations posted these warnings, "Comrades, Fascism lies in ambush; when the moment comes, let each one obey the given watchword." Those of us who did not belong to any party asked each other what was going to happen.

July 18th

The rumours which had been circulating were confirmed. The garrison in Africa had revolted. The communications with the rest of Spain were interrupted.

The chiefs of the General Staff of the Division, in complicity with Queipo, took its Commander, General Villa-Abraille, prisoner. Queipo immediately assumed the command, and, with the aid of the chiefs of the garrison, quartered the troops for lack of confidence in them. The first soldiers to come out were quotas of the Intendancy Corps; shortly after came the quotas of the other regiments. These, by reason of belonging to well-to-do families, inspired greater confidence in their chiefs. There was an exception; the colonel of the Regiment of Engineers refused to support the movement, and also advised that he would not bring the troops out to combat it. His attitude was one of neutrality; a few days later he was shot.

At 3 o'clock in the afternoon, the first skirmish took place; the Assault Guards, under the command of a lieutenant, placed a machine-gun in the Plaza Nueva. Captain Escribano, with a group of soldiers, warned them to remove it, and when the lieutenant refused, the soldiers fired. A number of discharges were exchanged, and some moments later the Guards surrendered.

In the aforesaid plaza are situated the buildings of the Telephone Company, the Town Hall, and, facing this, the Hotel Inglaterra, with a broad façade and little depth. Behind this building and separated by a narrow street, is the Civil Government building.

The soldiers attacked the telephone building, which was defended by the Assault Guards, who surrendered after a short resistance. Some moments later, the soldiers took possession of the Town Hall, and the Municipal Guards, who were inside, surrendered without combat.

Other Assault Guards, in order to defend the Civil Government building, took shelter in the Hotel Inglaterra. There was intense sharp-shooting. Shortly Commandant Garrigo arrived at the head of a group of soldiers, who placed two cannons of seven point five in the plaza, opening fire on the hotel. At the fifth discharge the Guards surrendered. The Civil Government House, with no possible defence, surrendered moments later. In it were the Governor, the Commandant of the Assault Guards, the Chief of Police, and some leaders of the Popular Front. Queipo promised to respect their lives if they surrendered at once. Nevertheless, the majority were shot. The Commandant of Assault Guards died with "Vivas" for the Republic. They promised the Chief of Police that they would pay his full salary to his wife, if he would deliver the file-index which had been removed from the Commissariat and which contained those of the so-called social brigade. In these files were the greater part of the socialist, communist, and C.N.T. leaders, and of a great many workmen who at some time had been arrested for some social question. The Chief of Police told where he had hidden them, and the insurgents took possession of them and immediately dedicated themselves to hunting up those who were listed therein.

The insurgents, at 6 o'clock in the afternoon, were masters of the centre of the city and of the barracks of the Assault Guards, situated in the Alameda de Hércules. It was owing to the adhesion of these that the insurgents were able to take possession of Seville with such rapidity. The police, for the most part, adhered to the movement, giving their service to it from the very first day.

Radio Seville, which had not yet fallen into the hands of the rebels, announced a general strike, asking the workers to assemble at their syndicates. There were constant calls for the peasants in the villages to come to Seville to defend the Republic. Soon after it was silenced. The rebels had taken possession of the transmitter.

The workers, complying with the watchword, gathered at their syndicates, where they uselessly asked for arms, as there was but a small number of guns and pistols to give them. They could not get to the Casa del Pueblo in Cuna Street, in the centre of the town, as the insurgents supplied with machine-guns, held the strategic places. With their inadequate supply of weapons, the workers held the outer quarters until the arrival of the Moors and Foreign Legion.

On that same day (the 18th) at 8 o'clock at night, Queipo spoke over the radio, saying that the movement had triumphed in all Spain. He exhorted the workers who resisted in the districts to surrender, and said, "Those who do not report for work on Monday, will be discharged: the directors of the syndicates will be shot if they do not give the order to resume work. This movement is not against the Republic, but against the Government of the Popular Front." He ended with a "Viva la República!" which was followed by the national hymn. Queipo continued for many nights to end his talk with this "Viva la República!" and the transmitter, for a considerable period of time, played several times a day the "Himno de Riego."

On that same day of the 18th, the first Fascist patrols appeared in the streets, wearing the blue shirts, and showing on the left arm a black band with the yoke and five arrows in red. From the first moment, they carried on their activities in absolute independence of the military.

During the following days, the situation was very confused. The rebels were in possession of the centre of the city. Queipo was unable to take the outer districts, even with cannons and machine-guns at his disposal, until the arrival of the Moors and the Foreign Legion. These came from Africa in airplanes which landed in Jerez de la Frontera (Cádiz). In order to transport them in greater numbers, they were tied to the wings of the planes.

In the Café Madrid, in Sierpes Street, I saw two Moors showing the marks which the cords had made on their bodies.

San Julián, San Bernardo, La Macarena, El Pumarejo, Triana, all the districts, with almost no arms, made a heroic defence. They had to be taken one by one. The Moors, employed as shock troops, entered hurling hand-grenades. In San Julián, the slaughter was tremendous. The rebels forced all the men whom they found in the houses to come into the street, and there, without ascertaining whether they had taken any part in the fight, they killed them.

The lower part of Triana was shot to pieces by cannons on the opposite bank of the river. The Moors, with savage ferocity, and in obedience to terrible orders which it seems incredible could have been given by Spanish soldiers against their own brothers, entered the houses from which they supposed that shots had come and killed with knives all the inhabitants, excepting not even the women and children. The Moors and the Foreign Legion, by the right of conquest, looted the dwellings of the humble workmen, who lacked direction and sufficient arms for their defence.

In the streets were to be seen a great number of dead bodies, which no one intended to remove. In the narrower streets, it was necessary to pile them up against the walls of the houses in order to allow passage-way for the automobiles, which, provided with machine-guns, circulated throughout the city. The occupants wore white handkerchiefs tied around the left arm; others tied them to the barrels of their muskets. The object was to distinguish the one from the other.

Seville in a few days was under total domination.

During the first days the Moors came from Africa in airplanes. Days later, protected by the Italian fleet, numerous and continuous expeditions crossed the Strait. They came to Seville in such great numbers that there were not enough places for lodging them. The buildings of the Plaza de España, and of the Park of Maria Luisa had to be outfitted for them, but they did not use these, as they preferred to live in the gardens, destroying that section of the park which they converted into an Arab settlement. They uprooted shrubs and hedges to build the bonfires, over which, in groups, they cooked their meals; all brought teapots which they kept continually over little fires, which extended in long files along the promenades; they washed their clothes in the ponds of the park; those who bathed did so in absolute nudity. The prostitutes and inverts were to be seen there at all hours; in plain daylight the most shameful scenes presented themselves. The guards had orders to interfere with them in no way; they were the absolute masters of the park. The Sevillians had to give up going to their beautiful gardens.

Queipo said over the radio, "The movement has triumphed in all Spain; I solemnly promise that those who cease their resistance have nothing to fear; the Foreign Legion and the Regular troops which have come from Africa will level to the ground the villages which do not lay down their arms." Every day he announced brilliant victories, and promised the triumphal entrance of the Nationalist troops into Madrid within a very brief time. He fixed upon different dates: first, it was July 25th, the festival of the Apostle Santiago, patron of Spain; then it was the day of the Virgin of the Kings, patroness of Seville; later, October 1st; and, finally, as a definite date, he guaranteed that Mola would speak from the Ministry of Government in Madrid before November 10th. He gave assurance that, as soon as the capital was taken, the end of the war would be a question of days.

Madrid Fights Back

*F*OR *many weeks the Madrileños had been obscurely aware that an officers' plot was in the making. Tension between the extreme right and extreme left was increasing daily, until it became almost palpable—a ghost putting on flesh and walking through the sun-dried streets of Madrid. There was an air of unreality about those July days. A car would backfire, and immediately there were rumors of another assassination. The Government under the liberal and ineffective Casares Quiroga maintained a kind of ironic detachment, unable to arrest the disease overwhelming the country. Only the Anarchists, busily organizing a building strike, seemed to be unaware that power-ful forces were at work to destroy the familiar life of the capital.*

The murder of Calvo Sotelo was followed by a declaration of war by the effete and cynical Gil Robles, but no one, least of all Franco, could envisage the kind of war that would emerge. "People felt," said Arturo Barea, "the fear of soldiers about to depart for the front." But there was also, very distinct and yet unreal, the fear that in some mysterious and incomprehensible way Madrid itself was the front, with the opposing armies already taking up their battle lines across a doomed city.

The women walked about in light summer dresses, the men were in shirt sleeves. Radios and gramophones were playing "The Music Goes Round and Round." There was a good deal of talk about the forthcoming Fair of St. John, the famous Verbena de San Juan, *a combined summer festival and amusement park which is the highlight of a Madrileño's summer. Meanwhile the Government radio kept announcing: "The situation is well in hand." The announcement was made a little too frequently to allay the people's fears.*

July 17th was a Friday. Everyone was looking forward hopefully to a long and peaceful weekend.

31

Here is the diary of Constancia de la Mora, the aristocratic grand-daughter of Antonio Maura, Prime Minister under King Alfonso XIII. Her husband, who bore the princely name of Ignacio Hidalgo de Cisneros, was a high officer in the Air Force.

July 17, 1936. Three o'clock.

A military uprising in Morocco. Ignacio had gone to the War Ministry. I was alone in the house. It was very hot. I pulled aside the blind and looked into the street. Down the block a little peddler pushed his cart. Otherwise nothing. The sun beat on the pavements. Madrid was quiet.

July 17, 1936. Four o'clock.

Ignacio would call very soon. He would say: "It is nothing. The traitors are all under arrest." Then he would leave day after tomorrow or the day after that for the seashore, to lie under the sun and watch the breakers foam over the rocks.

July 17, 1936. Five o'clock.

The house is so quiet, so empty. Now surely Ignacio will call very soon. A military uprising in Morocco. But suppose it was part of a great plot? Ignacio had expected it. Suppose the garrison in Madrid revolts? The people will defend the Republic. Spain will never be fascist—not while the people live.

July 17, 1936. Eight o'clock.

The heat hangs on. My face is damp with the hot winds. In the street there is no more movement now, people passing quickly, talking. I can hear their voices, but no words. Are they talking of the uprising? What do they say? . . .

July 17, 1936. Midnight.

How can it be that Ignacio has not called? He must know that I am sitting at home in the empty, quiet house, waiting for his voice to reassure me. He would have called, I know he would—if he had the chance. So he must be working furiously. Then the uprising is serious. . . .

July 18, 1936. Eleven o'clock.

The empty house trembles with the blatant loud ring of the telephone.

"Ignacio! Are you all right? What is happening? Are you not coming home? Is the uprising . . ."

His voice, sharp and staccato, cuts me off. "I am at the War Ministry now. I have been at the airport most of the night. I must keep all my loyal pilots standing by for orders."

"But what's . . ."

"Connie!" Ignacio's voice was loud. "I want you to promise me something."

"Yes, but . . ."

"I want you to absolutely promise to stay inside the house. Do you understand? Do not go out, under any circumstances."

I was bewildered. "Ignacio, why not, what's going on?"

But Ignacio hung up. I was furious. I had yet to learn that commonplace of wartime: that there are times when one cannot speak over the telephone.

July 18, 1936. Four o'clock.

I slept a little, awaking still fatigued. The heat grew. The radio in the house was broken. We could not find a mechanic to repair it. But the Government ordered all radios turned on permanently, and loud enough for neighbors to hear. Through our open windows floated the magnified voice of the Government announcer: *"People of Spain! Keep tuned in! Keep tuned in! Do not turn your radios off! Rumors are being circulated by traitors. Wild stories are causing panic and fear. The Government will broadcast day and night—learn the truth from this station. Keep tuned in! Keep tuned in!"*

Across the street from Freddie's house, a little soft drink and sandwich stand installed a radio. People sat sipping cool drinks at the small painted tables in the diminutive garden—listening. Crowds stood around the counter—listening.

Freddie and I could not sit in the empty house. We needed people around us. We walked out into the evening and sat quietly at one of the tables, listening to the blaring voice from the radio and listening to the talk of the people.

"The Republic has the situation in hand," the Government announcer said.

"Ha!" a little man sitting next to me told his stout, good-natured-looking wife. "This time we'll really give it to those vermin! The Army! Every general, every last one of them, ought to be shot." His wife nodded.

"President Azaña has moved from his residence at El Pardo to the National Palace in Madrid."

A tall, immaculately dressed dandy standing just in back of me snorted. "So! The Government has things in hand! But Azaña has to move. So!"

My neighbor stood up. "Say it again, you dirty Monarchist." The crowd turned from the loudspeaker. "Where's the king-lover?" somebody yelled. The well-dressed man slipped discreetly away.

"I can't make head or tail of it," Freddie said. "What in heaven's name is going on?"

I shook my head. If only Ignacio would come.

At midnight Freddie left me and I went home to bed. I fell asleep with the voice of the announcer still pounding at my ears.

Next morning I woke with a start. It was very early. Through my open windows floated the voice from my neighbor's radio.

"Attention! People of Spain! The Government will now briefly review the military situation."

I sat up in bed, wide awake. *"The rebellion against the Republic, led by a handful of traitorous generals, began with the Moorish troops. They persuaded their soldiers, by the use of the most vicious lies, to rise against the Republic. Some of the Moorish troops have been transported to the peninsula, where they are attacking—unsuccessfully —Republican troops.*

In the meantime, other members of this conspiracy against liberty have incited isolated regiments in the north and south to rise against the Republic. Fighting is still going on in these cities but we feel sure of the outcome. Málaga has been attacked and is in flames. Government forces and rebels are fighting in the streets of Barcelona."

I began dressing hastily. The news made more sense now. The plot had been carefully laid. Garrisons all over Spain apparently were to rise at the signal of the rebellion in Morocco. But the Rebels had not taken the Republicans completely by surprise. Comparatively few garrisons had risen. The Republican troops, barring accidents, would be able to handle the situation.

I ate my breakfast reading the headlines, feeling more confident by the moment. For I did not know, nor did Ignacio at the War Office, nor did the people of Spain know, that even as we all awoke and went to work that morning of July 19, 1936, at Berlin and Rome two dictators were giving the orders for the invasion of Spain by Fascist troops, airplanes, cruisers, transports, technicians, Army officers, ammunition, guns, and money. The unequal battle—Spain against Germany and Italy, with England and France and the United States handcuffing my country's fighting arms—had already begun. But we did not know it.

About ten o'clock, the Government broadcast the news that General Francisco Franco, the hated general who sent the Moors to rape and kill in the Asturias, had flown to Morocco from the Canary Islands where he had been stationed after his removal as Chief of Staff. Now the pieces of the plot were beginning to fit together. Ignacio had always said that Franco was a very ambitious man—General Goded was more intelligent; General Mola a better soldier; but Franco was the most ambitious.

Ignacio came home Sunday morning at five o'clock. He had not slept or eaten a proper meal since he left the house Thursday afternoon. He looked haggard, thin, and so tired that I took pity on him and put him to bed without a single question.

A few hours later I woke again to the sound of the radio. I closed our windows hastily. Ignacio must sleep. But I stole out into the street and listened. The Government of Casares had resigned. *"Martínez Barrio will head a new Government. Listen in! Keep tuned in! The names of the new Cabinet Ministers will be announced shortly."*

Ignacio woke in an hour. At breakfast, Freddie and I bombarded him with questions. Ignacio talked fast as he ate. The revolt was much more serious than anyone had expected at first—anyone except himself and most of the Republican Army officers in Spain. The plot was a careful one, designed to bring all the converging Rebel troops from the provinces into an attack on Madrid. The Government must stop this converging process. But the only forces that could be used with complete trust were the workers belonging to trade unions and Popular Front parties. The Republican Government, however, did not wish to arm the people. Therefore it had resigned, to be replaced by a more moderate government which intended to make peace with the Rebels.

"Peace?" I cried, jumping up from the table. "But that means Fascism! And the people will never . . ."

Ignacio grinned. "Don't get so excited, Connie," he said, gulping coffee. "I don't think it's all over yet—not by a long sight. Martínez Barrio doesn't realize the situation. He can't make peace with the Fascists. He doesn't know it yet, but he can't. You should see the crowds outside the War Ministry. Thousands of them. They have been there since Thursday night. Just standing quietly, or sleeping in the garden and on the curbs, holding their trade union cards in their hands. Waiting for arms, just waiting."

While the Government announced on the radio that the uprising had been crushed, some sixth sense told the Madrileños that it was only beginning. The people were crying out for arms, but none were given to them. The government of Casares Quiroga fell, to be replaced by a moderate liberal government formed by Martínez Barrio, the voluble Speaker of the Cortes. This government lasted only a few hours. A third government formed by José Giral took the immediate and irrevocable step of arming the people; and so it happened that truckloads of rifles left the Ministry of War on the morning of July 19 for the headquarters of the UGT and CNT, the Socialist and Anarchist trade unions. In this way power fell largely into the hands of the union leaders.

Meanwhile one large center of resistance was holding out. This was the Cuartel de la Montaña, the three-story barracks standing on a hill commanding the center of the city, the Gran Vía, and the Presidential Palace. Historically, the Cuartel de la Montaña had symbolized military domination of the city, and was detested by thousands of Madrileños for this reason. The barracks was taken by storm by Shock Police (Guardia de Asalto) *and by a vast crowd of unarmed Madrileños on the afternoon of July 20th.*

A young lawyer and journalist, Arturo Barea, saw the storming of the barracks and describes the fearful vengeance taken on the defenders.

The barracks, in reality three different barracks joined together, is a huge building on the crest of a hill. In front of it lies a wide glacis on which a whole regiment has room for its drill. The terrace slopes down to the Calle de Ferraz on one side and is cut short above the Northern Railway Station on the other. A thick stone parapet runs along its whole length, with a sheer drop of twenty feet to a lower glacis which separates the barracks from the public gardens of the Calle de Ferraz. At the back, the building looms high over the wide avenue of the Paseo de Rosales and the open country to the west and northwest. The Cuartel de la Montaña is a fortress.

Rifle shots were cracking from the direction of the barracks. At the corner of the Plaza de España and the Calle de Ferraz a group of Shock Police were loading their rifles in the shelter of a wall. A multitude of people were crouching and lying between the trees and benches of the gardens. A wave of furious shots and cries was surging from them, and from others I could not see, nearer to the barracks. There must have been many thousands ringing the edifice on its hill. The pavement on the other side was deserted.

A plane came flying towards the barracks at great altitude. People yelled: "It's one of ours!"

The day before, Sunday—that Sunday on which we had gone to the Sierra in the morning, hoping that the storm had blown over—groups of officers on the two airfields of Madrid had attempted an insurrection, but had been overpowered by the loyal forces.

The machine flew in a wide curve and banked down. I could not see it any longer. A few moments later the ground and the air shook. After dropping its bombs, the plane made off. The crowd went mad with joy, some of the people in the gardens stood up, waving and throwing their caps into the air. A man was making a pirouette when he fell, shot. The barracks was firing. The rattle of machine guns rose above all the other noises.

Shouting and screaming, a tight cluster of people appeared on the other side of the Plaza de España. When the mass arrived at the street corner, I saw that it had in its midst a lorry with a 7.5 centimeter gun. An officer of the Shock Police was trying to give orders on how to unload the cannon. The crowd never listened. Hundreds of people fell upon the lorry as though they wanted to devour it, and it disappeared beneath the human mass like a piece of rotting meat under a cluster of black flies. And then the gun was on the ground, lifted down on arms and shoulders. The officer shook himself, and shouted for silence.

"Now as soon as I've fired it off you're to carry it over there as quickly as you can, do you understand me?" He pointed to the other end of the gardens. "But don't kill yourselves. . . . We've got to make them believe that we've got plenty of guns. And off with all of you who aren't helping."

He fired off the field-gun and even before the barrel had come to rest the dense mass of men closed in and carried it one hundred, two hundred yards further on. Again the gun roared, and again it started on its crazy run over the paving stones. It left in its wake people hopping on one foot and screaming with pain: the wheels had rolled over men's feet. Machine-gun bullets were spraying the street very close to us. I took cover in the gardens and threw myself down behind a stout tree trunk, just behind two workers lying on the lawn.

Why the devil was I here—and without any kind of weapon in my pockets? I knew perfectly well that it was sheer useless folly. But how could I be anywhere else?

One of the two men in front of me raised himself on his elbows. He gripped a revolver with both hands and rested it against the tree trunk. It was an enormous, ancient revolver with a nickel-plated barrel and a sight that stuck out like a wart. The cartridge drum was a shapeless bulk above the two hands clutching the butt. The man pressed his face perilously close to the weapon and pulled the trigger, laboriously. A terrific bang shook him and a pall of stinging smoke made a halo round his head.

I almost leaped to my feet. We were at a distance of at least four hundred and fifty yards from the barracks, and the front of the building was completely screened by the trees of the gardens. What did that damned fellow think he was firing at?

His companion took him by the shoulder. "Now let me have a shot."

"No, I won't. It's my revolver."

The other swore: "Let me have a shot, by your mother!"

"No, I won't, I've told you so. If they bump me off the revolver is yours; if not, you can just lump it."

The other turned round. He had a clasp-knife in his hand, almost as big as a cleaver, and he brought it down on his friend's behind. "Give me the revolver, or I'll prick you!" He stabbed at his buttocks with the point of his knife.

The man with the revolver jumped and bellowed. "It's gone in!"

"Now you see—you let me have a shot or I'll puncture you."

"Here you are, but hold tight, it kicks."

"D'you think I'm an idiot?"

As though following a fixed ritual, the other raised himself on his elbows and clutched the butt with both hands, so deliberately and ceremoniously that it looked almost like a supplication. The nickel-plated barrel lifted slowly.

"Go on, get it over!" shouted the owner of the revolver.

The other turned his head.

"Now it's you who's got to wait. It's my turn. Now I'll show those bastards!"

Again we were shaken by the crash, again the acrid smoke clung to the ground around us.

The bangs of mortars and the rattle of machine guns went on at the barracks. From time to time the gun roared at our back, a shell made the air throb, and the explosion resounded somewhere in the distance. I looked at my watch: ten o'clock. Ten! It was impossible.

Just then a silence fell, followed by a pandemonium of cries and shouts. Through the confused noise rose the words: "Surrender! White flag!" People burgeoned from the ground. For the first time I saw that there were women as well. And all of them started running towards the barracks. They swept me along. I ran with them.

I could see the stone stairways in the center of the parapet which led from the lower to the upper glacis; they were black with tightly packed people. On the terrace above a dense mass of bodies blocked the exit.

A furious burst from the machine guns cut through the air. With an inhuman shriek, the crowds tried to scatter. The barracks spouted metal from its windows. Mortars sounded again, nearer now, with a dry crack. It lasted some minutes, while the wave of cries was more frightful than ever.

Who gave the order to attack?

A huge, solid mass of bodies moved forwards like a ram against the barracks, against the slope leading upwards from the Calle de Ferraz, against the stone stairs in the wall, against the wall itself. An immense cry rose from the multitude. The machine guns rattled, ceaselessly.

And then we knew in an instant, though no one told us, that the barracks was stormed. The figures in the windows disappeared in a flash, other figures whipped past the windows after them. The tide of screams and the firing now sounded inside the building. A Miliciano emerged in a window, raising a rifle high into the air and throwing it down outside. The multitude answered with a roar. I found myself part of a mass which pushed on towards the barracks. The glacis was strewn with bodies, many of them twitching and slithering in their own blood. And then I was in the barracks yard.

The three tiers of galleries enclosing the square yard were filled with running, yelling, gesticulating people who waved rifles and called senselessly to their friends down below. One group was chasing a soldier who forged ahead, crazed, but swerving aside whenever anyone crossed his path. They had run almost the whole round of the gallery when somebody tripped the soldier up. He fell. The group of people closed round him. When they separated, there was nothing to be seen from the yard where I was.

A giant of a man appeared in the highest gallery, bearing on his huge hands a soldier who threshed the air with his legs. The big man shouted:

"Here he comes!"

And he threw the soldier down into the yard. He fell, revolving through the air like a rag doll, and crashed on the stones with a dull thud. The giant lifted his arms.

"And now the next!"

A crowd had gathered in the corner of the arms depot. The rifles were there. One militiaman after the other came out, brandishing his new rifle, almost dancing with enthusiasm. Then there was a new rush at the door.

"Pistols—Pistols!"

The depot began to pour forth black boxes, passed from hand to hand over the heads. Each box contained a regulation pistol—a long-barreled Astra caliber 9—a spare cartridge frame, a ramrod, and a screwdriver. In a few minutes the stones of the yard were spattered with black and white patches—for the inside of the black boxes was white—and with grease-stained paper. The depot door was still spitting forth pistols.

It has been said that there were five thousand Astra pistols in the Cuartel de la Montaña. I do not know. But that day, empty black-and-white cases dotted the streets of Madrid. What was not found, however, was ammunition. It had been seized at once by the Shock Police.

I walked out of the barracks.

When I served my first few months in the Army, a conscript soldier destined for Morocco, it had been in these barracks; that was sixteen years ago.

I had a glimpse of the officers' mess in parting. Dead officers were lying there in wild disorder, some with their arms flung across the table, some on the ground, some over the window sills. And a few of them were young boys.

Outside on the glacis, under the glare of the sun, lay corpses in hundreds. It was quiet in the gardens.

Among those who hurled themselves at the Cuartel de la Montaña was Valentín Gonzáles, the son of a miner from Estremadura, who made his living as a road contractor. A born rebel, he soon came to hate the dominant role played by the Communists. Later he was to become famous as El Campesino, *"The Peasant," a general in command of an army.*

Here he sketches briefly the months which brought him to lie at last in the bed of King Alfonso XIII.

I was among the Republicans who stormed the Cuartel de la Montaña, the barracks which the Fascists had turned into their fortress. Later I joined the fighting for the airfield of Cuatro Vientos. And in the end I found myself with governmental forces operating in the town of Guadalajara, thirty miles from the capital.

And then came another nightmarish day. General Mola was reported to be marching on Madrid. I rounded up some twenty men, and we went to the mountain pass of Somosierra, the key point where Mola had to be stopped if he was to be stopped at all. It was my first command: twenty-nine men, two lorries, rifles, and one machine gun. I did not know it then, but this was the beginning of the famous Forty-Sixth Division, the "Campesino Division," the largest formation of shock troops in the Spanish Republican Army. But at the start our group did not carry my name. We adopted that of Chapaev, the great guerrilla fighter of the Russian Revolution. Thus we set out, not even in uniform, with our single machine gun, meaning to stop General Mola's regular soldiers. Fortunately we were not left alone. A column under Colonel Cuerva—who was killed two days later—joined us soon. Then Captain Galán, an active Communist who constituted himself my military adviser, put four hundred men under my command. It was not exactly a strong force to pit against trained soldiers, but it was enough. We beat Mola's troops back and not only made three hundred prisoners, but also took ammunition and lorries which were badly needed. Madrid was saved.

I had a head wound and was sent to a hospital. But I could not stay there idle while the fighting was going on outside. After two days I went back to my post, though it was another month before I could get rid of my bandages.

For my services at Somosierra I was given the rank of captain, in front of my unit in formation. The Communist Party were determined to profit by the distinction I had won; at the ceremony in Buitrago, the members of the Central Committee and even a representative of the Comintern were present.

I heard that the Fascists had captured Villavieja and held my brother a prisoner there. I moved on Villavieja, took the place back, and freed my brother. This feat brought me the offer of another promotion. I refused. As a lifelong antimilitarist I hated the officers of the army and all they stood for. My new rank of captain was quite enough.

Galán disagreed with me. He had been made a colonel in the meantime, thanks to one of those rapid promotions of the Civil War, caused mainly by the lack of high-ranking officers on our side. Galán wanted me to accept higher rank, possibly because he wished to see the higher command in the hands of Communists. Whatever the reason, he called two thousand militiamen together and proposed my promotion to them. By acclamation they voted me a major and the officer commanding the sector of Buitrago. This was a nomination by the fighting men themselves, and I accepted it.

Almost in spite of me, my command was growing. On August 6, Largo Caballero visited us, confirmed my rank on behalf of the government and—more important—provided uniforms for my militiamen. Now they really began to look like soldiers.

Galán urged me to make an appeal to the Castilian peasants, asking them to join the militia. I had doubts about it. If they had not risen already in defense of the Republic, why should they rise if I called them? Yet so it was. Nobody was more astonished than I when thousands of peasants responded to my appeal and volunteered. Why did they do it? Because they hated professional soldiers as much as I hated them, and would not listen to their appeals, not even to the appeals of those who had remained loyal to the Republican government. To me they listened because they knew I felt as they did. Because I was El Campesino, the peasant, one of them.

With the peasant volunteers I organized seven battalions. We had barracks of our own in Madrid. I used professional soldiers who had remained loyal as instructors and advisers, but I still did not trust them as leaders. They were with us now, but before that they had been soldiers, and therefore against us—wasn't our enemy in the field the military caste?

The war was going badly for us. From the start the Fascists had the help—solid, substantial help—from the Italians and Germans. We got no help from the Russians until two months after the outbreak of the fighting, and even then it was not on the same scale. And we did not get it for our own sake. But I did not see that at the time. I should have seen it, but I did not. I was blind.

Again Madrid was in danger. On November 4, Largo Caballero, the premier, who prepared for the transfer of his government to Valencia, asked General Miaja and myself to save the city. I took six battalions and posted them at the most dangerous and vulnerable spots.

The decisive days were November 6-9. But many people in our own camp did not realize that they might be decisive, because they had given Madrid up for lost. The world expected the fall of Madrid from one hour to the next. And the world should have been right; Madrid was ripe to fall. It should have fallen, if the men, women, and children had not united to save it, as no civilians had ever united in defense of their homes.

I am no talker; I am a doer. This time I had to talk. We held a mass rally in the largest theater of the capital, and I spoke to the crowd. I told them, "Stop crying. The Fascists won't enter Madrid. But if we want to stop them, you must turn out, all of you, men and women, children and old people, and dig trenches, and build fortifications round the town. People of Madrid, arise!"

We went out in lorries and collected everybody we found in cafés, theaters, and in the streets. And they came. They worked the whole night with an enthusiasm and a will to resist that might have shamed the government which had abandoned its capital.

The enemy expected to take Madrid on the tenth. Early that day, while I was inspecting the outposts with two of my officers, I saw two Fascist tanks coming up. We captured one of them, the other turned to flight. The lieutenant who commanded the captured tank carried plans for a simultaneous attack on Madrid from nine directions. Forewarned as we now were, we could meet the Fascists at every point. They were surprised by our resistance and withdrew. For the second time Madrid was saved.

The Russians had begun to play their game in Spain.

There was the famous Fifth Regiment. All the Communist, and more-or-less Communist, writers, journalists, and poets praised it to the skies. They called it unique, and it was unique.

From the beginning, it had been a Communist regiment. But for the first two months of the war, before the Russian intervention, it had been a regiment of Spanish Communists. Then it was a unit of militiamen. Its commander was Major Barbado, member of the Central Committee of the Party. Its political commissar was Enrique Castro. Like so many other old-time Communists, Castro was disillusioned by Moscow at a later stage; he has published a book which explains why he lost faith in Russian Communism.

One of the first steps after Russia began to take a hand in the Civil War was a change in the command of the Fifth Regiment. The Communists replaced Barbado by Lister, who was a typical Stalinist, always putting Russia first and Spain second—or perhaps nowhere. Like Modesto, the second of the two men on whom Russia mainly relied during the Civil War, Lister was Moscow trained in every sense. To complete their control of the Fifth Regiment, the Moscow Communists also used two leaders behind the scene. One was Major Orlov, personally delegated by Stalin, and the other, Major Carlos J. Contreras. Nowadays Contreras is known under another name; he is Vittorio Vidali, leader of the Communists in Trieste.

The Russians sought to establish the supremacy of reliable Communist detachments over all the military forces on the Spanish Republican side, through the Fifth Regiment, and also through the International Brigades which they controlled with the help of the Frenchman André Marty and the Italian Longo, who called himself Gallo in Spain. They saw to it that the Fifth was the best equipped regiment, and had ample funds, and that it enjoyed the advice and instruction of Russian technicians as well as of other foreign specialists operating under the close control of Russian agents. The Fifth Regiment was practically independent of the Defense Ministry. For that matter, it was practically independent of the Spanish Republican Government.

The Communists succeeded in terrorizing the professional soldiers who served with them. Those who played the Communist game were rewarded with promotions and glorified by the Communist press in Spain and abroad. Those who showed opposition were discarded, unless they had very strong political support. An example was the case of General Miaja. At the beginning he held out against the Communists; it was decided to remove him from his command. Then he learned of his danger and submitted to Communist direction. At once the Communist press made a favorite of him. Other officers took this object lesson to heart.

In spite of Russian determination to keep the Fifth Regiment under the control and direction of Moscow-trained leaders, it was made part of my command on the orders of Largo Caballero, with the approval of the Russian military advisers. My first shock brigade had been organized at Alcalá de Henares and included six battalions plus two companies of guerrillas. The Fifth Regiment was nominally added to this command. It was done at the time when the Russians made most of me, using my popularity with the masses they had not been able to reach otherwise. Ilya Ehrenburg wrote a series of articles about me, in which he called me "the Chapaev of the Spanish Revolution." Eventually my brigade became the Forty-Sixth Assault Division.

The arrangement by which the Fifth Regiment was in my command, but under the orders of Lister, offered more advantages to the Russian-trained Communists than to me. They were in a position to get the credit for my victories and let me take the blame for their blunders. For instance, when I took the Cerro de los Angeles, the Communist press celebrated it as Lister's victory. In fact, what he had done was to lose the position and retire to Perales de Tajuña, where he consoled himself by feasting. I had the job of regaining the ground he had lost; and then he emerged once again to reap the credit.

During that time the Russian agents, working mainly from the headquarters of the International Brigades at Madrid and Albacete, organized the execution not only of people who opposed the Communists directly, but also of those who showed reluctance in following their directives. And because the Fifth Regiment was on paper part of my command, they could pile the responsibility for a great number of those acts on me. They found it useful that the name of a commander who was a prominent Communist should inspire terror, behind the lines as well as at the front—and that this man was someone who did not belong to their inner circle. They looked further into the future than I did. I had been brought up in a school of terrorism. I did not shrink from violence. The reputation which was built up around my name did not bother me—then.

I am not pretending that I was not guilty of ugly things myself, or that I never caused needless sacrifice of human lives. I am a Spaniard. We look upon life as tragic. We despise death. The death of a bull in the ring, the death of a man in war, seems a fitting end to us. We do not torture our consciences about one or the other. Throughout the Spanish War, I held power over life and death in my hands. I do not say that I always used it wisely or even justly. I do not apologize for anything I have done.

It was a bitter war. It was not pretty on either side. But Republican excesses, such as they were, were nothing compared with Franco's. It was Franco who mobilized Moorish troops against his countrymen, and gave them free rein. And the excesses of which I may have been guilty myself were nothing compared with those of the Moscow Communists. I did not slaughter my comrades in arms for disagreeing with my political opinions.

Once the Communist caucus used me as a cover and made me arrest one of our supporters. This was when they thought Madrid lost. Modesto and Miaja called me in and told me that the colonel commanding the assault guards of the national palace—the former royal palace—had revolted against the government, and his men with him. This was astonishing news, for the assault guards, a body formed by the Republican Government in 1931, had been constantly loyal to it, in contrast to the reactionary civil guards. But I had no reason to doubt what Modesto and Miaja told me. At their request, I took some men with me and arrested the colonel and his guards. Then I handed him over to Modesto. Only later did I find out that there had been no such thing as a mutiny or revolt. The colonel's only fault was that he was neither a Communist nor the tool of Communists.

This incident left me in control of the royal palace, which had been the residence of Alfonso XIII. I found it disappointing, in spite of its enormous size. It lacked the magnificence I had expected. With my aides I went into the king's bedroom. It was decorated with splendid mirrors and gilt woodwork. Its chief piece of furniture was a huge screen. Across one of the walls stood the king's bed, also gilt, eight feet long and six feet wide, and in a recess above its head was a great crucifix.

"Well," I said to my aides, "who wants to sleep in the king's bed tonight?"

They seemed frightened by the idea, as if they felt a vague superstition. One of them said openly that it would bring bad luck.

"All right," I said, "in that case the bed of the king is for me."

And that night, El Campesino, the peasant, slept in the bed of Alfonso XIII, the last decadent sovereign of what had once been one of the most powerful empires of the world.

He had owned a very comfortable bed.

The Battle for Barcelona

*O*N *July 18, 1936, Barcelona felt immune from the conflict. All that was known for certain was that there had been a military uprising in Spanish Morocco. President Companys, the head of the Catalan Government, was not unduly alarmed by the urgent messages coming over the Madrid radio, for he was firmly convinced that General Llano de la Encomienda, in command of the garrison at Barcelona, was on the side of the Republic. An uprising in Barcelona led by the military seemed to be unthinkable. On that Saturday night, as he walked down the tree-lined avenue called the Ramblas, he was more concerned with the bloody clashes between extreme right and extreme left which had taken place every weekend since the elections earlier in the year. They were small clashes, but they were worrying.*

Companys himself had been President only for four months. Imprisoned after the Catalan nationalist uprising in October, 1934, which he had led, he was released in February when all political prisoners of the left were released. He was a lawyer, dark-faced, wiry, subtle and eloquent. In the early hours of the morning, walking with his friend, the poet Ventura Gassol, he came to the conclusion that the mood of Barcelona was one of confident watchfulness, and he returned to the Generalitat, the presidential palace, to sleep.

Yet there were disturbing signs. The Anarcho-Syndicalists had proclaimed a general strike, and all traffic was tied up. There were rumors of uprisings all over Spain. The Army, he knew, could not be relied upon in an emergency. At this moment, too, Barcelona was crowded with foreigners who had come to take part in the Olympic Games in the Montjuich stadium. The opening of the Olympic Games had been scheduled for the following morning.

The young journalist, Jaume Miravitlles, a member of the Catalan administration, kept a watchful eye on the military as he made the final arrangements for the Olympic Games:

The Olimpíada in Barcelona was conceived as a reply to the Olympic Games which were then being held in Germany. We felt that there was a great need for a gathering of athletes in a spirit of freedom and racial equality. All over Europe there were young liberals and socialists who regarded the games being held in Germany as a sham and a pretense, glorifying Hitler and the Nazis. They wanted to take part in games without the swastika banner floating overhead.

The date for the opening of the Olimpíada was set for Sunday, July 19th. Already hundreds of athletes had arrived in Barcelona, and we were faced with the problem of putting them up and finding beds for them. The first problem was easily solved: the school children were on vacation, and we were able to transform a group of schools near the Plaza de España into dormitories. The problem of finding 5,000 beds was more difficult. I went to General Llano de la Encomienda, the Captain-General of Barcelona. He offered to provide the beds, and congratulated us for bringing about the Olympic Games, "because it will assist the cause of liberty and freedom." He selected high-ranking officers of his staff to assist us, among them Captain Lizcano de la Rosa, Captain López Varela and Colonel López-Amor. They were so enthusiastic for the games that I trusted them completely. I reported their enthusiasm to President Companys, who suggested that a special commemoration medal struck in gold should be presented to the General and to his officers. These medals were presented to them on Saturday, July 18th.

The Army had offered beds, but there was still the problem of bringing them to the dormitories. The general strike paralyzed all transportation except the railways. Through the good offices of General Llano de la Encomienda the two railroad stations, the Estación de Francia and the Estación del Norte, were bursting with beds sent from all the garrisons of Spain. So there they were, filling up the railroad stations, and we had no means of transporting them to the dormitories.

We asked for help in transporting the beds, and the General promptly provided us with trucks and drivers. The Anarcho-Syndicalists regarded these truck drivers as strikebreakers. There were clashes and one truck driver was killed on the Saturday before the opening of the games.

On that same day President Companys called me into his office and showed me a leaflet which had come into his possession. "Soldiers of Spain," it began. "The scum of the earth is coming to attend the Olympic Games in Barcelona. Are we to be deprived of our beds for the benefit of these communist and socialist scum?"

Companys took the leaflet very seriously, and told me we would have to do everything to convince the people the games had no political meaning whatever. There must be no singing of the "Internationale" or "Bandera Rossa," no flying of revolutionary and political flags—only the national anthems of Spain and Catalonia were to be played, and only the Spanish Republican and Catalan flags were to be flown.

In the afternoon I went off to the stadium at Montjuich to talk to the athletes, telling them that everything would be done to prevent the games being used for political purposes. On no account was the Olimpíada to provide a pretext for a political plot. We had heard from Madrid about the uprising in Morocco. From Salamanca and Navarre more rumors were coming to us. We were beginning to wonder whether we would ever see the Olympic Games, which were to open in a few hours' time.

On that Saturday night, at ten o'clock, I went to see General de la Encomienda again. I told him it was my firm belief that the Army in Barcelona would have no part in Franco's uprising, and I hoped the games would open as scheduled. General de la Encomienda said he knew nothing about the uprising, that he was the representative of the legitimate government of Madrid, which was still in power, and that he would do everything he could to maintain stability in Catalonia. He spoke of his loyalty to the government of Catalonia, installed by the electoral will of the Catalan people, and he said he would support the government to the best of his ability. Then I spent some time talking with his staff, particularly with Lizcano de la Rosa, a good friend of mine and a very active sportsman.

"What do you think about it all, Lizcano?" I said.

"You can be absolutely sure the Army is on the side of the Madrid government," he answered. "Don't worry about the Olympic Games. We'll all be attending the inauguration tomorrow."

There was a good deal of discussion about the inauguration and various matters of organization, and it was two hours before I was able to leave the headquarters of the Captain-General. From there I went immediately to the offices of Radio Barcelona on the Calle Caspe, where I broadcast to the Catalan people, telling them that there was no doubt at all that the Olympic Games would be officially opened the following morning, without fail. "I can give you this assurance," I said, "because I have just spoken with General de la Encomienda and his officers, and they are all with us, and they will be attending the games tomorrow, wearing the gold medals presented to them by President Companys." The broadcast and conversations with friends lasted more than an hour, and I left the radio station between two and three o'clock in the morning. As director of the Olympic Games I had an apartment in the stadium at Montjuich, three or four miles away from the broadcasting station. I was walking along a quiet street, looking for a taxi, when some soldiers sprang out of the shadows. I was unceremoniously arrested, and taken to the nearby University building, filled with hundreds of other prisoners. They had all been arrested during the last quiet hour of the night.

I found my old friend, Ángel Pestaña, a syndicalist leader.

"What happened?" I asked. "What on earth is going on in Barcelona?"

"What has happened," he said calmly, "is that the Army has come out in open rebellion. They are taking positions all over the city in support of the Franco rebellion."

I could make nothing of all this. I thought of the officers I had left only a few hours before and General Llano de la Encomienda's sworn promise to defend the Republic. I thought of the Olympic Games and the care the Army had taken to find beds for the athletes. And then it occurred to me that the Army had played a trick on us, and soon all of us would be put up against a wall and shot.

I looked round at the other prisoners. Many of them had been arrested in their houses. The Army, by and large, had chosen its prisoners well. We sat there waiting, listening to the growing sound of gunfire in the night.

✺

The Army was, in fact, in open revolt, and General Llano de la Encomienda was its prisoner. About this time an artillery column

under Colonel López-Amor was marching toward the Plaza de Cata-
luña. An American observer, Lawrence Fernsworth, watched the
fighting late that night and the next morning.

From the top of the Ramblas I struck across the Plaza de Cataluña, a broad and beautifully flowered park, with its statues and
fountains banked in shrubbery, which here forms a spacious, roughly
circular plaza flanked by cafés, banks, restaurants, the American
consulate, the telephone building, which is a skyscraper ending in a
dome, and the military casino, among others. The Plaza de Cataluña
is a kind of central hub into which various avenues and paseos lead.
At the upper side the Paseo de Gracia cuts up through the center of
the newer and more open part of the town, just as from the lower
side the Ramblas cut through the older and more congested quarters.
In a way the Ramblas and the Paseo counterbalance each other.

"Will they dare? Will the military plotters dare come out of their
dark barracks where perhaps now they are getting the men drunk, the
better to handle them? Will they not be cowed by this show of resistance?"

Such were the questions which haunted me as I walked across the
plaza flecked with yellow globes of light from the lampposts. For it
seemed that the whole city was in arms against the danger that now
menaced the constituted government. Somehow I felt that this Saturday night's effervescence would pass, that Sunday would dawn bright
and clear, both rebellion and revolution vanished with the night. The
answer to my questions was "No."

I did not, therefore, feel greatly perturbed when I arrived near the
upper end of the Paseo de Garcia where it intersects with El Diagonal,
a swanky avenue so called because for several miles it cuts diagonally
across the upper part of the town straight as an arrow.

Diagonal, Paseo de Gracia, Plaza de Cataluña, and Ramblas constitute a strategical scheme of approach and access which always play
their roles on days of big parades, mass celebrations, rebellions, and
major and minor revolutions or strikes.

Now I found hundreds of Shock Police on guard here at this corner
of the Diagonal, some mounted, others afoot. More detachments were
seated drowsily about the terraces of some nearby cafés closed for
the night. It was a customary precaution to have the Shock Police out

in emergencies although I had never seen so many in one place. However, these precautions merely served to increase reassurance.

Tranquilly I turned off to the right to my house, which stood a block beyond. It was a quarter to four. From the direction of the sea the first harbingers of Sunday's dawn were already appearing.

I was tired and immediately dropped off to sleep. The sound of high-powered motorcars racing up and down the avenue broke through my slumbers. Then there was quiet. But it seemed I had been sleeping only a minute or so when shouting from the direction of the crossing of the Diagonal and the Paseo de Gracia wakened me. In reality I had been sleeping more than half an hour, and it was now four-thirty.

There were shouts from a mob and such cries as "Viva la República! Viva Azaña! Viva Cataluña!" Then there were a few shots, followed after an interval by more crackling of rifles and by revolver reports, not yet heavy or continuous.

I jumped out into the gallery facing the Diagonal. The street was deserted in the soft light of the heightening morning, except for a couple of one-horse garbage carts whose drivers had until then been quietly sweeping up the streets. Now they were frantically tugging at the bridles of their frightened horses as they found themselves caught in an increasing crossfire. With the shooting the shouting likewise grew louder. Mounted police galloped around the far corner of the block where the church stood, dashing toward the monument where I could now see the Shock Police darting cautiously back and forth and crouching, rifles aimed and spitting, in such shelter as the base of the monument afforded. Others were aiming from the tops of nearby buildings. Soon the firing was general.

A few riderless horses now galloped back wildly, in panic. Flocks of swallows, aroused out of their slumbers, swished, looped, and wheeled frantically into the picture, disappeared over housetops and returned to repeat the performance. They seemed to have gone mad. Flocks of pigeons, flying higher, performed similar antics. A howling dog tore through the street as if possessed.

Pandemonium was now general all around the block and in the adjacent streets. It was evident that a considerable battle was on. More horses, some mounted, others riderless, scurried back and forth. One policeman lost his cap, which lay in the street. Another fell off his horse, picked himself up, and ran to the wall of buildings for shelter. From the tops of the buildings opposite there was shooting by civilians, apparently sniping against the police.

Machine guns were entering the fray. Some of this shooting seemed to come from the bell tower of the fortresslike Romanesque church at the corner of my block, known as La Carmelita. Because of the diagonal slant of the street it was hidden from the front gallery view, but it protruded into the back patios so that from my back gallery I could have a grandstand view of the tower and most of the nave as well as the adjacent convent.

Still looking across the Diagonal now, watching the scene from behind the half-opened shutters, which folded and swung outward on hinges—for it seemed no longer prudent to stand in full view—I observed that all the shutters of the opposite houses were tightly closed and they seemed deserted except for the men shooting from the flat, parapeted roofs. Policemen had entered these buildings, and their blue uniforms could be seen moving behind the parapets and the chimneys, so that it was obvious they had driven out or killed off the snipers. Looking along the avenue, to the left toward the sea, I saw a column of artillery crossing, evidently bound toward the center of the city.

I was far from clear as to what was happening and still discounted the idea of a military rising. My first thought was that it was another Anarcho-Syndicalist revolution.

But by telephoning other journalists and my various sources I soon got an outline of the real facts. As by preconcerted signal, said my reports, the regiments quartered in the city had marched out from their various barracks and were now engaged in a full-fledged rebellion. A column several thousand strong had come down the Diagonal from Pedralbes bent on marching down the Paseo de Gracia to the Plaza de Cataluña. There some of them were to seize the telephone building and various strategic edifices, while others were to proceed down the Ramblas where reinforcements from other barracks would join them. The object was to capture the government buildings and the city hall which lay off the Ramblas to the left, just behind the cathedral. Farther on near the port were the general military headquarters and the palace of the civil governor. Other rebel regiments were engaged in an attempt to take these from the loyal defenders. From that direction already came the cannonading of artillery.

By that time I realized that a real revolution was on. I rushed to the front gallery and saw the blue-coated Shock Police engaged with men in khaki uniforms, evidently officers and soldiers. But it was apparent that most of the soldiers had been driven off and prevented from marching down the Paseo de Gracia. They were rushing and clashing in the streets along the sides and back of the block where my view was cut off.

My office opened on the back gallery and the din made it evident that the battle had shifted to the back streets near here. Across a roof I caught a glimpse of a pitched battle in the street. But more immediately interesting was the fact that bullets were now flying furiously in both directions across the open space on which I looked. On the back street a dismantled printing plant, four or five stories high, ran almost across the block. Invisible men were stationed in it and shooting in the direction of the tall, square bell tower rising from a rear corner of the church and looking into the court. From a square niche near the top of the tower a machine gun was spitting furiously. Bullets from the hidden riflemen spattered around this opening digging into the masonry and scattering splinters. Bullets came so close to my gallery that I could hear them whistle. One came very near to me and at the same time I heard shouts seemingly from beyond the church tower. Two civil guards were waving to me to get off the gallery, which simultaneously I had decided would be a good thing to do. An attack was evidently being made from both sides, but the church tower was impregnable to anything short of artillery fire. Like many another church and its tower, this one had evidently been built after the manner of a fortress with well planned intention. What puzzled me was how the rebels had managed to gain entry to the church with so many shock police everywhere on guard. Later it developed they had entered the church with their machine guns and an ample supply of ammunitions the evening before.

The fighting died down and then came a lull—almost complete silence. It lasted some two hours.

A few people began to appear in the streets—families with their baskets of lunch. Barcelona folk have the habit of going into the country on Sundays via the electric lines for a day by a stream. Droves of them can be seen every fine Sunday morning beginning about five o'clock. Revolution and turmoil seldom deter them. But today there were only a few, evidently trusting that the electric line was still running; trusting also to escape the turmoil. You could never tell about these revolutions. Sometimes it would be all over after the first spurt. At other times the lull was merely the prelude to the renewal of battle with redoubled intensity. . . . Later some of the would-be picnickers came straggling back and you knew that exit from the city was cut off. The pedestrians who crossed the streets held both hands high in the air, in one a white handkerchief to show they were noncombatants.

At about seven o'clock I went out to inspect the scene and get about the city as much as I could. I met a Catalan friend on a similar mission. We inspected the nearer end of the street in which the explosions had been and saw that most of the trees on one side had been splintered off four or five feet from the ground.

"Looks bad," said my friend. "They must have come along here throwing bombs. That would mean that the Anarchists are on the rampage, trying to create terror under cover of the military uprising and seize the power for themselves."

Over by the monument I saw dead horses lying about and splotches of blood drying on the pavement where the wounded had been taken away. The stone walls of many buildings were broken and chipped by bullets. Empty cartridges and bandoliers were lying about everywhere. Against a wall the Guardia de Asalto, as the Shock Police are called, had already placed a bouquet of flowers where one of their comrades had fallen. During two and one half years thereafter, whenever I passed that place, there were fresh flowers in an earthenware vase by the wall.

To the left from the Paseo de Gracia, where one of the side streets ran in the direction of the Ritz, was a field piece in the hands of the citizen militia. On the way toward it I came across ten dead horses piled on top of each other along the curb and on the sidewalk. It was a ghastly sight. The field gun had been captured from the artillery column that I had seen marching toward the center of town a few hours before. From militiamen and others I now learned what had happened.

The officers of the artillery column had professed to be favorable to the republic and had come out to defend it against the rebels. This ruse was repeated in various parts of the city during the day and for a time it worked. On this pretense the officers had induced a lorry of armed Anarchists to lead the forces through the street, thereby guaranteeing its safety. However, when the officers considered themselves sufficiently advanced and safe, they disarmed the Anarchists and continued onward to join their fellow rebels.

But when they arrived near the Ritz they were rushed by Shock Police and citizens. Many citizens went into the fray armed with staves or only with their bare hands. The officers scurried to shelter in a doorway. Little valiance was shown anywhere by officers. Cowardice and treachery were the outstanding characteristics of their movement. The treachery had begun when they first harangued the enlisted men in the barracks, telling them that the republic was endangered by an Anarchist-Communist uprising and that the army was going out to defend the Republic. They then plied the troops with liquor to give them false courage and make them easier to handle. Most of the soldiers now on the march were quite drunk.

When the officers of this particular column rushed for shelter a sergeant tried to save it against the loyalists' attacks. The rear finally surrendered while the front continued fighting. Several guns had been captured by the loyal forces. A lone policeman manning a machine gun played havoc with the front of the column, shooting horses from under them—the same horses that a few moments ago I had seen lying dead. In this way the entire column was routed.

I did not go down to the field gun because the men in charge waved me off and some armed civilians told me it would be dangerous to advance as bullets were flying.

Then I went down to the Plaza de Cataluña. Here the fighting was resumed with intensity. The well-known Hotel Colón, facing the plaza, had become a rebel stronghold, and was being used as a base in an attempt to capture the telephone building. A brisk machine-gun fire was going on across the plaza.

It was particularly brisk from the military casino and clubhouse to the left. You could see the rifles flash from the windows. A huge American flag was flying over the street from the American consulate diagonally across the plaza from the hotel. Somewhat earlier in the day the acting consul general, Lynn W. Franklyn, had managed to get to the consulate afoot and return, but that would be impossible now.

I decided to investigate the situation about the Plaza de la Universidad, another parklike square in front of the university building. It was about four blocks off. There seemed to be considerable fighting over that way and men were posted everywhere in the streets.

About two blocks from the university I was stopped by Shock Police stationed in a doorway who ordered me to go to the university, keeping my hands in the air. "Everyone who passes by here must go to the university to be investigated."

The university was apparently a loyal Republican stronghold. After reaching it through a gantlet of armed sentinels I was surprised to see a large number of army officers and soldiers. A major in a steel helmet, a tough rotund face black with unshaven bristles, in a hard-boiled manner demanded my documentation and other explanations. A sergeant was ordered to search me. The major's manner continued far from pleasant but he told me I could proceed, keeping my hands in the air and turning sharply to the right at the university corner. I was stopped briefly at various places in the streets by sentinels who seemed mere boys and all of whom cautioned me of danger.

I could not quite understand this spectacle of Shock Police and citizen militia cooperating with the army. Had the Shock Police gone over to the rebels? Such swift changes sometimes occurred. Or were these troops aiding the government?

But it was the same old story, as I learned later. The troops, whose officers pretended to be loyal, had gained access to the university and won the cooperation of the loyal forces to further their rebellion. The young armed sentinels I encountered as I left were Carlist rebels working with the army. By this ruse the army conspirators were able to have some important Republican personages walk unwittingly into their nets. Later, when their treachery was discovered, they had to appeal to these same prisoners to save their own lives.

Although fighting was still going on, and would continue for the next two or three days, it became evident by late afternoon that the constituted government was the victor.

The Catalan Government was able to announce on July 22nd that "the battle for Barcelona had been won by the armed people." The battle was won, but among the many exhausting and dangerous results was the huge supply of weapons which had fallen into the hands of

the Anarchists. Henceforth their power rivaled that of the govern-
ment, which was compelled to take orders from the Anarchist leaders.
President Companys was to remain in the Generalitat until the end
of the war, but only by the exercise of an almost superhuman skill in
walking a tightrope.

Inevitably there were reprisals. The Army leaders were put on trial
and shot. Among them was General Manuel Goded, Captain-General
of the Balearic Islands, with headquarters in Palma, Majorca, who
was ordered by Franco to assume command in Catalonia.

Jaume Miravitlles, who became Secretary-General of the Central
Committee of the Anti-Fascist Militia shortly after being released
from his prison in the University building, describes the fate of the
Army leaders:

General Goded was a small, thin man with gray eyes and the very
fair skin to be found among Spanish aristocrats. Contemptuous of
politicians, he believed firmly that only the Army could produce men
capable of ruling the country. To us, he was always icily polite. We
came to know him well, for on the second day of the fighting in Barcelona he flew from Palma to take command in Catalonia, and he
was arrested by our *milicianos* as he stepped off the plane.

No one could blame him for not knowing the real situation. We
did not know it ourselves. Thirty-six hours passed before we were
able to bring some order into the situation with the creation of the
Central Committee of the Anti-Fascist Militia, representing all the
major parties in Catalonia. As the representative of Esquerra, the
Catalan nationalist party headed by Companys, I was appointed
Secretary-General of the Committee. There were no Communists on
the committee, for the Communist Party was weak in Catalonia, poll-
ing only 900 votes in the election of 1933. Buenaventura Durruti was
one of the three members appointed by the FAI, the Anarchist Party.
The Catalan nationalists came to the committee meetings armed with
fountain pens. Durruti and his associates were armed with hand
grenades, revolvers and tommy guns. Fighting was still going on, and
we could hear machine-gun fire.

Once I wrote an article saying there was little difference between
Fascists and FAIists. Durruti, a magnificent, ferocious specimen of

a man, remembered the article well. He came up to me, put his great fists on my shoulders, and said: "So you're Miravitlles. Be careful! Don't play with fire! It may cost you a great deal."

So, in this atmosphere of tension and threats, the Central Committee of the Anti-Fascist Militia opened its proceedings.

Meanwhile General Goded was our prisoner, and his capture was a matter of considerable importance. In those days there still seemed to be a possibility of stamping out the insurrection. The people of Madrid had taken the Montaña barracks by storm, Bilbao had declared for the Republic, and we were clearly winning in Barcelona. The fate of Saragossa, Oviedo and Seville was still in doubt, but the news looked hopeful. President Companys was hoping to use General Goded as a trump card to force the surrender of the rebels all over Spain.

Because of his rank and prestige General Goded was not thrown into prison, but kept as a personal prisoner in the palace of the Generalitat. There were many meetings between Goded and Companys. Sometimes the General's coldness and his affection of superiority would melt a little, and he would discuss Spanish history and lament the social catastrophes which from time to time were visited upon Spain. We saw him often, for he sat with us at the President's table, a strange visitor from the enemy camp. During the course of our conversations there was never any direct reference to his status. Was he under arrest? Was he an official resident in the palace of the Generalitat? Would he be liberated after a while and permitted to leave the country? Nobody referred to these subjects. In a passive kind of way we had the feeling that his life would probably be spared. We had not counted on the power of the Anarchists.

From the beginning Companys worked on Goded to make him admit the failure of the insurrectionary movement. I was present when Companys said: "You know, my General, that the *coup d'état* has failed. Madrid, Bilbao and Barcelona have declared for the Republic, and you must be perfectly aware that no political movement in Spain can resist the power of that historical triangle. I advise you to tell your friends to put down their arms."

Goded listened politely. I had the feeling that he would resist a public declaration of failure with the last atom of his strength.

"I did the same thing," Companys went on, "after our rebellion of October 6, 1934. After one night of shooting and hundreds of dead lying in the streets of Barcelona I realized that victory was hopeless, and that continuing the fight would only mean many more sacrifices by the people. I went to the radio and told the Catalans to accept defeat and to return to their homes. I am advising you to do the same, speaking not as a politician but as a human being. When a rebellion is lost, it is a crime to go on fighting."

They were very different—the President and the General. They were both in their fifties, but that is all they had in common. They were like people from different universes. The General was pale, the President was olive-skinned. The General was austere and tight-lipped, the President voluble and quick-witted. Companys was a liberal, a romantic, a lawyer who had defended Anarchists in the courts without fee, and had been thrown into jail many times under the dictatorship of Primo de Rivera. Women worshipped him, and the masses were spellbound by his speeches. He was warm, friendly, cordial. The General looked at him from the heights of his aristocratic disdain, and at first he refused to accept all the President's arguments. The General regarded the question of surrender as one affecting his military honor, and he was not particularly impressed by the argument that if the fighting went on there would be needless victims. After all, he was a soldier.

But gradually he mellowed. There were a few places in Barcelona where the rebels were still holding out. He offered to telephone to the commanders of these garrisons, ordering them to lay down their arms. This was not precisely what Companys had in mind. He wanted a public declaration, not a private message to isolated garrisons. He wanted a declaration of such scope that it could be broadcast throughout Spain and be a decisive factor in the war. This conversation lasted two or three hours. Repeatedly General Goded affirmed that his tradition of military honor prevented him from making a public declaration urging the rebels to surrender. He would not do it. He would resist to the very end.

There were five of us in the room: Companys, Goded, Tarradellas, Gassol and myself. It was fascinating to watch the General's face while his sense of honor struggled with his sense of humanity. Thin and pale, with courtly manners, hating us with a cold and bitter hatred, he weighed the evidence of defeat in his mind. Companys brought more arguments in an effort to sway him. Finally the General capitulated. He offered to make the broadcast we wanted, and a transmitter was set up inside the Generalitat. In a clear voice heavy with emotion he said: "I, General Goded, am talking to you, not as a prisoner but as a Spaniard, and I urge you to accept defeat and lay down your arms." His short and very moving speech was recorded on gramophone records and sent to radio stations all over the country, wherever the Republican Government was still in power. It was broadcast repeatedly in Madrid, Valencia, and Bilbao. The speech caused consternation among the rebels, and its effectiveness was proved the very next day when garrisons in Valencia and Madrid, which had been fighting, offered to surrender.

President Companys always believed that General Goded's life should be spared because he had performed an act so contradictory to his sense of honor and because the consequences of his speech were momentous and led to the saving of so many lives, at least momentarily. Companys felt that it was a question of honor to spare him, no matter what the consequences. But within forty-eight hours of the outbreak, the government of Catalonia no longer governed. Anarchist and socialist armed bands had captured the military supplies of the garrisons, and the city was in their hands. An authentic revolutionary force, aided by the dregs of society which infest every large port, was in command, and the government of President Companys was like a small island in a sea of violence, unable to exert its power, at the mercy of vast forces released by the revolution.

When the Anarchists came to learn that Goded was the personal prisoner of the President and living in the presidential palace, they demanded his surrender. The President at first refused, feeling that Goded had given effective assistance to the cause of liberty through his speech. The Anarchists however saw in Goded only the symbol of the reactionary forces of the enemy, and demanded that he should be put on trial. For some days the fate of Goded wavered in the balance, but when the Anarchists threatened to murder the President and all the members of his government unless Goded was surrendered to them, and when it appeared that the Anarchist threats had to be taken seriously, Goded was surrendered to them. He was removed to a prison ship in the harbor, and later put on trial for his life.

Companys knew he was only President in name. He told us: "A

government is a very complex body clinging together by custom and tradition. When a revolutionary movement arises, then the chief of the government is no longer the effective ruler. He presses a button, but nothing happens. He gives an order, but no one obeys. I tried to save the life of General Goded, but at this particular moment of revolutionary history I was powerless. We could have fought the Anarchists, but how would that have helped us to win the war against Franco?"

General Goded was shot at the fortress of Montjuich in September. About the same time four other officers were shot. These were the men who led the insurrection, the same men with whom I had worked to organize the Olimpíada Popular—Foix, Lizcano de la Rosa, López-Amor, López Varela. I knew all of them well, but I was closest to Lizcano de la Rosa, the handsome young officer in charge of training the Mozos de Escuadra. This was a group of about four hundred soldiers forming an elite corps and serving in their traditional costume as a kind of presidential guard.

When I heard that these officers were in prison, I immediately went to see them. On the evening before the insurrection they had spoken of their complete loyalty to the Republic and they were loud in their protestations of friendship. I had trusted them, and now I was bitter.

"Why did you do this to me?" I asked Lizcano de la Rosa. "I am not reproaching you for being on the other side of the barricades, because civil war is after all a national tradition. I am hurt, because we were friends, and you used our friendship to hoodwink me."

He was quiet for a while, and then he said: "In a war of this kind we must use all means—even friendship—to attain our ends. The most important of our weapons was surprise. If we had failed to hoodwink you, we would have been betraying our revolution."

So I left him, and put him out of my mind. At the inevitable trial he was sentenced to death, together with the other three officers, and I would have heard no more of the matter if he had not sent to me on the day before the execution a message saying: "You are the only friend I have left in the world. Please be with me during the last moments of my life." I could not refuse the request. I attended the execution.

The prisoners were brought ashore from the prison ship at six o'clock in the morning. They wore their officers' uniforms, but without insignia. They wore open collars, and were bareheaded. Lizcano de la Rosa came up to me and said: "Jaume, I am very happy to see you here." His manner, his voice, the way he looked at me showed that he was a man of courage, but there was a rictus on his face which was already the rictus of death, and his skin was green, absolutely green. He was being faithful to the long-standing Spanish tradition of the condemned man who says: "Dear God, give my flesh the strength not to betray my soul."

With the others he was taken by truck to the fortress of Montjuich. A military guard, officers of the militia, and members of the government accompanied the truck. Fifty yards from the wall they were removed from the truck. They could see the coffins, painted black, in which they would be buried.

Three of them stood against the wall, a fourth sat in a chair. This officer, who had been severely wounded, was López Varela. First in the line was Lizcano de la Rosa, then came López-Amor, then López Varela, then Foix. The last was perhaps the most impressive, for he looked at us with an expression of absolute contempt, very calm and smoking a cigarette. I am sure he felt he was dying for a worthy cause and regarded all the rest of us as the representatives of the Devil. He possessed an enviable serenity.

The man in the chair was praying and telling the beads of the rosary in his hands.

The right arm of López-Amor was flung up in the Fascist salute. He was the colonel who had led the insurrectionary forces through the streets of Barcelona.

In front of the condemned men stood the firing squad, and behind the firing squad were now gathered hundreds of *milicianos* and representatives from the unions.

At the moment when the officer gave the order to fire, Lizcano de la Rosa, who had been gazing at me in a way which suggested that he wanted to perpetuate his whole life in a single look, shouted: *"Viva España!"* and all the *milicianos* shouted back: *"Viva!"* and these cries were suddenly interrupted by a fantastic fusillade, as the *milicianos* joined the seven men of the firing squad in shooting at the condemned men. Everyone seemed to be shooting at the four officers. And when the shooting was over, the condemned men could no longer be recognized, they were shot to pieces, and it was almost impossible to put their bodies, which now possessed the consistency of a liquid, into the waiting coffins.

I was standing only ten yards from the wall. I was sorry and sick at heart, and walked away.

The Alcázar

*S*OME *forty miles from Madrid, on a great bluff bordered on three sides by the Tagus, stands the ancient city of Toledo, famous for its great Cathedral, its swordsmiths, and the paintings of El Greco. On the highest ground of the city there used to stand the medieval palace-fortress called the Alcázar. With its four towers and vast courtyards, it dominated the city and all the plain around. Here, on July 18th, a small force of Nationalists numbering about 1,300 men, of whom about 800 were Civil Guards, took refuge under the command of Colonel José Moscardó, the director of the Escuela Central de Gimnasia. With them went some 600 women and children, and perhaps 250 left-wing hostages who were later shot.*

The heroic defense of the Cadets of the Alcázar became legendary, but according to Colonel Moscardó's own account of the siege there were never more than 40 Cadets in the building. From the beginning the defense seemed hopeless. Repeatedly the Republican forces under Colonel Asensio attempted to take the fortress by storm. They tried to starve out the defenders, and carved mines in the rock beneath the fortress walls in an effort to blow it up. They sprayed the walls with gasoline, and tossed hand grenades at them, and kept up a constant fire. They turned the Alcázar into rubble, but the defenders continued their resistance in the underground galleries. Finally, on September 27th, a Nationalist column under Colonel José Enrique Varela succeeded in raising the siege. No prisoners were taken, and the streets were soon running with blood down to the city gates.

The following account of the siege of the Alcázar is given in Colonel Moscardó's own words:

On July 18th I was in Madrid, preparing to go to Berlin for the Olympic Games as director of the School of Gymnastics. While in Madrid I received news of the revolt of the African garrisons—the signal for the beginning of our Sacred Crusade. So I immediately gave up the idea of journeying to Berlin and returned quickly to Toledo, where I arrived at about three o'clock in the afternoon. At once I circulated orders for everyone to take up their positions, as we had previously arranged.

I established my headquarters in the building of the Military Government, though during the day we met in the Alcázar. The military government building had direct communication with the Alcázar without passing through the streets of the town.

We immediately undertook to organize the many volunteers and the occupation of the strategical points of the town. Among these strategic points was the armaments factory garrisoned by a Madrid regiment, reinforced at my orders by Civil Guards. The School of Gymnastics, which lies outside Toledo on the road to Madrid, was garrisoned by students, and this too was reinforced by the Civil Guards.

On the evening of July 18th the Communist deputy "La Pasionaria" broadcast a speech summoning the masses to march under arms through the streets. When this broadcast came to an end, the Reds in Toledo marched out of their meeting places in the direction of the central square, the Plaza de Zocodover. From the streets leading into this square they began shooting at the Civil Guards, who were standing in the doorways. They wounded three. The shots could be heard in the Alcázar, and I went down with a number of officers, all armed, to the square. I repelled the aggressors, caused the deaths of two of them, and there were also several wounded: these were abandoned by the enemy. I was next informed that members of the Falange and the Acción Popular were surrounded in a building owned by the latter. I ordered that they should be liberated, and this was done. They were taken to the Alcázar, where we proceeded to arm and organize.

A special situation existed between the Civil Governor and the Army: a declaration of war was therefore unnecessary. We continued to organize the occupation and defence of Toledo according to plan. By July 21st, with the aid of trucks coming from all the district centers, we were able to concentrate in Toledo all the forces from the Civil Guard headquarters throughout the province. The Civil Guards were able to bring their wives and household goods.

I was informed by telephone from the Civil Governor of Toledo that a socialist deputy had arrived with an order from the Central Government placing him in charge of arming the cavalry students and the Civil Guard. While this matter was still under consideration he was ordered to go up to the Alcázar. However, the deputy thought it wiser to return immediately to Madrid. No doubt he believed it unlikely that his mission would be crowned with success, and there was also of course the real danger that he would be held as a hostage. By this time the authorities in Madrid had become suspicious of the attitude of the military government in Toledo. Meanwhile, there was still no declaration of war. From the War Office in Madrid there came telephoned orders to form a convoy of all the ammunition at the armaments factory. The convoy was to be escorted by two hundred Civil Guards.

To gain time, I asked for orders in writing. The man on the telephone said he was Sarabia (the minister of war) in person, but I answered that he might be somebody else, and that this matter was of such far-reaching importance that I insisted on absolute certainty regarding the person and the order. All this exasperated the authorities in Madrid, who gave orders over the telephone in every imaginable tone. In view of the existing tension the declaration of a state of war was decided upon on the 21st, when the ammunition was of course transferred to the Alcázar. From that moment began the siege of the Alcázar. The Civil Governor, together with his entire family and some persons with left-wing political tendencies, were held as hostages.

In spite of the declaration of a state of war, a Red airplane appeared and threw down on the city proclamations addressed to the troops, telling them they were free and no longer owed obedience to their commanders and could return to their own homes. These proclamations had no effect whatsoever. Another airplane came over and threw several bombs on the Alcázar and its surroundings.

Next, the outposts were attacked by forces sent from Madrid under the command of General Riquelme, who was ordered to occupy Toledo and force us into submission.

The School of Gymnastics, which lies on the Madrid road, was not at all suited for defence. The men concentrated there were accordingly transferred to the María Cristina Orphanage, where there were a number of students and professors. Later, in the face of growing pressure from the enemy, it became necessary to transfer all of them to the Talavera Hospital where conditions for defence were more favorable. Resistance was maintained at these outposts until lack of food and ammunition made it impossible. Then, in the most perfect order, first evacuating the sick and the aged, these forces retired to the Alcázar in the afternoon of the 22nd, having resisted the army of Madrid which was supplied with all the implements of war including artillery and bombers. During the last forty-eight hours of its resistance, this detachment fought alone. Meanwhile the armaments factory had surrendered to a corporal sent to parley by General Riquelme. Together with the hospital this armaments factory formed our advance line, and as there existed no means of communication with the factory the hospital provided our only connecting link. The factory had better defences and disposed of more forces than the hospital. We thought it was still in our possession even after it had surrendered to the enemy without a struggle.

The personnel assembled in the Alcázar comprised:

MEN

Commanders and other officers	100
Civil Guards	800
Cadets (Academies)	150
Cadets (School of Gymnastics)	40
Falange, Acción Popular and others	200

In all, there were some 1,300, of whom 1,200 were in charge of defence, while the non-combatants attending to the other services took no part in defence.

To this garrison must be added:

Women	550
Children	50

These consisted mainly of the families of the Civil Guards and of some professors of the Academy, and a number of Toledans who sought refuge at the Alcázar: the total population of the fortress amounting to some two thousand souls.

MATERIAL

For the defence of the Alcázar we depended upon the armaments of the Civil Guards, of the Academy, the School of Gymnastics, the Assault Guards, and the Special Security Police, who together had about one thousand, two hundred rifles and muskets. The Academy had two mountain guns with a supply of fifty shells. There were thirteen Hotchkiss 7 mm. machine-guns, and thirteen quick-firing guns of the same make and caliber, all of them being used in the instruction of the cadets. There was a 55 mm. mortar.

We had the ammunition from the Alcázar, and the ammunition transferred from the armament factory, altogether amounting to some 800,000 cartridges for rifles and machine-guns; fifty 7 cm. shells; fifty Valero mortar shells of 51 cm.; four cases of Lafitte hand grenades; one case of incendiary hand grenades No. 25, and some 100 small bombs, and one electric explosive charge. As for defensive material against gas attacks there was none. The students of chemistry from the Academy disposed of twenty-five gas masks, but each one was a different model, and most of them were of no practical use at all.

Material for fortification. There were only a few pickaxes and shovels belonging to the Academy, for no engineering school was attached to it.

Material for communications. During the first days we used the automatic telephone, but after the beginning of the siege this was cut by the enemy. Later, for use inside the fortress, we installed some military field lines connecting the most important points. The Civil Guards were able to bring the transmitting radio station from their headquarters, but it ceased to work after the electricity was cut, since we had no batteries.

Material for establishing communication with outside was available in the Academy, but without electricity the field radios could not be used. With great effort we succeeded in combining all the car batteries and setting up a receiving station with auriculars, which permitted us to get news from outside.

For sanitary material we used the stores from the Academy infirmary and the drugs from the military stores within the defence lines. We had sufficient supplies until a comparatively advanced stage of the siege, and at the end there were even some bandages and cotton wool left over.

PROVISIONS

These were scarce from the beginning. Normally the Academy had a considerable stock of provisions, but because of the decrease of infantry and cavalry cadets to about seventy, and because the National Movement took place during the summer vacations, supplies were very low, there being only small quantities of the most necessary things such as beans, peas, rice, olive oil, salt, sugar, coffee, spices, etc. Apart from these there were some bottles of good wine, tins of anchovy, asparagus, and mussels.

Because these provisions were insufficient to solve our food problem, I ordered that none of them should be touched except as compensation for those who had worked excessively hard or in case of illness, when some of the stronger wine, the vermouth, or the tinned food might be provided. There was a sufficient supply of bread to last five or six days. There was no Commissariat, but we had a contract with a private bakery. As soon as the siege began, of course the bakery ceased to supply us with provisions.

Water was rationed in order to avoid any waste. There was however enough in the different cisterns of the Alcázar to ensure the necessary supply of this vital element. Nevertheless it was continually inspected and removed to different places in order to avoid its loss through artillery or air bombardment.

We had first planned to overcome the bread shortage by eating up the supply of inferior wheat used to feed cattle, and this we had already begun to do, counting on our stores of barley for cattle in case of need. Fortunately we discovered a deposit of wheat belonging to a Bank on the eastern side of the Alcázar. There were two thousand sacks of wheat, of ninety kilograms each, of excellent quality. With this providential find, together with the horses and mules belonging to the Academy and the Civil Guards, we hoped to solve the food problem—though in a very precarious manner—until the end of the siege. The bread ration, allowing for the dimensions of the field oven, did not reach 180 grams per person owing to the large number of mouths to feed and the small amount we were able to grind in a corn mill we found in the Administration Museum.

As the siege went on, the meat had to be severely rationed, and when the siege ended we were left with one horse and five mules. These would have supplied us with scanty rations for another six days at the most.

We were concentrated within the Alcázar from July 18th, and after that date no one went down into the town except on rare and urgent occasions, but the beginning of the siege really dated from July 22nd, when the last forces on duty outside the perimeter retired into the Alcázar. Some guards failed to retreat, because the Reds were already in Toledo.

The last day of the siege was September 28th 1936. On that day the Nationalist troops entered Toledo and we left the Alcázar. On the previous day, however, some of the liberating forces, including a company of Regulars from Tetuán and the Fifth Regiment of the Legion, had already entered. They spent the night in the Alcázar.

From the beginning of the siege crossfire from rifles and machine-guns was nearly incessant, though of varying intensity. It increased towards midday and diminished towards evening.

We suffered two military assaults intended to carry the enemy within the Alcázar. On one of these assaults, on September 18th, the enemy succeeded in climbing the ruins of the north façade where they fastened a red flag. Driven back, they renewed the assault three times, but with diminishing strength each time. Finally they desisted, and the attack died down. There was only the daily crossfire, a little heavier than usual.

The artillery, too, kept up an almost permanent fire. During the first days the enemy employed a battery of 7.5 cm., which they soon increased to one of 10.5 cm. But seeing the small material effect they were causing on the Alcázar, they brought up two pieces of 15.5 cm. which they placed in the Dehesa de Pinedo some 3,500 meters from the Alcázar and close to the road from Madrid.

At first they fired only during the day: at seven o'clock in the morning, then about noon, and finally about half-past five in the afternoon. The duration of each barrage was about an hour.

As the siege continued and the resistance inside the Alcázar did not diminish, the Reds increased the number of their pieces of artillery as well as the intensity of their fire. Finally, they continued the bombardment at night, and for this purpose they illuminated the Alcázar by means of powerful searchlights.

Towards the end of the siege they were using two 10.5 cm. batteries, and two 7.5 cm. batteries. There were some light 7 cm. cannon, two of 15.5 cm. mounted in the Dehesa de Pinedo, five of 15.5 cm. in Los Alijares. Besides these they employed two anti-aircraft guns, one an army piece, the other a naval gun. All of these were used for firing on the Alcázar.

On or about August 18th they began to fire with the 15.5 cm. pieces from Pinedo, and within three days they fired 98 shells. During the last days of the siege they fired as many as 478 shells in a single day, the total number of 15.5 cm. strikes effected during the siege being calculated pretty exactly at 3,500, and there were some 10,000 shells fired from the smaller guns. They never attacked with mortars. Occasionally they shot a few mortar shells onto the east terrace and one or two into the central courtyard. Had they known how to employ this weapon, they could have caused far greater damage to the defenders, but either they did not understand how to use it or else they were unable to calculate its effects.

The enemy aviation attacked the Alcázar almost daily, though with only a few planes. They dropped bombs of 12 and 50 kilograms which caused little material damage except in the case of the Capuchin monastery which entirely disappeared as a result of the aerial bombardment.

Beside the bombs they threw cans filled with gasoline: the idea was to set fire to the Alcázar. These attempts were fruitless. After eight attacks of this kind, they gave up.

They also attacked us with tear gas bombs dropped from planes onto the inner courtyard or onto the roofs and adjoining streets. These bombs caused considerable annoyance; but annoyance gave place to joy when we learned they were not poison gas bombs, as we had feared.

They also employed every kind of incendiary weapon and inflammable liquid, and these were thrown with slings from the Hospital of Santa Cruz. They fell on the military administration building, the pavilions of the courtyard, the drug-store and the stables belonging to the Academy, which formed a single building within the defence perimeter. They also sprayed gasoline through hoses, directing the jets of gasoline on the barracks and on the north façade of the Alcázar, without gaining any important advantage.

Because they were unable to destroy the fine spirit of patriotism of those who defended the Alcázar and the honor of Spain, the enemy finally resorted to underground warfare. They could mine the Alcázar with impunity, for we possessed no means of preventing them.

In all they constructed three mines. One started from a house in Juan Labrador Street and then branched off. Another ended under the southwest tower of the Alcázar. A third was dug under the foundations of the west façade, very near the carriage entrance. They charged these mines with 3,000 kilograms of powder each, and after evacuating the civil population to the nearby mountains, they detonated them electrically on September 18th 1936, causing enormous damage to the building. Miraculously there were only five casualties among the defenders. They had planned the final storming of the Alcázar on this day, and everything was therefore prepared with the greatest care.

The artillery preparations began at six in the morning when the 15.5 cm. batteries on Alicares hill fired some 90 projectiles against the east façade in the hope that the women, children and sick persons lodged there would be forced to transfer to the opposite or western side. At 6:21 A.M., believing that the artillery attack had produced the desired effect, they sprang the mines. Five minutes later, when the gases were dispersed, they threw themselves with all available force against the fortress, attacking in two directions. The first attack took place against the north façade which they reached by taking a zigzag path under cover of the ruins of the Hotel Imperial. The second attack was directed against the south wing, where the mess rooms and food stores were kept. They evidently believed that the defenders were at the end of their resources. Not for an instant, however, did any of the defenders leave their posts, and we drove the enemy back in spirited counter-attacks during the course of that memorable day.

Then they constructed another mine and sprang it on September 27th when our troops were already on the heights commanding Toledo from the north. Because our troops were advancing, and there was little time for the work, they made use of a sewer which opens on Pabellones Street and approaches the Alcázar by way of the north-east tower. However, they were unable to arrive at the foundations, for the mine was too short. It had no effect. It certainly produced a crater of some 30 meters in width and 4 meters in depth, but there were no casualties on our side.

While the defenders were concentrated within the Alcázar, they were called upon daily to surrender. These messages were received by telephone. The first to call up was General Pozas who, as soon as he realized that neither the ammunition supplies nor the two hundred Civil Guards were leaving the fortress, threatened to destroy the Alcázar completely "with not one stone left standing." Then on July 21st General Riquelme telephoned and demanded an immediate surrender. He also demanded an explanation of our attitude. I replied that we took the position of all honorable men in view of the disasters which the Marxist government was bringing down on Spain, and that we were absolutely in accord with General Franco and wholly unwilling to see the ammunition belonging to the Academy and the Civil Guards delivered up to the rabble, to serve as weapons against us. General Riquelme insisted that our attitude was absurd, and promised to take active steps in the matter. I told the General that we preferred to die than to see the Alcázar transformed into a dung heap, as he proposed, by surrendering it to the enemies of our country. On the following day Barnés, the Minister of Education, tried to shake us from our patriotic duty by saying that resistance on our part would cause great damage to the city of Toledo, "this precious jewel," and we should bear this in mind, since it was certain that if we continued with our present attitude, violent measures would have to be adopted. He said he hoped things would not come to this, and he looked upon our attitude with sympathy, "considering it rather childish than otherwise." I replied that we could not conceivably change our attitude, and we would refuse to surrender to anybody or anything, in our determination to save the country by our efforts.

On the afternoon of July 23rd the telephone rang. I was summoned. I lifted the receiver and heard the commander of the Toledo militia speaking in a thundering voice.

"I hold you responsible for all the crimes and all that is happening in Toledo," he said. "I give you ten minutes to surrender the Alcázar. If you do not surrender, I shall have your son Luis, who is standing here beside me, shot."

"I don't believe it," I said.

"To prove my words, he will now come to the telephone."

I heard my son say: "Father!"

"What is it, my boy?"

"Nothing. They say if you don't surrender, they will shoot me."

"Well then, commend your soul to God and die like a true patriot, crying 'Long live Christ the King' and 'Long live Spain.' "

"I give you a hearty embrace, Father."

I said to the commander of the militia: "You may save yourself the truce of ten minutes which you gave me, and shoot my son. The Alcázar will never surrender!"

During the following days a number of civilians and members of the Civil Guard including a lieutenant—these were people who were unable to join us—tried to speak to us from the street. We paid little attention to them, as they always referred to our unconditional surrender.

On September 8th 1936, at about six o'clock in the evening, we heard from a megaphone posted on one of the houses of the south façade that a certain Major Rojo desired to speak to me. Imagining he was a "Red" Major, we paid no attention to him, saying that we refused to speak to anybody. Then it was explained that the Major was D. Vicente Rojo, a famous professor at the Infantry Academy. I told my A.D.C. to confirm his identity, and he replied that he was quite sure this was the professor, for he had spoken to him across the lines, and being the bearer of a commission from the Government of the Republic, he wanted to meet me. He asked us to appoint an hour on the following day when the meeting could take place. We replied that he might come at nine in the morning, and that according to the rules and regulations of war he would be received as an emissary, and there must be a suspension of hostilities on both sides from nine to ten o'clock, and that he should present himself at the south façade, approaching the Alcázar from the place where he was now speaking.

And in fact on the next day, September 9th, at 9 A.M., we received a message by megaphone that the appointed hour had arrived and Major Rojo was coming across for the parley. A moment later Major Rojo appeared, wearing his major's badge, dressed in khaki overalls, with field cap and service belt. Below the badge he wore the colors of the Republican flag.

He halted in the middle of the street and was told from the windows to proceed in the direction of the carriage entrance through which he could enter into the Alcázar. On his arrival he was received by two officers who had been his former colleagues at the Academy and who had been his friends.

That morning orders were given to the men, women and children living in the basements, commanding them to preserve a strict silence when Major Rojo passed through their quarters on his way to our office. We did not want him to guess the number of people there.

At the carriage entrance the officers appointed to receive him bandaged his eyes and then led him to my quarters. They took care to make him lose his bearings, for he had been an instructor at the Alcázar over a long period and knew the fortress well.

When he was brought into my presence, I ordered the bandage removed from his eyes. He saluted me, but I did not shake his hand. I observed a cold and correct military attitude. He asked me to let the officers who had accompanied him remain with us. I agreed to this request. About halfway through the interview I called in my aide-de-camp.

He told me he brought the conditions for surrender offered by the Defence Committee of Toledo, and handed them to me. The conditions were to the effect that they would respect the lives of all, and that we should come out in groups of five in the following order— women, children, aged, sick and wounded, and finally the soldiers and the Civil Guards, who would lay down their arms in a place assigned. According to the last clause the commanders and officers would come out in order and *would be judged by the Tribunals of the People according to the part they had taken in the Movement.*

I rejected these conditions in writing. I told him that I had never felt more greatly honored than when defending the garrison of the Alcázar, and I undertook to maintain the defence of the fortress and the honor of Spain. I told him I would far sooner die than surrender.

Afterwards we asked him a few private questions, which he answered very briefly, offering us very little satisfaction.

What interested us most, of course, was the direction taken by the mine, for we hoped to penetrate it and destroy it. We had in fact excavated in two places without knowing which direction it took, and we had failed to find it. The enemy, knowing our intentions, had meanwhile redoubled his vigilance and intensified his efforts. When we mentioned the mine, he said he had not seen it, but had learned that the "Reds" thought we had succeeded in getting pretty close to it during our excavations.

I also asked him about the progress of our troops from the north and south. He told us they were advancing, but very slowly. This was especially true, according to the Major, of the troops under General Mola. He said the enemy, meaning ourselves, was very short of ammunition.

One of his colleagues suggested he ought to stay within the Alcázar. He said he had a wife and children in Madrid, and they would be killed if he did not return. We told him that we too had our families in Toledo, but with the honor of the country at stake we had never doubted for a moment about the side we would fight for. But it became apparent that he had no intention of staying with us, and we did not insist further.

A question of acute importance to the population inside the Alcázar was how to obtain the services of a priest. A priest was required to administer to the dying and to satisfy the spiritual needs of the people defending the fortress. Accordingly I asked him to request the Government in our name to send a priest to share our fate. I suggested it might be possible to send a priest who had been condemned to death. He promised to do this as soon as he returned to Madrid.

We then asked him a few more private questions and we asked some private favors. At the conclusion of the armistice he was again blindfolded and conducted with the same formalities and by the same officers through the carriage entrance out of the Alcázar. To those accompanying him, he said with visible emotion: "Good luck!" and "*Viva España!*"

On the following day, September 10th, towards evening we learned from one of the houses on the south façade that the government had acceded to my request for a priest, and a certain Canon Vázquez Camarasa had been sent from Madrid to minister to us. He begged us to arrange the time and place of his arrival. We told him we would treat him in the same way as we treated Major Rojo, as an emissary. Orders would be given by both sides to suspend hostilities. Once more the hour for the parley was set at 9 o'clock in the morning. He was to enter the Alcázar by the same gate. All this was agreed to. They also suggested that he should remain within the Alcázar for two hours. I replied that he was needed for at least three hours. There was some discussion with the enemy commanders, but eventually they agreed to this.

I asked my officers whether any of them knew Canon Vázquez Camarasa personally. In this way I hoped to avoid any subterfuges. There was one officer who knew him, and another who had heard him preach a short while ago. Both were sure they could identify him. So I ordered the officer who knew him to receive him next day and accompany him to my quarters.

On the following day, September 11th, after notification received from the enemy, Canon Vázquez Camarasa made his appearance. He was dressed correctly in civilian clothes and carried a crucifix in one hand. From our windows he was directed to the carriage entrance, where the officer I have already mentioned received him, bandaged his eyes, and led him to my quarters. I received him in company with my aide-de-camp and several other officers.

We asked him about the situation in Madrid, and he told us that things were almost normal. There were still lines of people in front of shops, but they were short and the people were served rapidly. The churches were closed and respected. His own house, he told us, had been ransacked, but on the following day, although he had taken no action, his possessions were returned to him, and there was a notice declaring his house protected by the C.N.T. He said the militiamen accompanying him had treated him with every respect, though they knew him to be a priest. In an absent-minded manner, as though entirely unconscious of the importance of the question, he asked how many people were in the Alcázar. I said that I deeply respected him as a priest, but could give him no information on the matter, whereupon with an exaggerated show of mortification, as though he had only just realized the impertinence of the question, he apologized for his indiscretion. He then celebrated Holy Mass and gave us a brief sermon in which he spoke of the glory which would be ours in the next world, though not in this, for it was his firm conviction that we would be defeated.

Because of the absolute impossibility of hearing individual confessions he gave a general absolution. It was a moment of inexpressible emotion for all of us. He then celebrated Holy Communion, using the Sacred Hosts kept by the Sisters of Charity of the Alcázar. The Sisters of Charity, many ladies, and several officers including my aide-de-camp participated. Finally there was a magnificent procession full of religious fervor and patriotism, as the Sacred Host was carried to those who were seriously wounded. There, in the infirmary, there occurred scenes of exalted and indescribable patriotism.

When his spiritual mission came to an end, we returned to my quarters. I soon discovered the real motive which brought him to me. Among other things he said he understood perfectly why we defended ourselves against attacks from outside the fortress, but he failed to understand why innocent women and children should be forced to face the dangers and privations of a siege. Immediately I realized his intention to invoke questions of conscience, and to persuade me to evacuate women and children, and in fact this was the principal object of his visit to the Alcázar. So I sent for one of the women. Speaking for all the others, she told him she felt perfectly safe among the gentlemen defending the fortress, whose fate the women were prepared to share, whatever the outcome of the siege. And hearing this firm and valiant declaration, he knew that nothing more was to be gained in that direction.

Several of the men consulted him on spiritual matters, and spent some time alone with him. Those who had families in Madrid wrote out their addresses for him, so that he could communicate with the families and let them know that they were in good health. He readily offered to perform this service for them. But it struck me that all this was highly dangerous, for it meant putting hostages into the hands of the "Reds," who would take full advantage of these hostages for their own purposes. Therefore, with as much tact as I could muster, I asked for the notes he had written, and he gave them to me immediately.

We knew the kind of man we had to deal with, and so we deliberately showed him the inner courtyard, so that he could see what condition it was in. He was profoundly impressed by the sight, and said that by defending ourselves we were as much responsible for the destruction as the attackers. It was of course an inopportune and unpatriotic sentiment which we tolerated, coming as it did from a priest. It revealed his sympathy for the cause we were fighting against.

Taking advantage of the cease-fire, several of our men went out on the street and talked to the "Reds," who suggested that with a little good will on both sides things could be arranged, for inevitably we would be forced to surrender, etc. etc. We rejected all these insinuations. During the cease-fire, one of the "Reds" shot at a window where several of our men were looking out, killing one of them. I protested to the people in the street, and they agreed with me that the cease-fire was being broken, putting the blame on "one of the many rascals who like to butcher people." They said all the men on guard had been notified of the cease-fire, and they promised to make an investigation and punish the offender. When the cease-fire was over, the priest left the Alcázar with the same formalities which characterized his entrance. The enemy, which had ceased fire a few moments before he entered the fortress at nine o'clock in the morning, resumed their fire a few minutes after he left.

On July 23rd and 24th the "Reds" announced by radio the fall of the Alcázar. The illustrated papers published faked photographs showing the defenders leaving the main entrance in groups, with their hands above their heads. As all this was false but might nevertheless deceive the Nationalist High Command (the truth was that the morale of the defenders was excellent, and there was never a moment when we considered surrendering or acting in any other way than to uphold the honor of Spain and selling our lives at the highest price), I decided to send a liaison officer to General Mola in the Sierra de Guadarrama with a short note informing him that we were continuing to defend the Alcázar and would never surrender.

Because of the difficulty of the mission, I needed a man of quite extraordinary ability, and indeed there was only one chance in a hundred of a successful conclusion to the mission. I was still debating the choice of a suitable man when Infantry Captain D. Luis Alba Navas, a professor at the School of Gymnastics and an officer serving under my orders in the Alcázar, volunteered for the mission. I immediately accepted his offer, for he was a man of proven courage and intelligence and he was familiar with the country to be traversed. He was moreover a man whose personal tastes were directed towards hunting and fishing, and these brought him in contact with the country folk, whom he attracted by a naturally kind and simple disposition. All of these qualities were combined with a vast ability to deal with practical matters.

He was given blue overalls, a hundred pesetas, and a pistol which he wore on a cord hanging from his neck. He also was given a Communist Party membership card which belonged to one of our hostages.

Luckily the card did not mention the profession of the owner, and we filled it in. He became "a fisherman."

He left the Alcázar at midnight by way of the iron gate leading to the New Bridge over the Tagus. He swam the river till he came to the stream known as "La Degollada," then following the hills along the left bank until he reached the armaments factory. Here he recrossed the river and made for the open country, at last reaching Burijon, some forty kilometers from Toledo. At Burijon he called on the Red Committee and demanded a car to take him to the Province of Ávila. He explained that he was on a secret mission. The committee granted the request, and he was about to get into the car when one of the bystanders, who happened to be a former student in the School of Gymnastics, exclaimed: "What are you doing here, captain?" He meant no harm. Calmly, in the most natural way imaginable, the captain said he was no captain, but some doubt having arisen among the "Reds," they arrested him and brought him before a judge at Torrijos. Then they decided to send him by car to Toledo. On the way, when they came to Venta del Hoyo, they met some cars coming in the opposite direction. There were some "Red" officers from Vargas in these cars, and they asked where the prisoner was being taken. When they discovered who the prisoner was, they came to the conclusion that his rank and popularity among the lower classes in Toledo would certainly prevent him from being shot, and they decided to kill him on the spot. This they did, and while the prisoner was still lying handcuffed on the ground, they gave him the *coup de grâce,* abandoning his body on the road. It was learned later that two days afterward the body was removed to the armaments factory and thence to Madrid, where it was paraded through the streets. To this day no one knows the last resting place of the heroic captain, who did not hesitate to sacrifice his life for the honor of his country in an enterprise with so little hope of success.

On July 17th this officer became a father for the fourth time. Yet his love for his wife and four children, all of them in Toledo, did not for one moment divert him from the fulfillment of a duty voluntarily assumed. The deed has been rewarded with the Laureate Cross of San Fernando.

On September 18th Cayetano Caridad, a corporal of the Civil Guard, met a glorious and heroic death. As a youth he had worked in the Río Tinto mines, and so we gave him the task of detecting the enemy mine. When he found the approximate point of danger, he ordered everyone evacuated, but remained behind to make further observations. When the explosion occurred, he was buried in the ruins. More than once this corporal said he would die willingly in the mine if he could save the lives of his companions.

I have mentioned the most conspicuous deeds, but many similar deeds took place during the siege. The garrison of the Alcázar possessed a blind belief in inevitable triumph, and was animated by a spirit of the highest patriotism.

The Massacres

THERE were massacres on both sides. In that strange primitive war, there seemed to be an echo of the wars fought by the ancient Spaniards against the Romans with no quarter given by either side. Caesar speaks of whole legions perishing, and whole cities being sacked and everyone in them put to the sword. In Spain the modern habit of massacre began.

Since the rage to massacre is always a form of suicide, it would seem that the Spaniards were embarked on a determined campaign of suicide. The logical conclusion of the Spanish Civil War was a country empty of people. A million lives were lost, but not in war. Most of the killings took place beside bullet-marked walls, in prisons, in bull rings and in cemeteries. With extraordinary patience the Spaniards explored the meaning of the word "murder." Only the Basques, who had lived in their small corner of Spain since time began, were incapable of committing atrocities.

Here are two accounts of massacres. In both cases the writer appeared on the scene after the massacre was over. The murders take place off stage, as in a Greek tragedy, and are perhaps all the more terrible for this reason.

The first account was written by Jay Allen in a report to the Chicago Tribune.

I have come from Badajoz, several miles away in Spain. I have been up on the roof to look back. There was a fire. They are burning bodies. Four thousand men and women have died at Badajoz since General Francisco Franco's Rebel Foreign Legionnaires and Moors climbed over the bodies of their own dead through its many times blood-drenched walls.

I tried to sleep. But you can't sleep on a soiled lumpy bed in a room at the temperature of a Turkish bath, with mosquitoes and bedbugs tormenting you, and with memories of what you have seen tormenting you, with the smell of blood in your very hair, and with a woman sobbing in the room next door.

"What's wrong?" I asked the sleepy yokel who prowls around the place at night as a guard.

"She's Spanish. She came thinking her husband had escaped from Badajoz."

"Well, didn't he?"

"Yes," he said, and he looked at me, not sure whether to go on. "Yes, and they sent him back. He was shot this morning."

"But who sent him back?"

I knew but asked nevertheless.

"Our international police."

I have seen shame and indignation in human eyes before, but not like this. And suddenly this sleepy, sweaty being, whose very presence had been an added misery, took on the dignity and nobility that a fine dog has and human beings most often have not.

I gave it up. I came down into the filthy patio, with its chickens, rabbits and pigs, to write this and get it over with.

To begin at the beginning. I had heard dark rumors in Lisbon. Everybody there spies on everybody else. When I left my hotel at 4:00 P.M. August 23, I said I was going to Estoril to try my luck at roulette. Several people noted that down, and I hope they enjoyed their evening at Estoril.

I went to the Plaza de Rocio instead. I took the first taxi. I drove around and around and finally picked up a Portuguese friend who knows his business.

We went to the ferry that crosses the Tagus. Once on the other side we told the chauffeur, "Elvas." He looked mildly surprised. Elvas was 250 kilometers (about 150 miles) away. We streaked through an engaging country of sandy hills, cork oaks, peasants with sideburns and women with little bowler hats. It was 8:30 o'clock when we pulled up the hill into Elvas, "the lock nobody ever opened." But Elvas knows humiliation now.

It had been nine days since Badajoz fell on August 14th. The Rebel armies had gone on—to a nasty defeat at Medellín, if my information was correct, as it sometimes is—and newspapermen, hand-fed and closely watched, had gone on in their wake.

Nine days is a long time in newspaper work; Badajoz is practically ancient history, but Badajoz is one of those damned spots the truth about which will not be out so soon. And so I did not mind being nine days late, if my newspaper didn't.

I know Badajoz. I had been there four times in the last year to do research on a book I am working on and to try to study the operations of the agrarian reform that might have saved the Spanish Republic— a republic that, whatever it is, gave Spain schools and hope, neither of which it had known for centuries.

We began to hear the truth before we were out of the car. Two Portuguese drummers standing at the door of the hotel knew my friend. Portugal, as usual, is on the eve of a revolution. The people seemed to know who the "others" are. That is why I took my friend along.

They whispered. This was the upshot—thousands of Republicans, Socialist and Communist militiamen and militiawomen were butchered after the fall of Badajoz for the crime of defending their Republic against the onslaught of the Generals and the landowners.

Between fifty and one hundred have been shot every day since. The Moors and Foreign Legionnaires are looting. But blackest of all: The Portuguese "International Police," in defiance of international usage, are turning back scores and hundreds of Republican refugees to certain death by Rebel firing squads.

This very day (August 23) a car flying the red and yellow banner of the Rebels arrived here. In it were three Falangists (Fascists). They were accompanied by a Portuguese lieutenant. They tore through the narrow streets to the hospital where Señor Granado, Republican Civil Governor of Badajoz, was lying. Señor Granado with his military commander, Colonel Puigdengola, ran out on the Loyalist militia two days before the fall of Badajoz.

The Fascists ran up the stairs, strode down a corridor with guns drawn, and into the governor's room. The governor was out of his mind with the horror of the thing. The director of the hospital, Dr. Pabgeno, threw himself over his helpless patient and howled for help. So he saved a life.

We drove to Camp Maior, which is only seven kilometers (about four miles) from Badajoz on the Portuguese side. A talkative frontier policeman said: "Of course, we are handing them back. They are dangerous for us. We can't have Reds in Portugal at such a moment."

"What about the right of asylum?"

"Oh," he said. "Badajoz asks extradition."

"There is no such thing as extradition for a political offense."

"It's being done all up and down the frontier on orders from Lisbon," he said belligerently.

We cleared out. We drove back to Elvas. I met friends who are as much Portuguese and vice versa.

"Do you want to go to Badajoz?" they asked.

"No," I said, "because the Portuguese say their frontier is closed and I would be hung up."

But they offered to take me through and back again without complications. So we started. Suddenly we drove out of the lane on to a bridge that leads across the Guadiana River into the town of Badajoz. Now we were in Spain. My friends were known. The extra person in the car (myself) passed unnoticed. We were not stopped.

We drove straight to the Plaza. Here yesterday there was a ceremonial, symbolical shooting. Seven leading Republicans of the Popular Front, shot with a band and everything before three thousand people. To prove that Rebel generals didn't shoot only workers and peasants. There is no favoritism to be shown between the Popular Fronters.

Every other shop seemed to have been wrecked. The conquerors looted as they went. All this week in Badajoz, Portuguese have been buying watches and jewelry for practically nothing. Most shops belong to the Rightists. It is the war tax they pay for salvation, a Rebel officer told me grimly. We passed a big dry goods shop that seems to have been through an earthquake. "La Campaña," my friends said. "It belongs to Don Mariano, a leading Azañista. It was sacked yesterday after Mariano was shot."

We drove by the office of the Agrarian Reform, where in June I saw the Chief Engineer, Jorge Montojo, distributing land, incurring naturally the hatred of the landowners, and because he was a technician following strictly bourgeois canons of law, the enmity of the Socialists, too. He had taken arms in defense of the Republic, and so—

Suddenly we saw two Falangists halt a strapping fellow in a workman's blouse and hold him while a third pulled back his shirt, baring his right shoulder. The black and blue marks of a rifle butt could be seen. Even after a week they showed. The report was unfavorable. To the bull ring with him.

We drove out along the walls to the ring in question. Its sandstone walls looked over the fertile valley of Guadiana. It is a fine ring of white plaster and red brick. I saw Juan Belmonte, bullfight idol, here once on the eve of the fight, on a night like this, when he came down to watch the bulls brought in. This night the fodder for tomorrow's show was being brought in, too. Files of men, arms in the air.

They were young, mostly peasants in blue blouses, mechanics in jumpers. "The Reds." They are still being rounded up. At four o'clock in the morning they are turned out into the ring through the gate by which the initial parade of the bullfight enters. There machine guns await them.

After the first night the blood was supposed to be palm deep on the far side of the lane. I don't doubt it. Eighteen hundred men—there were women, too—were mowed down there in some twelve hours. There is more blood than you would think in eighteen hundred bodies.

In a bullfight when the beast or some unlucky horse bleeds copiously, "wise monkeys" come along and scatter fresh sand. Yet on hot afternoons you smell blood. It is all very invigorating. It was a hot night. There was a smell. I can't describe it and won't describe it. The "wise monkeys" will have a lot of work to do to make this ring respectable for a ceremonial slaughter bullfight. As for me, no more bullfights—ever.

We passed a corner.

"Until yesterday there was a pool blackened with blood here," said my friends. "All the loyal military were shot here and their bodies left for days as an example."

They were told to come out, so they rushed out of the house to greet the conquerors and were shot down and their houses looted. The Moors played no favorites.

Back at the Plaza. During the executions here, Mario Pires went off his head. (Mario Pires is a Portuguese correspondent who had been entirely favorable to the Franco Rebellion before his visit to

Badajoz.) He had tried to save a pretty fifteen-year-old girl caught with a rifle in her hands. The Moor was adamant. Mario saw her shot. Now he is under medical care at Lisbon.

I know there are horrors on the other side aplenty. Almendra Lejo, Rightist, was crucified, drenched with gasoline, and burned alive. I know people who saw charred bodies. I know that. I know hundreds and even thousands of innocent persons died at the hands of the revengeful masses. But I know who it was who rose to "save Spain" and so aroused the masses to a defense that is as savage as it is valiant.

"But they didn't burn the jail." I had read in the Lisbon and Seville papers that they had. "No, the brothers Plá prevented it."

I knew Luis and Carlos Plá, rich young men of good family, who had the best garage in southwestern Spain. They were Socialists because they said the Socialist Party was the only instrument which could break the power of Spain's feudal masters.

They harangued the crowd that wanted to burn the three hundred Rightists in the jail just before they entered, saying they were going to die in defense of our Republic, but they were not assassins. They themselves opened the doors to let these people escape.

"What happened to the Plás?"

"Shot."

"Why?"

No answer.

There is no answer. All these people could have been allowed to escape to Portugal three miles away, but they weren't.

On the moon-drenched streets there was a smell of jasmin, but I had another smell in my nostrils. Sweet, too horribly sweet. So back to Elvas.

There in the white Plaza by a fountain, a youth leaning against the wall with his feet crossed was playing his guitar and a soft tenor sang a melting Portuguese love song.

At Badajoz in June boys still sang beneath balconies. It will be a long time before they do again.

Suddenly through the square shot a car with a red and yellow flag. We halted. Our drummers came to meet us.

"They are searching the hotel."

"For whom?"

"Don't know."

We shall go away, as soon as it is light. People who ask questions are not popular near this frontier, if it can be called a frontier.

Arturo Barea writes more cautiously, but just as fearfully. His massacre is smaller, but is repeated endlessly. Better than anyone else he has described the authentic terror of being in Madrid.

Ángel lived on the ground floor of a small tenement house stuck between two brothels. His flat was a single big room divided into a bedroom, dining-room and kitchen by thin partition walls. There was nothing in the bedroom but a double bed and a night table. The kitchen was half the size of the bedroom. Light and air entered through the door and through a barred window which opened on to a courtyard three yards square, containing the lavatory for all the tenants of the ground floor and the water tap for the whole house. The room, now deserted, smelled of mildew and urine. I waited for Ángel while he changed in the bedroom.

Suddenly, an explosion shook the house. Ángel came out, still struggling into his coat. Piercing cries and the patter of feet sounded outside. Ángel and I went out into the street. People were running wildly. A few yards away, several women were lying on the ground and shrieking. One of them was dragging herself along on a belly torn to bleeding tatters. The walls of the houses and the paving stones were spattered with blood. Then we were all running towards the injured.

In the last house of the wide stretch of the street was a clinic for nursing mothers. At that hour there had been a queue of women, most of them carrying a child, waiting for the distribution of milk. A few yards further down, prostitutes had been following their trade. A bomb had fallen in the middle of the street and sprayed the mothers and the streetwalkers. A woman propped up on her bleeding arm stump gave a scream and let herself drop heavily. Near me was a bundle of petticoats with a leg sticking out, bent at an impossible angle over a swollen belly. My head was swimming, I vomited into the gutter. A militiaman beside me cursed and was sick. Then he began to tremble and broke out into spasmodic laughter. Someone gave me a glass of neat brandy and I poured it down my throat. Ángel had disappeared. Some men were busy picking up the wounded and the dead and carrying them into the clinic. A man stuck his head out of the gate, white hair and spectacles over a bloodstained surgeon's overall, stamped his foot, and yelled: "No more room! Take them to Encomienda!"

Shrieks sounded from the Plaza del Progreso. Ángel was beside me, his coat and hands splashed with blood.

"Another bomb in the Plaza del Progreso!"

Groups of people came running down the street in frenzied fear, pairs of men carrying someone between them, women with children in their arms, all screaming and shrieking. I saw nothing but arms and legs and bloodstains in motion, and the street rocked before my eyes.

"Go to Encomienda! There's been one here too."

The whirling mass of arms and legs disappeared through the Calle de Esgrima.

We went back to Ángel's flat and washed. Ángel changed again. When we came out of the house, the neighbors told us that a plane had flown low over Madrid from north to south, dropping bombs all along the course. It had left a trail of blood from the Puerta de Toledo to Cuatro Caminos. By accident or because the pilot guided himself by the open spaces, most of the bombs had fallen in public squares and many children had been hit.

That was the 7th of August 1936. That evening and that night, Fascists were firing from windows and from skylights. Many hundreds were arrested. There were mass executions of suspects during the night.

Antonio sent for me while I was at home in the evening. The local branch of the Communist Party was organizing pickets to paint the street lamps blue and to see to the blackout. Rafael, Ángel, and I went. We worked in small groups, each protected by two armed Milicianos; but it was an almost hopeless task to improvise a blackout in August, in Madrid. Shuttered houses were stifling. It was impossible to stay in any public place with the shutters closed. We had to compromise. People were to avoid the rooms facing on the street and stay in the inner rooms, using only candles. It was easy to paint the street lamps blue, with a mixture of water, aniline dye, and plaster;

only a few tenuous, white rays filtered through. We turned off every other lamp.

The streets looked ghostly in our wake, night black, with white dots on the pavements and blue, sickly blobs of light a little higher up in the dark. Sometimes the front of a house was lighted by the fugitive glow of a candle carried through a room in the house opposite, which turned a balcony into a yellow square of light, streaked by the black lines of the railing, and leaped distorted along the walls. The people thronged the streets as they did every night, but they were only half visible in the penumbra, shapeless black bulks from which voices came and, at intervals, the dazzling spark of a lighter or a little red glow from a cigarette outlining a few heads.

Some lorries arrived carrying Milicianos returning from the Sierra and from Toledo. Their headlights were switched on; the crowds caught in their beams looked livid and naked. The cry went up: "The lights—turn out the lights!"

Brakes screeched, and the lorries rolled slowly on amid the sound of breaking chairs and pitchers. The red light of the rear lamps glowed like a bloodshot eye. In the darkness it was as though bloodshot monsters were panting there, about to spring.

By midnight the whole quarter lay in deep shadow. In the Calle de la Primavera we stopped under a street lamp which had been forgotten. One of us climbed up, while another reached him the brush soaked in blue dye. A shot cracked, a bullet ricocheted on the wall above the lamp. Somebody had shot at us from one of the houses opposite. The people lounging in the street took refuge in doorways. We marched out the tenants from the four houses from which the shots might have come. The concierge and neighbors identified them one by one. Then we weeded out those who had been in the street from the others, and started to search each flat in turn. All the tenants surged after us and asked us to go into their flats with them; they wanted to clear themselves, and at the same time they were afraid that a stranger might have hidden in their rooms. We searched through attics and lofts full of cobwebs and old rags, we climbed up and down stairs, we caught dust and dirt on our clothes and banged against rafters and invisible nails. At four in the morning we had finished; we were filthy and sleepy, it was broad daylight, but we had not found the sniper. Somebody had brought a huge pitcher filled with steaming coffee and a bottle of brandy. We drank greedily.

One of the men said: "That bird's saved his skin." As though in answer, Ángel exclaimed: "Let's go to Mataderos and see the ones who were polished off this time."

At first I refused to go, and then I suddenly gave in. It was easier. I dug my fist into Ángel's ribs and said to him: "You're a brute— after what we saw yesterday afternoon, too!"

"God save us—come along, then you'll get rid of the bitter taste of seeing those mangled kids yesterday. Do you remember the woman with child, who had her leg doubled up on her navel? Well, she was still alive and she gave birth in the clinic. Then she died. A boy, it was. Nobody in the whole quarter knows her."

The executions had attracted far more people than I would have thought possible. Families with their children, excited and still drowsy with sleep, and militiamen with their girls were walking along the Paseo de la Delicias, all in the same direction. Requisitioned cars and lorries were passing by. Crowds and cars had collected at the entrance to the vegetable market and the slaughterhouses at the Glorieta. While carts and trucks with green vegetables came and went, militia pickets on duty meandered round and asked anyone who caught their fancy for his papers.

Behind the slaughterhouses a long brick wall and an avenue with stunted little trees. The sightseers ambled from one to the other and made humorous remarks; a pitying comment might have provoked suspicion.

I had expected the bodies. The sight did not shake me. There were about twenty of them. They were not mangled. I had seen far worse in Morocco and on the day before. But I was shaken by the collective brutality and cowardice of the spectators.

Vans which belonged to the City of Madrid arrived to collect the corpses. One of the drivers said: "Now they're going to water the place and make it nice and spruce for tonight." He chuckled. It rang like fear.

The Islands

*W*AR did not come to all the Balearic Islands. Minorca escaped, protected by its smallness and unimportance, but Majorca fell into the hands of an Italian expeditionary force and soon became a fief of Mussolini. Here Mussolini based the airplanes which took part in the remorseless and interminable bombing of the cities on Spain's Mediterranean coast, and here too the Fascist goon squads perfected the art of capricious mass murder.

One of the tragedies of the Spanish Civil War was the blunting of the sensibilities. So much blood flowed that indignation and horror soon gave way to weariness and acceptance. Only a few succeeded in maintaining a sense of outrage before the facts of murder. Among these was the French Catholic novelist, Georges Bernanos, who claimed descent from the family of Joan of Arc. He was living quietly in the house of rich Spanish friends at Palma de Majorca when he first heard of the mass arrests of peasants and watched the trucks loaded with doomed prisoners on their way to the cemeteries.

His book, The Great Cemeteries Under the Moon, *is not so much a record of what he saw as an impassioned plea against the dreadful futility of the murderous philosophy of Fascism. But here and there he writes of things seen and felt with a kind of luminous and accurate fury:*

I used to see on the Ramblas in Majorca trucks crowded with men. These trucks roared past with the sound of thunder, on a level with the many-colored terraces, lavishly equipped and gleaming, gay with the murmurs of a country fair. These trucks were gray with the dust of the road, gray too with the men who sat there four by four, their gray caps upside down on their knees and their hands lying gently along the seams of their trousers. They were rounded up every evening from forgotten villages, at the hour when they came from the fields; and they set off on their last journey, their shirts clinging to their shoulders with sweat, their arms still full of the day's toil, leaving the soup on the table and a woman who had arrived too late at the garden gate, with a little bundle of possessions twisted in a new napkin: *A Dios! recuerdos!*

By an extraordinary combination of circumstances, Bernanos was staying in the house of the Marqués de Zayas, the chief of the Majorcan Falangists and the man most responsible for the slayings. In mid-August the Spanish Marqués surrendered his powers to a Blackshirt commoner, Arconovaldo Bonaccorsi, a bearded and barrel-chested adventurer, who called himself General Count Aldo Rossi. Here Bernanos describes Bonaccorsi's descent upon the island:

The newcomer was neither a general, nor a count, nor was he called Rossi: he was simply an Italian official belonging to the Blackshirts. One fine morning we saw him arriving in a scarlet three-engined plane. His first visit was to the military governor, nominated by General Goded. He was received politely by the governor and his officers. Hammering the table with his fist, he made a speech declaring that he was the herald of the spirit of Fascism, and a few days later the general together with his entire staff was thrown into the prison of San Carlos, while Count Rossi assumed effective control of the Falange. Wearing a black shirt with an enormous white cross blazoned on the breast, he drove through the villages, taking the wheel of his racing car, while other cars filled with men armed to the teeth followed in clouds of dust. Every morning the newspapers provided complete descriptions of these oratorical journeys, where in an extraordinary mixture of the languages of Majorca, Italy and Spain, the Count, flanked by the local mayor and curate, announced his Crusade. No doubt the Italian government possessed some less garish collaborators in Palma than this huge ruffian who, while wiping his hands on the tablecloth during a dinner with a great lady of Palma society, declared that he had to have at least "one woman a day." But the particular mission entrusted with him agreed well with his genius. His mission was the organization of terror.

From then on every night teams recruited by him operated in the villages and in the suburbs of Palma. Wherever these men demonstrated their zeal, the scene was nearly always the same. There was the same discreet knock on the door of a comfortable apartment or of a thatched cottage, the same trampling of feet in a garden filled with shadows or funereal whispering on the landing, with some poor devil listening through the wall, ear pressed against a keyhole, heart shaking with terror.—"Follow us!" The same words to the woman driven out of her mind, her hands trembling as she gathers together those small familiar possessions put down a few moments before, and the noise of the motor still filling the air with its thunder out there, in the street. "I shouldn't wake the children, should I? It wouldn't be any use. You are taking me to prison, señor?" *"Perfectamente,"* says the killer, who sometimes is only twenty years old. And then the climb into the truck, where two or three comrades have already taken their places, equally resigned, equally melancholy, with a vagueness in their eyes. . . . *Hombre!* The truck makes a grinding noise and starts off. As long as it keeps to the main road, there is still a gleam of hope. But already they are slowing down, over the rough, bumpy hollow of a small earth road. "Get out!" So they jump out, line up, kiss a medal or only a thumbnail. Bang! Bang! Bang! The bodies are arranged along the slope where the gravedigger will find them the next day, head shattered and the nape of the neck lying on a hideous cushion of black coagulated blood. I speak of the gravedigger because they are very careful to do what has to be done close to a cemetery. The local mayor will inscribe in his records: "So-and-so, died of cerebral congestion . . ."

The first phase of the process of liquidation lasted for four months. During the course of these four months the stranger who was chiefly responsible for these killings sat in the place of honor during all the religious celebrations. He was usually accompanied by a chaplain recruited locally, wearing boots and breeches, with a white cross on his chest, pistols in his belt. (This priest, as it happened, was later shot by the military.) No one was permitted to remain in doubt about the discretionary powers of the Italian general. I know a poor priest who humbly begged him to spare the lives of three young women prisoners who had come from Mexico. He had heard their confessions and believed them to be good people. "Very well," said the Count, who was about to go to bed, "I will discuss the matter with my pillow." The following day he ordered his men to kill the women.

So it was that right up to December the sunken roads of the island, in the neighborhood of the cemeteries, regularly received their mournful harvest of people whose thoughts found no merit in the eyes of the authorities. They were workers and peasants, but they were also middle-class people, druggists, lawyers. When I asked a doctor friend for the film taken some time before by a radiologist who was one of his colleagues—he was the only radiologist in Palma—he replied smiling: "I wonder whether we shall ever find it. . . . Poor X was taken on a little journey a few days ago . . ." These facts are known to everyone.

And when these liquidations and summary executions were over, it was still necessary to think about the prisons. As you may imagine, they were full. The concentration camps were also full. So were those ships from which the guns had been removed, those sinister prison hulks which, with excessive caution, were illuminated each night by the ominous scorings of the searchlights—those searchlights which I saw, alas, from my bed. There followed the second phase—the liquidation of the prisons.

A great number of these suspects, both men and women, could not be put on trial according to martial law because they had committed no crimes which could be judged by a military court. So they were released in groups according to their place of origin. On the way to their homes, the cargo was tossed into a ditch.

I know all about this. . . . Shall I go on? How many were killed? Fifty? A hundred? Five hundred? The number I am about to give was given me by one of the chiefs in charge of the Terror in Palma. The number mentioned by the people is, of course, rather different. It hardly matters. At the beginning of March 1937, after seven months of civil war, there were 3,000 assassinations. Seven months consist of 210 days: an average of 15 executions a day. May I add that this small island can easily be crossed from one end to the other in two hours? A curious motorist, at the price of a little fatigue, might easily have been able to win a bet over whether one could see fifteen heads being shattered in a single day. These figures are not unknown to His Eminence the Bishop of Palma.

I imagine it has cost you a good deal to read this. I assure you it has cost me more to write it. It cost me even more to see it happening and to hear it. Perhaps less than you think? . . . We kept going, my wife and I, not by bravado, nor even with the hope of being very useful—there was so little we could do—but chiefly because there arose in us a feeling of profound solidarity with those good people who shared our hopes and illusions, whose numbers increased daily as they found themselves confronted by the mounting evidence which they tried so hard to disbelieve, until at last they came to share our agony. They were not free; nor were we. I am thinking now of some young Falangists and Requetés, and of some old priests. There was one old priest who, for having uttered a few imprudent words, was forced to swallow a liter of castor oil under the threat of death. It might have been, if I had lived intimately with the men of the left, that their way of protesting would have released in me certain partisan reflexes which I would not always have been able to master. But men are bound more closely together by pity and shame, lies and sadness, than by revolt and hate. So one awakens on a harassed morning, one goes about one's business, and on the road, or beside a table in a café, or on the threshold of a church, one meets people whom previously one had thought on the side of the massacrers, and suddenly, with tears in their eyes, they say: "It's too much! I can't take it any more! This is what they have just done!" I am thinking of the mayor of a small town whose wife succeeded in hiding him in a cistern. Whenever there was an alarm the poor man squeezed at the bottom of a niche in the cistern only a few inches from the water. One day in December they took him from the cistern, shivering with fever. They shot him in the stomach and took him to the cemetery. He was in no hurry to die, and so his executioners who were drinking a little way away and getting drunk, returned to watch him. They thrust the neck of the brandy bottle in his mouth, and afterwards they smashed the bottle over his head. These facts are well-known. I do not fear any contradiction. The atmosphere of the Terror is not in the least what you thought it would be. The first impression is one of an enormous misunderstanding in which everything is confounded, the good and the bad, the guilty and the innocent, enthusiasm and cruelty, all inextricably confused. Did I really see it? Did I really understand what was happening? They tell you it is about to end, it has already ended. You breathe again. You breathe, in fact, until the next massacre, coming with surprising suddenness, takes place. Time passes. And then what happens? Shall I tell you? There come priests and soldiers and a flag which is all red and gold—not gold as a medium of exchange, nor is there blood for sale. . . . It is so hard to see before one's eyes the vilification of precisely those things one is born to love.

In mid-December the incredible red-bearded Arconovaldo Bonaccorsi vanished from Majorca as mysteriously as he came. The Terror continued. It lacked the ghastly flamboyance which the Blackshirt officer gave to it, but became more methodical. Until the end of the Civil War Majorca remained wholly under Italian influence. It became a training ground, a supply depot, and an airfield serving Italian troops in Spain.

Ibiza, the third of the Balearic Islands and the one closest to the mainland of Spain, suffered a similar fate. At the beginning of the Civil War the island was invaded by an expeditionary force led by Captain Alfredo Bayo in command of a small Republican fleet. Sympathizers of Franco were arrested and jailed. A few days later Captain Bayo made an ineffectual attack on Majorca and sailed back to Barcelona with nothing accomplished, vanishing into obscurity. Years later he reappeared as military adviser to Fidel Castro in Cuba.

The Ibizans were left to their fate. Italian planes bombed the island and showered down leaflets ordering the people to surrender to the rebel forces. Elliot Paul, then living at Santa Eulalia del Río, describes his last tragic hours on the island and his escape on a German gunboat:

At noon on Sunday, September 13, four planes appeared suddenly over Ibiza and dropped bombs on the crowd of women and children who were promenading on the waterfront and the *paseo*. There was no warning, no attempt to destroy anything of military importance. A small tobacco shop was wrecked, a gasoline pump near the shore, several fishing vessels moored to the wharf, a clubhouse. Of the fifty-five Ibicencos who were killed, forty-two were women or children under ten years old. In the evening, just as the work of caring for the wounded and sorting out the dead was at its height, one of the younger fascist prisoners in the fortress remarked to the anarchist guards:

"Our turn is coming now."

Horrified by the outrage to the women and children and inflamed by the fascist's insolence, the guards seized a submachine-gun and shot down the speaker and the men around him. The alarm was given and more anarchists rushed in from the barracks. They quickly decided to execute all the prisoners that night, in groups of five. When the prisoners refused to come out in the yard, machine-guns were turned on them in the building, and those who were not killed by bullets were despatched with bayonets. The anarchists then marched to the hospital, pulled Abel Matutes whimpering from his bed, and shot him. The bodies of some of the prisoners were loaded on a truck and buried in a common trench, others were left in the fortress. The anarchists then made ready for departure with two large passenger boats and ordered the members of the Ibiza militia to embark with them. The militiamen in the outlying towns heard of what was happening and hurried to Ibiza, insisting that they should not be left behind to be butchered. They were taken aboard.

Early next morning, unwilling to believe the stories that were spreading through Santa Eulalia, I started to walk to Ibiza. Flora, who had until that moment been firm in her decision that our duty lay with our friends on the island and that having joined our cause with theirs we could not desert them, at last said that she was ready to go. I decided to send a telegram to all the consulates in Barcelona, if it were possible. At that time we did not know what had happened, but our *Cuartel* was completely deserted. That was alarming enough. We had heard the bombardment but had had no direct news from the port. Half the inhabitants of Santa Eulalia had again taken to the woods.

"There is a white flag over the fortress in Ibiza," the Barberet told me.

"Who put it there? By what authority?" I asked, so angrily that he froze up immediately and said he did not know.

Before I had progressed far toward Ibiza, an automobile overtook me. I had not seen one in motion for weeks. In it was Dr. Torres and he offered to give me a lift as far as the intersection of the San Miguel road. He was on his way to Santa Gertrudis, and the driver kept telling him he had not enough gasoline to get there and return. He decided to drive to Ibiza, get gasoline there if he could, then return to Santa Eulalia via Santa Gertrudis. We chugged along, got near enough to the port to see the white flag, and met a survivor of the massacre who had been left for dead. He was in a hysterical condition. He tried to tell what had happened but was unable to control himself. One of the militiamen who had been left behind came along and told the doctor there was not a drop of gasoline in the city.

"Then we'll go straight back," Dr. Torres said to the driver. "I don't want to be seen in town. There'll be too much work to do."

Too disgusted to say goodbye and thank him for the lift, I continued on foot. What I found in that formerly most beautiful and prosperous and hospitable city is too bleak for words to convey. The inner harbor, smashed fishing boats, and fish, belly up and stinking. At the corner, the wreck of the tobacco shop and the gasoline pump. Bloodstains on all the walls. On the broad *paseo,* one building still inhabited. There stood old Carmen, wife of Sergeant Ortiz, her arm around the shoulder of a woman in black, and very gently lifting the blanket from a donkey cart-load of corpses to find one the other woman might claim. I walked alone through the old Roman gates to the walled city and through narrow slits of street and up stairways to the fortress. About a hundred bodies were still lying on the floor, and the first I recognized was that of Francisco Ribas, the boy I had promised to save. Ex-Captain Nicoláu's head, or rather the top of his head, had been blown off. Francisco Guasch and old Bonéd had fallen side by side. In one another's arms were the seraph-faced young priest and the priest who looked like a butcher-boy, and in that muddy lake of corpses and blood he looked more than ever like a butcher-boy of a slaughter-house of man's most evil dreams.

Alone, I stood in that frightful hall, too numb to be saddened or horrified, faint from the unspeakable smell, alone in the ancient town the sight of which had always raised such thankful emotion in my heart, alone in blaming or not blaming or what or who, alone in yesterday's riddled hopes and illusions, unable to be sick, to vomit, to weep, to tear my hair, unable to Santa Eulalia or Spain or the workers of the world, to stay or go away or not do either. Later I snapped out of it, and numbly and dutifully, as being the only man alive for miles around who tapped nightmares on typewriters, I found the fascist boy survivor and the militia boy remainder, and separately and together I listened and asked and prodded my numb brain and obtained what facts I have written of events I did not actually see but only heard and smelled the morning following, as other mornings and events will be following following ever.

Of the two hundred and thirty-nine in the fortress, perhaps five were innocent, and of the fifty-five dead in the streets *all* were innocent, and the port was innocent, and the island and my town, and honest people everywhere.

I, having mounted the hill of silent terror of the ghosts of Spaniards and Moors, and descended to the death of fishes, communed with corpses, talked with boys—I walked up the empty *paseo* to where the corpse cart stood and the door was marked Red Cross. The woman in black was simply sitting there, perhaps waiting for another cartload. Old Carmen greeted me in her excellent Castillano, and her gruff-voiced husband stood up to shake hands.

"Terrible, terrible, Señor Paul," he said. No more. Only a face for Mantegna.

I told him I wanted to send telegrams, and he regretted that the telegraph office was not in operation. It had died when the city had died. There was nothing to do but to walk back to Santa Eulalia. I left money with the old man, and the text of telegrams to the consulates, and he promised to send the messages whenever, if ever, it was possible again.

I got home after dark, although a San Carlos man, one of whose relatives had been killed by the fascist bombers, overtook me before I had walked many miles. There are many hours of that day I cannot seem to account for or dislodge from the mortar of my memory. I told Flora, Pep Torres, Erica Braussen a few of my facts, and we spent the evening somehow, and listlessly went to bed.

The next morning Santa Eulalia was practically deserted. Not a house in town, now, that did not have its emptiness and death or slaughter and desolation in prospect. Some fascist planes flew over, but dropped no bombs. Eulalia Noguera came to us for the first time since her brother's death and said that Cosmi, her uncle Mateo, Carlos, Pep Salvador and in all seventeen of the best Santa Eulalia men had set sail for some unknown destination before dawn that day in the schooner *Isabel Matutes*. We rejoiced that they had got away. In fact, with so many good men safe I began not to feel completely numb again and to see that much more would be happening and that, if there were no end to injustice and hate and bloodshed and emptying of inhabited buildings, there simply was no end.

At quarter of twelve that day a Belgian resident of Santa Eulalia sought me out and told me there was a destroyer in Ibiza harbor and that a peasant had told him it was German. An Englishwoman in Ibiza had told the Belgian that Sergeant Oritz had told her that an American and his family wanted to be taken off. I thanked him, and thinking rapidly but with no definiteness I hurried to the house where Erica Braussen was staying. Flora was there with her. Erica turned pale when I said I thought the destroyer was of the German navy. I simply told them what the Belgian had told me. We must do something about it, we all agreed. I suggested that Erica write a note in German to the Commander of the gunboat, letting him know that there were Germans and Americans in distress in Santa Eulalia and asking him to call at our harbor. For pen and ink we hurried down the hill to Cosmi's café, and there, to my surprise, I found Cosmi. He and the other Republican leaders had been unable to get away the night before. He was disappointed, but quite resigned to an early death. I told him about our plan.

"I wish I could go," he said simply.

My brain began to function again. I knew Cosmi spoke French fluently, with an Algerian accent.

"Could you go as our cook?"

"I'll try. I had a French passport once, during the War," he said.

Quickly we consulted Erica and she wrote the note in German. Cosmi said he would go at once to Ibiza, if we could find him a bicycle, deliver the note to the German Commander and ask to be taken aboard. It was a slim chance, but not much slimmer than the one Erica was taking in placing herself within reach of the German authorities.

"Will you tell them that I am a governess, that I work for you?" she asked.

"Of course," I said.

Then I went back up the slope to ask Señora Guasch for the loan of her son's bicycle. I have never seen a widow with more thirst for revenge in her eyes, but they softened and she courteously granted my request. Within ten minutes Cosmi, collarless, sockless, with a dirty shirt and torn trousers, was speeding toward Ibiza. To make a favorable impression on the German Commander, we had set forth in the note that Cosmi, Algerian-French cook in my house, had lost his clothes and of course all his papers when communists had raided the town.

Flora, Erica and I thought so little of our chances that we did not begin packing, but ate a long and leisurely lunch. But as we were finishing dessert, a boy came running to us. An auto was in front of Cosmi's to take us off, would wait ten minutes. Hastily we threw a few things into suitcases, Eulalia, Pep, and Juanito helping, and carried them across the plaza, past the Royalty, Andrés' café, the post office, to Cosmi's. The driver told us the German destroyer could not come to Santa Eulalia because the Commander had no orders to that effect, but that the German officers, on receiving the note Cosmi had delivered, had taken gasoline from their launch and filled the tank of the nearest auto which had been standing on the pier. The destroyer was to leave Ibiza at two-thirty, call at San Antonio an hour later, and leave San Antonio about four-thirty. Because the English warships had refused to transport dogs, I assumed the Germans would not take Moritz along, and sadly I handed the leash to Eulalia Noguera, hoping Moritz would protect her, as she promised to care for him.

"He shall eat exactly as if you were here," Eulalia said, which was worth more than a library filled with treaties with Italy and Germany.

A small group of women were standing fearfully on the edge of the plaza as we passed, suitcases in hand. We stopped to say goodbye to them. I remember particularly Antonia and her three small daughters who had been born in America. In front of Cosmi's was a disconsolate group of men, those who were too tired and discouraged to take shelter from air raids. Pedro of the Royalty had tears in his eyes. Ferrer for once spoke in a low tone of voice, but cordially. Rigoberto, haggard, approached us. I have never seen such complete despair.

"One cowardly act after another," he said. "The only reason I am not leaving is because I cannot. Goodbye."

I told them we would go to some town near the border, where we would get money from America, and return as soon as it was possible. The suitcases were piled in, we seated ourselves as best we could, and the auto started moving through the empty town and on across a landscape from which the light had died. It was certain that the fascists were coming, and as we rode along I could not forget Ferrer, Pep Salvador, Captain Juan, Carlos, old Miguel Tur, our communist potter at Calla Llonga, Guarapiñada, all the men who were marked for slaughter. I had asked Pep Torres to try to get away with us, but sadly he had refused.

When we reached the tangent from which the port and the walled city could be seen, the destroyer was lying at anchor in the harbor. Stink of decaying fish. We skirted the cove and the wrecks of fishing vessels, zigzagged through smashed remnants of walls and approached a small group of Ibicenco men and some German officers and sailors. The young German in command, soft-voiced and with the gentlest manners, came forward to receive us and spoke in English. Ramón was standing near by, but no sight of Cosmi. I did not dare to enquire. I gave Ramón all the *pesetas* I had left and asked him to pass them on to Pep Torres. We stepped into the waiting launch as our suitcases were loaded into a tender, nodded to our fellow-passengers and the propeller began churning. Two poodles yapped and a Sealyham growled. It seemed that the Germans were tolerant of dogs. Too late. Extinction of propeller. And as we drifted neatly to the gangplank I saw Cosmi reclining in an easy chair.

"Ah, *la famille*," he said, for the benefit of all and sundry. Trust Cosmi to be exactly there and calmer than any of us.

They made us all comfortable on the quarter deck, and the English-speaking officer smiled and asked us please to be careful as we were going to make thirty miles an hour. There was some delay, tense for me because of Cosmi. I remained at his side, and then a miracle took place for the benefit of Cosmi and me, a sign in the sea and the sky. For there was, yes, unmistakably sailing and passing not fifty yards astern, the *Isabel Matutes,* and silently, almost impossibly thankful, we saw who it was at the wheel—Mateo, and waving to us, clowning, Cosmi's brother Pep Salvador, and bashfully smiling, Captain Juan and young Carlos. Also Fernando, the honeymooning schoolmaster quite brideless. A dozen others. And safely, before our eyes and the noncomprehending kind eyes of our German officers and crew, those good men sailed away to open stretches of the sea, to choose their own destination, and not to be shot against the wall. At the rail, Cosmi in his dirty shirt and torn trousers. Did they see us? I think so. And of the dead empty city (white flag) and stench of fishes and our orange peel of town life and promise, we counted seventeen good men sailing to safety and the future, and if only our German craft would start and get clear, perhaps there would be a future after all.

Cosmi, smiling and inscrutable, and at last propeller, and swinging, now moving, elastic of distance, and we turned, not to pass Santa Eulalia and Arabie and Cosmi's wife, small son and life's savings and shores and coves of dreams, but the other way.

Long Live Death!
Death to the Intelligence!

*L*ONG *ago the Spaniards have observed in themselves a strange in-*
fatuation for death. The Carlists went into war singing of "Death,
the Bride," and the Anarchists' battle cry was "Viva la Muerte!" But
it was left to the extreme fascists to combine the cry of "Long live
Death!" with the equally preposterous cry of "Death to the Intelli-
gence!" General Millán Astray, the founder of the Spanish Foreign
Legion, seemed in himself to be the personification and physical
representative of all these mindless cries.

He was a very odd man indeed. He had one eye, one leg, one arm,
and most of his fingers had been shot away. He was proud and vain,
wildly excitable, and incapable of coherent speech. Like the ferocious
and dedicated Anarchists, whom he resembled, he seemed to belong,
long before his death, to the world of the dead; and his ghostly voice
was forever summoning men to death's kingdom.

On August 15, 1936, on the Feast of the Assumption, an extraor-
dinary meeting of the generals took place in Seville to honor the
Monarchist flag which was now substituted for the flag of the Republic.
Here Don Antonio Bahamonde describes the antics of General
Millán Astray and goes on to describe the Falangists' dreams of
empire:

For the substitution of the monarchical flag for the republican,
festivals were organized with flourish of drums and patriotic harangues.

To preside over this great event, the Chief ("Caudillo") and Millán
Astray came to Seville. The authorities, with Cardinal Ilundáin in the

front, went to receive the *Caudillo*. Queipo refused to go, saying, "If Franco wants to see me, he knows where I am." Franco, upon not seeing Queipo, made no allusion to it. He went directly to his liaison quarters established in the Palace of Llandury. A few moments later he set out for the Town Hall, where the ceremony was to take place. When the *Caudillo* arrived there, Queipo was not to be seen. The situation was very strained; we were assembled for more than ten minutes when Queipo arrived. He exchanged with Franco some superficial phrases in the hearing of all, and then went to the central balcony, where the ceremony was to be performed. The plaza was swarming with Falangists, "Requetés," "Pelayos," and "Arrows," who applauded him when he appeared on the balcony. When silence was established, the republican flag was lowered and the monarchical flag hoisted to the strains of the Royal March. The *Caudillo* came forward on the balcony, embraced the flag and kissed it many times, and, raising his voice, shouted in loud cries, "Here it is, it is yours; they wanted to rob us of it." Cardinal Ilundáin kissed it with great unction. Queipo, Millán Astray, and all of us in attendance, did the same. The crowd called upon Franco to speak. Finally he spoke: "This is our flag, the authentic one, and one to which we have all sworn, for which our forefathers died, a hundred times covered with glory." He added a number of vulgar phrases and ended weeping. Then Queipo spoke. He brought a prepared speech in which he gave the history of the colours of the flag and of the different standards which we Spaniards have had, losing himself completely in these disquisitions without finding an ending. His friends spent an uncomfortable time; we saw no end. It was thoroughly ridiculous. He went so far as to talk of the Egyptians. Finally, he recalled the colours of red and gold, and compared them with the blood of our soldiers, generously shed, and with the Andalusian soil, golden with the harvests of our fields, and ended, as usual, with an allusion to the Marxist rabble. During the harangue, Franco, exchanging looks with Millán Astray, with difficulty suppressed his laughter. Afterwards Queipo said that his intense emotion had not permitted him to develop his discourse as he had planned.

Millán Astray, gesticulating like a man possessed, shouted, "We have no fear of them. Let them come; let them come and see what we are capable of under the shadow of this flag." A voice was heard, "Viva Millán Astray!" He replied, "What's that? No vivas for Millán

Astray. But let everyone shout with me, with all the force you are capable of, 'Hail death! Hail death! Hail death!' " The mob chorused the cries. He added, "Now let the 'reds' come. Death to them all!" And he ended by hurling his cap over the crowd with a completely crazy gesture in his effort to electrify them.

In the reception rooms of the Town Hall a cocktail was served. Franco and Queipo exchanged a few words and went into an office, from which they set out for the Division. The *Caudillo* was obliged to arrange matters. Queipo was radiant.

The flags, the propaganda posters of the various organizations, and the photographs of Queipo, were to be seen everywhere: on the barricades, on the façades, in the tram-cars, in the cabs. The Falange, employing every possible means, succeeded in having its colours predominate over all the rest. It put up monumental flags, which covered entire façades; it posted in the most central places enormous posters, which said, "The Falange calls you; now or never." "With us, or against us? There is no middle course. Falange awaits you."

The Requeté, in constant strife with the Falange, put up, in the available places nearest to the Falange posters, their bi-coloured banners with the royal crown, bearing this inscription, "If you are a good Spaniard, love your country and her glorious traditions, enlist with the Requeté." Others said, "Our flag is the only flag; the flag of Spain; our colours are always the same."

The civilian militia, on their part, issued posters with blue letters on white cloth, and the inscription, "Long live the sons of the Fatherland!" They made these of various sizes. They forced even the most modest houses to acquire them and to exhibit them on the balconies. There was not a family in the entire "liberated" territory who did not buy them.

The merchants sell an infinite number of articles which bear the patriotic emblems, in an unrestrained fury of ostentatious patriotism. All emulate each other in an exhibitionism that is grotesque.

There were placards posted up which said, "He who wears no uniform is unworthy of being a Spaniard. The country will call to account all those who have refused their aid. Enlist in the militia before it is too late."

Girls from the women's section of the Falange, accompanied by Falangists who watched in the doors, went into the cafés and similar establishments, and, approaching the tables where there were young men without uniform, asked them to which militia they belonged. If the one thus questioned replied that he belonged to none, they took out of a little basket a woman's chemise in miniature, the size for a doll, and said, "Put this little shirt on. You will look very pretty in it. It is the garment that you should wear." I have witnessed this scene a number of times in the Britz Café and in Gayange. Some took it as a joke, others turned livid; but, sad as it is to confess it, I never saw anyone react fittingly to so base an insult. Their fear of the Falangists who were watching the scene from outside restrained them.

The place of preference in the show-windows was occupied by the photograph of General Queipo. The merchant is obliged to acquire it. It bears the date of July 18th, and the reproduction of the General's signature. It very frequently happens that it is the families of those who have been shot, who are thus obliged to buy the photograph and the posters which glorify the movement. Any number of reproductions of the General's photograph have been made on the most diverse objects: ashtrays, vases, mirrors, etc. The show-windows are adorned with the likeness of Queipo in all sizes and postures.

The photograph of Franco is to be seen in but few places. Queipo, within his own territory, displaces him and annuls his personality. The liaison quarters of Franco tried to impose him but without success. More recently they have obliged the impresarios to exhibit the photograph of the *Caudillo* during the performance for a period of five minutes, while the Royal March is played and the audience remains standing with the arm raised in the Fascist salute.

Very conspicuous posters with the spread eagle and the repeated word, "Empire, Empire," are displayed above the others. This empire constitutes an obsession for the Falange. They say that Spain is athirst—for empire. In my conversations with representative Falangists, I have asked them where this empire is, and in what manner they would make it. The only answer they could make me was that Spain has Imperial destinies, and that she will again be what she was in the time of Charles V. They assure me that the paths of Falange lead to empire.

❁

On both sides of the battle lines men lived among their embattled dreams. The Nationalists dreamed of empire, the Communists of a mechanical and self-regulating Marxist state, the Anarchists of their libertarian cooperatives, while the poor peasants dreamed of being left alone. They were all vain dreams, and very dangerous.

Among those who had put dreams behind them and looked with clear eyes at the world as it is, was Don Miguel de Unamuno, the author of The Tragic Sense of Life. *He was seventy-two when the Civil War broke out, and for thirty-five years he had been Rector of the University of Salamanca. From the beginning of the uprising he had clearly demonstrated his distaste for the methods of the Nationalists, but he was too old, and too ill, to take up a public position against Franco. Quietly he continued to perform his duties as head of the university in spite of the rising clamor for his arrest.*

A month after the meeting of the generals in Seville to honor the new Monarchist flag, Miguel de Unamuno confronted Millán Astray. It is one of the great confrontations of history, the completely civilized man confronting the pure nihilist. Unamuno's public declaration in favor of life and civilized values was the last public statement he ever made, for he died a few weeks later.

The Ceremonial Hall in the University of Salamanca is a spacious chamber, used only on formal occasions, solemn, austere, the walls hung with tapestries. Through the huge windows enters a shimmering flood of iridescent light which deepens the amber glow of the century-old plinth stones.

This was the setting.

The play was enacted on 12 October 1936 when Spanish Fascism was in its first triumphant stage. The morning was half spent. The patriotic festival of the Hispanic Race was being celebrated.

There they were on the presidential dais: the purple calotte, the amethyst ring and the flashing pectoral cross of the Most Illustrious Doctor Plá y Daniel, Bishop of the Diocese; the lacklustre robes of the Magistrates; the profuse glitter of military gold braid side by side with the crosses and medals exhibited on presumptuously bulging chests; the morning coat, set off by black satin lapels, of His Excellency the Civil Governor of the Province; and all these surrounded —was it to honour or to overwhelm?—the man whose pride in his incorruptible Spanish conscience was steadfast and straight: Miguel de Unamuno y Jugo, the Rector.

From the front wall, the allegorical picture of the Republic had gone, and there shone from under a canopy the Caudillo's effigy in plump insolence. To the left and right, on crimson-covered divans, the silk of the doctors' gowns and their mortarboards with gay tassels in red, yellow, light blue and dark blue, symbolizing Law, Medicine, Letters and Science.

A few ladies were scattered among the learned men; in a prominent place, Doña Carmen Pola de Franco, the distinguished spouse of the Man of Providence.

From a packed audience which faced the dais of the elect, with its protective balustrade of dark polished wood, there rose the confused murmur of expectancy. At the far end of the long hall glinted the rounded brasses of a military band, ready to play the obligatory hymns.

The ceremony began. Don Miguel opened it with the ritual formula, spoken in that unforgettable voice of his, thin and clear. Then Don Francisco Maldonado stepped on to the platform, short, fat, Professor of Literature and Salamancan landowner. With affected, baroque diction and vast erudition, he delivered a colourless and circumstantial address. At the end, he expressed his hope for a better future, with kindly and sincere emotion. He descended the steps among cheers and applause, bowed to the dais and returned to his seat. He was followed on the speaker's platform by Don José María Ramós Loscertales of Saragossa, tall and lean, with fluid gestures, flashing eyes, sober and precise of speech, his sensitive face in perpetual motion, expressing a subtle and enigmatic irony. He spoke of the mortal struggle raging at the time—yet another circumstantial speech. Its thesis: the energies of Spain at white-heat in a crucible of passion—and like gold from the crucible, Spain would emerge in the end, purified and without stain, in her true colours which rejected the taints artificially imposed on her. Clamorous ovation.

And then rose General Millán Astray. With ostentatious humility, he preferred to speak from his own place. His appearance was impressive. The General is thin, of an emaciation which pretends to slimness. He has lost one eye and one arm. His face and his body bear the indelible tattoo of horrible scars. These savage mutilations and gashes evoke a sinister personality; his angry and rancorous bearing kills any compassion his mutilations might have inspired.

He had been the organizer of the *Tercio,* the Spanish Foreign Legion for operations in Africa; he had been the creator of an iron, inexorable discipline to which the reckless fugitives from other social discipline submitted of their own free will. He had gained those wounds which to many seemed glorious, to some over-exploited, and to all horribly impressive, in those fantastic Moroccan campaigns which had been Spain's bitter nightmare under the regretted aegis of King Alphonso XIII, called "The African" in his day. Yet the unquestionable nimbus which surrounded the figure of the General was due to the gruesome originality, to the mysterious paradox of his battle-cry: *"Viva la Muerte!"*—"Long live Death!"

Barely had Millán Astray risen to his feet when his strident voice rang out, as though bursting from that heroic chest bedizened with a galaxy of crosses, the testimonials and rewards of gallantry.

First of all he said that more than one-half of all Spaniards were criminals, guilty of armed rebellion and high treason. To remove any ambiguity, he went on to explain that by these rebels and traitors he meant the citizens who were loyal to the Government.

In a sudden flash of intuition, a member of the audience was inspired so as to grasp the faultless logic of a slogan which common minds had thought the product of an epileptic brain. With fervor, he shouted:

"Viva, viva la Muerte!"—"Long live Death!" .

Impervious, the General continued his fiery speech:

"Catalonia and the Basque country—the Basque country and Catalonia—are two cancers in the body of the nation. Fascism, which is Spain's health-bringer, will know how to exterminate them both, cutting into the live, healthy flesh like a resolute surgeon free from false sentimentality. And since the healthy flesh is the soil, the diseased flesh the people who dwell on it, Fascism and the Army will eradicate the people and restore the soil to the sacred national realm. . . ."

He made a pause and cast a despotic glance over the audience. And he saw that he held them in thrall, hypnotized to a man. Never had any of his harangues so subjugated the will of his listeners. Obviously, he was in his element. . . . He had conquered the University! And carried away himself, he continued, blind to the subtle and withering smile of disdain on the lips of the Rector.

"Every Socialist, every Republican, every one of them without exception—and needless to say every Communist—is a rebel against the National Government which will very soon be recognized by the totalitarian States who are aiding us, in spite of France—democratic France—and perfidious England.

"And then, or even sooner, when Franco wants it, and with the help of the gallant Moors who, though they wrecked my body only yesterday, today deserve the gratitude of my soul, for they are fighting for Spain against the Spaniards . . . I mean, the bad Spaniards . . . because they are giving their lives in defence of Spain's sacred religion, as is proved by their attending field mass, escorting the Caudillo and pinning holy medallions and Sacred Hearts to their burnooses . . ."

The General lost himself in the maze of his own vehement outburst. He hesitated, irritated and defiant at the same time. In these straits, an enthusiastic Fascist came to his rescue and shouted:

"Arriba España!"

The crowd bowed their heads in resignation. The man went on, undaunted:

"Spain!"

Mechanically, the crowd responded: "One!"

"Spain!" he repeated.

"Great!" chorused the obedient public.

"Spain!" the Blue Shirt insisted, implacably.

"Free!" they all replied, cowed.

There was an obvious lack of warmth and listlessness in these artificially produced responses. Several Blue Shirts rose to their feet as though pushed by invisible springs, and raised their right arms stiffly in the Roman salute. And they hailed the sepia-colored photograph on the front wall:

"Franco!"

The public rose reluctantly and chanted parrot-like:

"Franco! Franco! Franco!"

But Franco's image did not stir. Neither did the Rector.

Don Miguel did not rise to his feet. And the public fell silent and sat down again.

All eyes were fastened in tense anxiety on the noble head, on the pale, serene brow framed by snow-white hair. The uncertain expression of his eyes was hidden by the glitter of his spectacles.

Between the fine curve of his nose and the silver of his Quixote-like beard, his mouth was twisted in a bitter grimace of undisguised contempt. People began to grow uneasy. A few suddenly felt a recrudescence of their old rancorous abhorrence. Some admired the serene fearlessness of the Master and feared for his safety. The majority were gripped by the voluptuous thrill of imminent tragedy.

At last, Don Miguel rose slowly. The silence was an enormous void. Into this void, Don Miguel began to pour the stream of his speech, as though savouring each measured word. This is the essence of what he said:

"All of you are hanging on my words. You all know me, and are aware that I am unable to remain silent. I have not learnt to do so in seventy-three years of my life. And now I do not wish to learn it any more. At times, to be silent is to lie. For silence can be interpreted as acquiescence. I could not survive a divorce between my conscience and my word, always well-mated partners.

"I will be brief. Truth is most true when naked, free of embellishment and verbiage.

"I want to comment on the speech—to give it that name—of General Millán Astray who is here among us."

The General stiffened provocatively.

"Let us waive the personal affront implied by the sudden outburst of vituperation against Basques and Catalans in general. I was born in Bilbao, in the midst of the bombardments of the Second Carlist War. Later, I wedded myself to this city of Salamanca which I love deeply, yet never forgetting my native town. The Bishop, whether he likes it or not, is a Catalan from Barcelona."

He made a pause. Faces had grown pale. The short silence was tense and dramatic. Expectation neared its peak.

"Just now, I heard a necrophilous and senseless cry: 'Long live Death!' To me it sounds the equivalent of *'Muera la Vida!'*—'To Death with Life!' And I, who have spent my life shaping paradoxes which aroused the uncomprehending anger of the others, I must tell you, as an expert authority, that this outlandish paradox is repellent to me. Since it was proclaimed in homage to the last speaker, I can only explain it to myself by supposing that it was addressed to him, though in an excessively strange and tortuous form, as a testimonial to his being himself a symbol of death.

"And now, another matter. General Millán Astray is a cripple. Let it be said without any slighting undertone. He is a war invalid. So was Cervantes. But extremes do not make the rule: they escape it. Unfortunately, there are all too many cripples in Spain now. And soon, there will be even more of them if God does not come to our aid. It pains me to think that General Millán Astray should dictate the pattern of mass-psychology.

"That would be appalling. A cripple who lacks the spiritual greatness of Cervantes—a man, not a superman, virile and complete, in spite of his mutilations—a cripple, I said, who lacks that loftiness of mind, is wont to seek ominous relief in seeing mutilation around him."

His words rang out crystal clear. The heavy silence gave them resonance.

"General Millán Astray is not one of the select minds, even though he is unpopular, or rather, for that very reason. Because he *is* unpopular. General Millán Astray would like to create Spain anew—a negative creation—in his own image and likeness. And for that reason he wishes to see Spain crippled, as he unwittingly made clear."

At this point General Millán Astray could stand it no longer and shouted wildly:

"Muera la Inteligencia!"—"To death with Intelligence!"

"No, long live intelligence! To death with bad intellectuals!" corrected Don José María Permán, a journalist from Cadiz. A few voices seconded him, many hands were clenched to check an imprudent impulse to applaud the aged Rector. The Blue Shirts felt tempted to become violent, true to totalitarian procedure. But a most unusual realization of their numerical inferiority strangled this impulse at birth. Arguments flared up round the names of academicians who had disappeared or been shot. Irritated "sh's" came from various sides. Some gowned figures had gathered round Don Miguel, some Blue Shirts round their vilified hero.

At last the clamour died down like the sound of surf on the beach, and the groups dispersed. Don Miguel again became visible to the assembly, very erect, his arms folded and his gaze fixed straight ahead, like the statue of a stoic. Once more his word dominated the hall.

"This is the temple of intellect. And I am its high priest. It is you who are profaning its sacred precincts.

"I have always, whatever the proverb may say, been a prophet in my own land. You will win, but you will not convince. You will win, because you possess more than enough brute force, but you will not convince, because to convince means to persuade. And in order to persuade you would need what you lack—reason and right in the struggle. I consider it futile to exhort you to think of Spain. I have finished."

The controversies flamed up again, interrupted by sudden waves of unanimous silence.

Then Don Esteban Madruga, Professor of Common Law, a straightforward and truly good man, took Don Miguel by the arm, offered his other arm to Doña Carmen Pola de Franco, and led them out of the room. Unamuno walked with perfect dignity, pale and calm. Franco's wife was so stunned that she walked like an automaton.

The Junta in Burgos was consulted. Franco's orders came: they were inexorable. If the offence was considered grave enough, the Rector of Salamanca was to be executed without delay. The offence was indeed considered to be so, but somebody who was better advised realized that such an act would fatally injure the prestige of the nascent "Movement of Salvation." It was therefore never carried out.

Don Miguel retired to his home. His house was kept surrounded by the police.

And shortly afterwards, thus guarded, Miguel de Unamuno died suddenly on the last day of 1936, a victim of a stroke of the brain, achieving lasting peace.

Two Heroes

*T*HE *chief fault of José Antonio Primo de Rivera was that he was always attempting to vindicate the dictatorship imposed on Spain by his father. He had a classic profile, an engaging smile, dark brilliant eyes, and a faint air of perpetual bewilderment. He was, until his arrest in March 1936, the head of the militant Fascist organization called the* Falange Española, *and from prison he succeeded in maintaining some control over his Fascist followers. On June 5, 1936, he was removed to the prison at Alicante. He seems to have had no complicity in the officers' uprising and to have disliked most of the generals who took part, but since his Fascist organization obviously served the interests of the extreme right, it was inevitable that he should be brought to trial.*

The trial opened in Alicante on November 16, 1936. His brother Miguel, and his brother's wife, Margarita Larios, were also on trial. José Antonio was permitted to be his own defense lawyer. He made an admirable defense, demolished most of the arguments leveled against him, and dealt calmly with the arguments which showed that he had long been planning a revolution to take over the country. In his defense José Antonio could point to his announced program to give land to the peasants and bring about wide-ranging social reforms. He could explain away the curious discovery of pistols in his cell, but he could not explain away his own legend.

He maintained his calm during the violent speeches of the public prosecutor. The Alicante newspaper El Día, *under banner headlines reading* JOSÉ ANTONIO CONDEMNED TO DIE, *wrote an admiring account of his court behavior. "He listened to the prosecutor as though listening to rain. It seemed not to concern him. He went on reading, writing and arranging his papers without the least affectation and without a trace of nervousness." But he collapsed when the death sentence was read to him. His last words were a plea for clemency. "I am not one of those who say they despise life when they are in a situation like mine," he said. "Life is not a firework one lets off at the end of a garden party."*

His sister Carmen, arrested as a material witness, attended the trial and visited him on his last night. Here is the account she wrote some months later:

I was in Alicante in those early days of November. So far nothing had happened to disturb our personal tranquillity. Just when we were feeling confident that the fury of the Reds would not be turned against us, José Antonio, Miguel and Margarita were put on trial. The death penalty was demanded.

For us they were days of unbearable anguish. Almost every day we were called upon to give our testimonies. The trial date was set, and José Antonio asked the court for permission to act as his own defense council, and also for permission to defend his brother. There were some objections, but finally permission was granted.

He was handed the indictment, and in only a few hours he prepared one of the most brilliant defenses ever heard in any court.

Up to this time all trials had taken place in the auditorium of the city hall, but it was decided to hold our trial in the prison itself to avoid transporting the defendants back and forth. It was a public trial. Margarita Larios was detained with us at the reformatory, and every day of the trial she was driven to the prison.

The lives of three of my loved ones were hanging precariously in the balance. For me the suffering was terrible, and was not made easier by the fact that I also was a prisoner. The hours passed slowly without news, without sensation, unconsolingly. Only when Margarita returned to the reformatory at night did we learn what had happened.

The trial lasted three days. On the night of the third day there was no sign of Margarita. Even in the early hours of the morning there was no sign of her. We were terrified by the slightest sound. The wardress came in and went out again, mercifully hiding from us whatever news she had picked up from outside. "They are still deliberating," she said. Hours and hours passed. At last, some time after three o'clock in the morning, Margarita arrived.

We did not dare to direct questions at her. Without uttering a word, she entered the cell, embraced us, and burst into tears. We understood everything. As well as she could, she told us what happened. After deliberating for six hours the judges polled their verdict, and six black balls resting on the judges' bench testified to the verdict.

"José Antonio was more magnificent than he has ever been," she told us. "You cannot imagine the attention and respect with which the public listened to him. He won the sympathy of everyone. And when at the very end he realized that he was the only one to receive the death penalty, he turned to us with infinite joy written on his face and said: 'You are safe!' "

On the following day we did everything we could to secure a pardon for him. We were told it was necessary to provide depositions requesting a pardon.

The warden of our prison told us José Antonio had asked for three things should his sentence be carried out: a priest, a notary, and permission to say farewell to his family. All three requests were granted. We asked the warden not to send us to him except as a last resort, so as to spare us from what inevitably must be considered a most painful experience. About nine o'clock on the night of November 19th—a very late hour in a prison—we heard light tapping on the cell door.

"Get ready to go to the provincial prison," the warden said.

We knew then that the sentence had been confirmed.

"Is there no hope?" we asked.

"We do not know yet, but it is better for you to go now. Permission for you to go has been granted for this visit."

We continued to try to deceive each other, for he was unable to convince us that this would be our last visit. I was the more cowardly, for I could not prevent myself from crying. His aunt, María, was in the reformatory with me.

"Don't cry," they told me. "You will be giving José Antonio a harder time."

So I set my face and was strong, and we went to the provincial prison.

A prison is always a terrifying place to those who are not accustomed to it, and so it is difficult to describe what we went through that night.

We entered through a half-closed door and crossed the central courtyard. Dimly lit bulbs showed the way, and strange shadows hovered over the walls. Two men accompanied us.

"Wait in there," they said, and they left us in a room.

Soon they came back for us, and we were taken deeper into the prison. We reached a cell where there was only one bed. Less than two minutes passed, and then at the end of a gallery we saw the figure of José Antonio advancing towards us with two Red militiamen on either side of him, and several others behind.

It is impossible for me to describe what I lived through during these moments, for words are inadequate to describe such emotions. Our adored brother was coming towards us for the last time. In spite of his great talents he had been unable to save his life.

Seeing us, he smiled, and without losing his composure for even a moment he embraced us. I was crushed between my emotions and the effort to restrain them, and burst into tears. Then he kissed me with all his soul, at the same time saying:

"Don't cry, Carmen. There is still hope."

"No, it's not possible, José . . ." I said. "It is not possible that they could do this to you."

"It is understandable," he said. "So many of the Falange have fallen that it is quite understandable that I, their leader, should also fall. There is still hope. I have a three to seven chance—" He turned to the warden accompanying us and said: "Have you brought them here because my pardon has been denied? It would seem so."

"No," the warden said. "Confirmation of the sentence has not yet arrived."

The subject changed at once, and he asked us about Fernando.[1]

We did not know then that Fernando was the first to give his life. We had been told he was in Seville, and this information we passed on to him."

"Then he has survived," José Antonio said, "and now I alone—"

There was a vast joy in his voice at the thought of being the only one to die.

Turning to Aunt María, he said:

"You must not worry, Aunt María. I have made my confession and I am at peace. Besides, ever since this terrible thing began, I have

---

[1] Fernando Primo de Rivera, José Antonio's brother, died in the Model Prison in Madrid on August 23, 1936.

een preparing myself for just such a moment. I prayed daily and ecited the rosary. Then, too, I have been well fed. If you are sentenced to death, there is nothing better than being well cared for. Instead of the usual mess of food, I have been given garlic soup with eggs and excellent meat."

He had grown thinner. The Reds who witnessed the interview id not miss a single word, and their faces mirrored admiration for a man who, on the threshold of death, possessed such stout courage.

I had brought a crucifix, and gave it to him.

"Simply by looking at it, full pardon is given to you at the hour of eath," I said. "I bring it to you just in case—"

With great pleasure he took the crucifix and showed it to those anding around.

Because they might think I gave him something else, he said: "You e, it is only a crucifix she has given me. It gives me very great happiness, for I did not have one," he added, turning to me.

About twenty minutes passed, and then the warden suggested it as time for us to leave.

"They will come back, won't they?" José Antonio said, "unless e sentence is carried out immediately."

Although he must have been certain we would never come back, e warden agreed. José Antonio embraced us for the last time, and en went back to his cell. Turning, we waved goodbye "for a little hile." Then we were led out of the prison.

On the next day, November 20th, at twenty minutes to seven clock in the morning, we ourselves heard the volley which ended s life. The execution took place in the courtyard of the provincial ison.

His last words, spoken in farewell to the warden shortly before they me for him, were:

"Warden, if I have done anything to disturb or annoy you, forgive !"

the night before his execution he wrote out a long testament, iding his property between his brothers and sisters, and defending role as head of the Falange Española. He asked pardon for any od he may have shed and called upon God to accept his life as a rifice "in compensation for the vanity and pride which constituted great a part of my life," and he forgave his executioners.

Dead, he became a legend. He became el Ausente, *"the absent one,'*
the mysterious symbol of Spanish rebirth. He had been one of the
very few who might have rivaled Franco in power.

Buenaventura Durruti was a man of a very different stamp, bu
he also became a legend, regarded with something approaching aw
by the surviving Anarchists. Ten days after the execution of Jos
Antonio Primo de Rivera he died mysteriously. He seems to hav
died at the hands of one of his own followers.

Durruti was born on July 14, 1896, on the anniversary of the storm
ing of the Bastille. His father was a railwayman and a militant socia
ist, and the son became even more militant than the father. In th
railway strike of 1917 it was rumored that the young Durruti we
responsible for blowing up bridges and setting fire to trains. Later I
took part in a plot to kill King Alfonso XIII. By 1932 he was tl
acknowledged leader of the Anarchists in Barcelona.

He was a heavy-set, powerful man, dark-skinned, dark-eyed, full
animal magnetism. He took part in the fighting during the uprising
Barcelona, and when Madrid seemed about to fall, he lead a colun
of Anarchists in its defense. Here a Catalan describes how he die

When the "Durruti Column" left Barcelona, there was extraor
nary enthusiasm. The black and red flags waved, bands were playir
and flowers were thrown at him from the windows. We never sa
him alive again.

Madrid was in grave danger, and the column was thrown into t
thick of the fighting in the Casa del Campo. To everyone's surpr
the Anarchists panicked. They were not trained for this kind of wa
Durruti tried to remedy the situation with summary court-martia
Some of his closest friends were shot. He was utterly merciless.

Suddenly in Barcelona there came the news that he was dead. V
heard that he had been killed as he was stepping from his car o
side his headquarters after returning from the front. We heard tl
the fatal shot had been fired by a sharpshooter belonging to t
Guardia Civil who had fired from a window two thousand feet aw

The shot, which penetrated his heart, had grazed none of those who were standing close to him.

The funeral took place in Barcelona. It was a dark cloudy day, and Barcelona was given over to collective hysteria. People knelt in the streets as the cortege passed with its honor guard of anarchists in battle dress. They wept openly. Half a million people were gathered in the streets, and none were dry-eyed. For Barcelona, Durruti was a symbol of the triumph of the anarchist idea, and it was almost beyond belief that he could be dead.

There was a strange silence in the city that day. The red and black anarchist flags waved listlessly. No sun shone on the cortege. I have never known a more silent or more solemn or sadder day.

Speeches were made over the flower-draped coffin, and later that day he was buried. He was not forgotten.

About a year later an exhibition honoring the heroic resistance of Madrid was held in the Plaza de Cataluña. Here, among other objects, was exhibited the shirt worn by Durruti at the time of his death. It was displayed in a glass case. People crowded round it, observing carefully the bullet-hole with its scorched edges. I was there when I heard someone saying that it was inconceivable that this bullet-hole could have been made by a man firing from two thousand feet. That night I sent specialists from the medico-forensic laboratory to examine the shirt. They reported the unanimous conclusion that the shot had been fired from a few inches away.

Some days later I had dinner with Señora Durruti, a Frenchwoman. "How did he die?" I asked her. "Surely you know the truth."

"Yes, I know it."

"Then what happened?"

She looked straight at me.

"Until the day I die," she said, "I will accept the official explanation that he was shot by a Guardia Civil from an upper window."

Then in a lower voice she said: "But I know he was killed by one of those standing beside him. It was an act of vengeance."

Madrid in November

AGAIN and again Franco promised to take Madrid by storm, and again and again he was repulsed. All the weapons of intimidation and terror were employed to make Madrid surrender, and Madrid refused to surrender. The Government abandoned Madrid for the safety of Valencia, and the Madrileños seemed to be relieved by the absence of a government for which they had shown very little fondness. The supreme authority in Madrid was no longer the Government, but General José Miaja, who looked and often behaved like a wise old peasant, and who was perfectly capable of leaving his desk at the Ministry of War to take part in the fighting in the Casa del Campo.

Under Miaja the Madrileños were prepared to go on fighting to the end, but no one, not even Miaja, knew what the city would have to suffer before the winter came to an end. In November Franco launched a massive attack on the city, which was repulsed with the help of the International Brigade. The cold damp winter began, the bombs fell, the people went hungry, and the Fifth Column, Franco's supporters, drove about the city, shooting at random to inspire terror. But the Madrileños had explored the landscape of terror so thoroughly that they had even discovered the places where terror no longer inspires any emotion except familiarity.

Here Arturo Barea describes the familiar landscape:

In those days of November 1936, the people of Madrid, all of them together, and every single individual by himself, lived in constant danger of death.

The enemy stood at the gates of the city and could break in at any moment. Shells fell in the streets. Bombers flew over the roofs and dropped their deadly loads, unpunished. We were in a war and in a besieged town; but the war was a civil war and the besieged town held enemies in its midst. No one knew for certain who was a loyal friend and who a dangerous hidden enemy. No one was safe from denunciation and error, from the shot of an overexcited Miliciano or of a masked assassin dashing past in a car and spraying the pavement with machine-gun bullets. What food there was might disappear overnight. The air of the town was laden with tension, unrest, distrust, physical fear, and challenge, as it was laden with the unreasoning, embittered will to fight on. We walked side by side, arm in arm, with Death.

November was cold, damp, and hung with fogs. Death was filthy.

The shell which killed the old street seller at the corner of the Telefónica flung one of her legs far away from the body into the middle of the street. November caught it, smeared its slime and mud on what had been a woman's leg, and turned it into the dirty tatters of a beggar.

The fires dripped soot. It dissolved in the dampness and became a black viscous liquid that stuck to one's soles, clung to one's hands, hair, face, and shirt collar, and stayed there.

Buildings slit open by bombs exhibited shattered, fog-soaked rooms with swelling, shapeless furniture and fabrics, their dyes oozing out in turgid dribbles, as though the catastrophe had happened years before and the ruins stayed abandoned ever since. In the houses of the living, the fog billowed through the broken window panes in chill wads.

Have you ever leaned by night over the curbstone of an old well where the waters sleep far down? Everything is black and silent and you cannot see the bottom. The silence is dense, it rises from the bowels of the earth and smells of mold. When you speak a word, a hoarse echo answers from the deep. If you go on watching and listening, you will hear the velvet padding of slimy beasts on the walls of the shaft. Suddenly one of the beasts drops into the water. The water catches a spark of light from somewhere and dazzles you with a fugitive, livid, steely flash, as though of a naked knife blade. You turn away from the well with a cold shudder.

That is how it felt to look down into the street from one of the windows high up on the Telefónica.

At times the silence filled with dreaded sounds, that silence of a dead town, was ripped, and the shaft of the well came alive with piercing screams. Bundles of light swept through the street alongside the screeching sirens mounted on motorcycles, and the drone of bombers invaded the sky. The nightly slaughter began. The building quivered in its roots, the windows rattled, the electric lights waxed and waned. And then everything was choked and drowned in a pandemonium of hisses and explosions, of red, green, and blue glares, of twisting, gigantic shadows cast by crashing walls and disemboweled houses, of madly tolling fire bells, of whistles, of shouts, of cries. The broken glass showering down on the pavement tinkled musically, almost merrily.

By all accounts November 19th was the most terrifying of all the days endured by the Madrileños. Here is an account by Mikhail Koltzov, a former editor of Pravda, *a notorious* bon vivant, *and a brilliant correspondent. He was shot by orders from Stalin on his return to Russia, and has been recently rehabilitated.*

November 19th

These last two days were the worst this unhappy city has ever suffered.

Madrid is burning. A light glows in the streets, heat pours out of the streets, but it is not daylight, and not summer, but a November night. As I walk through the city enormous fires from all sides, and wherever I turn, light my way.

Madrid is burning, set on fire by German airplanes. Public buildings, hotels, hospitals, schools, all are burning. The residences of the people are in flames. The firemen cannot cope with the fires. They are completely exhausted. Even if they were five times as many, they would be unable to put out the flames. With the help of volunteers they are trying to prevent further disasters—explosions and mass deaths. They have quickly cut off gas-mains, removed gasoline stores, and isolated burning buildings.

With blind fury the Fascists are determined to break the resistance of Madrid. They are determined to wipe the capital of Spain from the face of the earth, to destroy her habitations, and at the very least to compel the defenders to surrender the city so that the million people living here shall be spared. What is happening now could destroy the sanity of sane men. I cannot vouch for the psychic health of all adult Madrileños, but I know that in this city many are suffering from nervous collapse.

The suffering of Madrid has by no means come to an end. The Fascist High Command is continuing to bombard Madrid with increasing fury. They have concentrated all their aviation here. Twenty Junkers with thirty supporting fighters bombarded the city today—there were fifty planes in the air at one time. The Republican air force is numerically weaker, and their courage cannot always compensate for the numerical superiority of the enemy. However, our "snub-nosed" brought down two Junkers and two fighters today.

Every three or four hours the bombardment is renewed. After each bombing there are more and more blazing ruins, more and more heaps of bloody flesh. The prayers, screams and lamentations of the people rise from the street. Those sharp-sighted, quietly murderous men manning their dark grey, steely planes circle the city, and the rumble of death can be heard above the defenceless roofs. The victims are removed from the streets. The cold winter air pours into the houses—there are few unbroken windows left. And then everything begins again from the beginning. What seemed to be an ominous shape of the future, recorded only in books, has become fact. Before the eyes of the whole world, on the threshold of 1937, Fascist militarism is destroying an enormous European city, the capital of Spain.

A two hundred kilogram bomb can destroy a five-story building: it can even reach down into the building's cellar. Such bombs have been falling in dozens. The Fascists have dropped three hundred kilogram and even heavier bombs capable of destroying eight-story buildings. The Fascists do not have to employ these heavy bombs in order to destroy the thin, fragile walls of the workmen's dwellings. A few incendiary bombs are enough to reduce an entire working-class area to flames in ten minutes.

Late at night we wandered out into the streets. Yesterday the Fascist planes had to use flares to find their way about the city. Today the burning city lights their way. These murderers are drunk with the spectacle of the flames as they fly about freely, dropping more and more bombs on more and more human beings.

The marketplace on the Plaza Carmen has become a blazing

inferno. Suffocating smoke, the acrid smell of olive-oil, burnt fish . . . These market-products, brought here with so much labor, have all perished, and tomorrow most of the Madrileños will have to go hungry. Walls, beams and girders crash to the ground. An enormous pillar of flame lights up all the surrounding houses. Squeezing her hands together, silently weeping, the poetess María Teresa León looks out at the burning city. Glassy and motionless, like lenses, are the eyes of Rafael Alberti. Madrid burns, and it would seem likely that if she burns much longer there will be nothing left. Certainly, today, it seems that nothing will be left.

The palace of the Duke of Alba is burning. It lies on a hill in a beautiful park, and is filled to the brim with books, works of art, whole galleries of paintings. When I visited the palace towards the end of October the Workers' Militia proudly explained how they had posted guards over these relics from the ancient past, guarding everything from the most important statues, paintings and tapestries to the veriest baubles. Even the Duke's old gloves are being protected. The Duke however has fled to London, and from there he has been heard complaining of Red vandalism—this at a time when the guards are carefully wiping the dust from the backs of his books. German airmen dropped incendiary bombs on his palace—not just one, but many. Now all his treasures are shrivelling and burning to cinders in the flames, or would be burning, if the worker-guards at the risk of their lives did not rescue them from the flames and lay them out on the grass—ancient weapons, paintings, mediaeval armor, costly folios from his library. What a picture for those who want conscientiously to determine which class is defending culture and which class is destroying it! . . .

All this while the rebels have been ferociously storming the University City. They have brought up great numbers of reinforcements, artillery, mortars. They have suffered, especially among the Moroccans, huge and terrible losses. The squares in the University City are piled with corpses.

The diplomatic corps are beginning to show some signs of life. One cannot say it is out of pure affection for the Republican Government or the people of Madrid. The nerves of the diplomats are giving way. Bombs from Junkers do not choose where they will fall. They have destroyed a French Lycée in University City, though it was clearly marked with a huge and brand-new Nationalist flag. Several bombs have fallen close to the British Embassy. Representatives of France and England have been inspecting the damage in the city, especially the hospitals. They have published a note of protest against the bombing. All the acceptable words are included in the note—"humanity," "defenceless population," "the horrors of destruction," "the rights of man." Only one small detail is missing: there is no address. For some reason the note was sent only to the editors of the Madrid newspapers.

November 20th

Rain has been falling since morning. It is something of a relief—enemy planes have not come over. The Militia and the International Brigade and the Santa Christina almshouse. But the three attacks produced no result.

November 21st

It rained again all day . . .

Mikhail Koltzov was at heart a cynic, with no very deep beliefs. Louis Delaprée, the correspondent of the conservative Paris-Soir, *was a man of a different stamp altogether, wildly passionate in his beliefs, and with no trace of cynicism. All his life he carried on a dangerous love affair with humanity.*

Delaprée wrote French extremely well, but the vigor of his style vanishes in any ordinary translation. I have preferred to reproduce his words in the strange and oddly moving translation made by a Spaniard in Madrid with the help of a dictionary. His tormented English curiously reflects the torment of those times.

Gloom over Madrid is so thick that one thinks it could be cut with a knife. We do not see the sky, but from the sky they see us.

Rustling noise, buzzing, thunder, in an impressive crescendo; it is the rebel airplanes. In the bosom of this darkness, the fighting planes of the government cannot persecute them. Defenceless, we hear above us this deep and musical vibration, herald of death.

Some suppressed detonations, then others, heart-rending.

Glasses moan, sweetly.

The windows open, under an invisible thrust.

And all those noises that will soon become familiar: the stamping of the fugitives, the shrill bells of the ambulances that take away the wounded, the sobs of the women who plunge their heads into their handkerchiefs beside you, the men who go up and down, clacking their heels as they walk to give themselves evidence that they have no fear.

And above all, above all, that noise of the heart going faster, faster.

The first bombs devastate the provincial hospital and San Carlos Hospital.

The old men whose strength is not altogether gone, fling themselves out of the dormitories, jostle on the stairs, stoop in the bottom of the caves, wrangle fiercely for "the best places" with all their declining strength. The invalids and sick let themselves fall on the floor and hide themselves under the beds. Five or six will be found tomorrow morning, in this same spot; they have gone mad and it is necessary to have recourse to violent means in order to pull them out of those ludicrous refuges.

Bombs continue to rain all over the quarter comprised between the square of the Cortes, Atocha station and León Street.

In San Agustín Street, a house, dug from top to bottom by a projectile, like the soil by the colter of the plough, burns and communicates the fire to the house opposite.

The Palace Hotel, where one thousand wounded are sheltered, has it been aimed at? I do not know. But four points of fall encircle it mathematically. The breath of the explosions has broken glasses one centimetre thick. As in San Carlos Hospital, men throw themselves under their bed and try to escape. Dressings of wounds are unfastened, wounds are reopened.

An incendiary bomb falls on top of the French Embassy, Villalar Street, luckily it can be timely quenched. But all the buildings all round blaze like torches. At 5 A.M. the street is still in flames.

A horrible confusion fills the night lit by deadly fulgurations. One knocks against litters. One runs against wounded who, in the glowing of the fire, look at their blood flowing on the asphalt.

At the junction of Alcalá and Gran Vía, a hand clings to my leg. I free myself and lighting a match, I bend over the being who gave that drowned's clasping. It is a young woman, the nose already pinched by the approach of death. I do not know where she has been wounded, but her dressing-gown is red with blood. She mutters:

"See! see what they have done."

And her hand sketches a vague gesture. Another match.

"See! see . . ."

The bloodless hand continues to point something out to my attention. I think at first it is the pool of blood that expands over the pavement.

"Look . . ."

I bend down still and I see on the waste of glasses a little child crushed.

The hand, white as marble, calls heaven to witness and falls again.

A match yet. My comrade Flash of the "Journal," who has come up to me, stoops like me over the wounded:

"She is dead," says he.

It is true. Her last sigh and one spasm have discomposed her dressing-gown. A harrowing wound, delved one should say by a sadist's knife, rends the body from the left breast to the right hip.

An ambulance passes slowly. We call. A man comes down. The luminous sheaf of an electric torch lights the corpse.

"Dead," says the man, briefly. "We shall collect tomorrow. The wounded first."

He notices the child's corpse, which on the causeway risks to be crushed for the second time. His hands adroitly remove the broken glass, take the little corpse and place it on the woman's heart, close to her right breast intact. A last flash of the torch shows us the little childish head on this motherly heart, and everything falls into the night again.

A whole town is full of scenes like that; of similar spectacles that seem to have been invented with delight by a hideous genius, by a demiurge necromancer. I have painted a bit longly that one because it was my first contact, no longer with the abstract bombardment without corpses that I shunned as anyone else in the tortured town, but with the very realities of this carnage.

How could one forget the image of that child lying dead on the breast of a dead woman, in the middle of a pool of black blood?

The day after was worse. That night had only been a general rehearsal.

The enemy's squadrons appeared at three o'clock in the morning. (Madrid was still bandaging its wounded, and counting its dead.) At 8 o'clock and 7 o'clock A.M. and 3:30 P.M. they came back. It was a well done work, a copious and carefully dosed watering of all central borroughs. San Miguel market, the Red Cross hospital, Marqués Urquijo Avenue are crushed. The bombs make explosions all over the place, at Martín de los Hijos and San Marcos Street, there were already three hundred odd dead on the roll.

The aerial bombardment, which undoubtably has been deemed insufficient, is joined by artillery bombardment.

In the telephonic Central that raises over Madrid fifteen stories of American skyscraper and two other—the last ones—of Spanish baroque, six shells of 75 land and by a miracle none explodes. A culot of 155 goes in the great room of the standard but it does not burst either.

The building has been shaken, as under a thrust. But nobody stirs. The girls with the helmets continue to set their pins, the reporters go on calling London or Paris.

Unhappily, in the rest of the city, there is no question of explosives of such a good composition. This bursts, thunders, rends and slays on all sides. The ambulances do not take a moment's rest from going over the streets, renewing their load of wounds and sufferings no sooner they have delivered at a hospital the previous one.

But night falls. Then the great butchery, the horror, the Apocalypse begins. The murdering planes incessantly perform evolutions in the sky dropping alternatively explosive bombs, incendiary bombs and torpedoes.

In the Puerta del Sol, at the end of Alcalá Street, a projectile falls into one of the entrances of the underground, cuts the causeway asunder and scoops out a funnel fifteen metres deep. In the Carrera de San Jerónimo an abyss gapes along the whole length of the street. From twenty focusses at the same time, fire begins to devour the city.

At the beginning of the bombardment, I happen to be with two comrades, near the little market of the Carmen. Three bombs, of which two are incendiary ones, fall near to us. Cowered underneath a porch, we see how the little sheds of the market take fire, lighting the desperate flight of men, women, children.

Making good use of a few minutes' lull, we run to the "Telefónica," the telephone central.

Seen from that magnificent observatory, the spectacle is one of unspeakable horror. A circle of flames converges towards the Gran Vía, with a majestic slowness. The houses are seen set on fire in the roofs first and then burning down to the ground-floor, and collapsing heavily within a glory of sparkles and flakes of fire. Some, burnt up, remain standing, high and sinister figures lit by the reflections of the fire that further away goes on with its business.

The firemen give up throwing water on these thousands of blazes. On the other hand the enemy's planes make their task impossible. These fly very low on the fires and when they see that the extinguishers are levelled, they drop two or three explosive bombs to teach how to behave to these firemen who have the ambition to fulfil their duty. A dozen of these brave men who tried to reach the burning Savoy Hotel are thus killed on top of their ladders and fall into the flames.

Nothing can be done. We must wait the end of this shower of murdering meteors, to wait till the dead and wounded will be numerous enough to quench the thirst of General Franco's gods.

Three hundred thousand persons run in the streets, seeking a shelter. Mothers go back towards the barrio that burns, towards the collapsed house to look for a child who now, though they do not know it, is no more than a little heap of ashes; children, mad with terror, call a mamma who has just been carbonized under the ruins. A whole people seeks a refuge against heaven's wrath and do not find it. From this night, with their mattresses, their alarm-clocks, their resigned souls, their lot of little brats, hungry and terrorized, they turn round in the sacked city; they turn round upon themselves, unable to flee from horror.

For fifteen hours Madrid is burning. Afterwards the fire becomes tired. We have a day of rest. The following night, the 18th, at 2:30, the slaughter is resumed, the fire renewed, hell takes hold of us again.

But what is the use of abiding any longer on the description of this martyrdom of Madrid, to enumerate the places where bombs have been dropped, to describe these mass murders? Horror itself becomes monotonous.

Before the end I want simply to propose five little subjects of meditation:

1. The bombardment has already killed about 2,000 noncombatants.

2. There was no military object within the perimeter that suffered the most.

3. Nobody—I say *nobody*—has seen the famous tracts thrown—it appears—by the rebel aircraft to warn the population that they should take refuge in the Salamanca borough.

4. This quarter already occupied cannot receive now more than twenty thousand persons. Now, there are a million human beings in Madrid.

5. The caves and underground refuges offering a minimum of security can only hold about one hundred thousand persons. Now, there are a million human beings in Madrid.

Death has therefore an easy prey.

Christ said: Forgive them, for they do not know what they are doing.

I think that after the massacre of innocents in Madrid, we must say: Do not forgive them, for they know what they are doing.

Undated

For thirty-six hours we have not been bombarded by the rebel squadrons. We do not owe this to an access of humanity of the besiegers for the artillery does not spare us, but to the state of the sky. It rains incessantly. Grey clouds weigh heavily on the ruins. With so low a ceiling, the planes remain on the aerodromes, keeping for another day their provisions of sudden death.

Undernourished, wan, prostrated, the civilian population avail themselves of this lull to organize their miserable defence against the fire of heaven. From all points of the town, streams of people are marching towards the Salamanca quarter where are to be found almost all the Embassies, except that of France.

This "barrio" of smart or opulent manoirs has been up to now spared by bombs and shells. There is a rumor that General Franco ordered his aviators some days ago to drop tracts warning the civilian population to take shelter in these "bourgeois" streets. Nobody has seen them, but everybody believes in the immunity of Salamanca. They go there then, by whole families, by crowds of emigrants. The fathers walk ahead of the rest of the family, carrying the mattresses on their heads. Behind them the children splashing in the muddy streets, without a laugh, without a smile, with somnambulists' eyes, with worn out faces of little old men. Women constitute the rearguard, dragging handcarts full of old things, baskets, chairs and cages. Little donkeys, terribly overloaded, trot in the midst of these removals in which the old picaresque of Spain has been ousted by the sinister images of the worst haunted Goyas.

Old men limp, not to lose the column out of sight, crying with fatigue and misery.

When these migrating tribes arrive in Salamanca, they stop, and despair falls like a mask of ashes on all faces. The place is engaged. Thousands of persons encamp in the wind, under the rain. Hearths have been set up again with kitchen utensils, mattresses and beds. Only, about these abstract abodes there are no walls, above there is no ceiling.

Twenty thousand persons live in such a way under the rain, in the cold. The houses are already filled up and the lobbies and caves and dog-huts.

Those who are late look with envious eyes at these open-air installations, entreat to have a little corner left to them and beg two square metres of sticky paving-stones or asphalt to lodge their family there. But it is impossible to close the ranks any more. So, the poor people go back or establish themselves as near as possible to the "taboo" quarter.

Certain people who are not Madrileños began to flee two months ago. I have made the acquaintance of an old peasant of Badajoz region who previously sought refuge in Talavera, then in Toledo, before coming to strand on this shore.

His two sons have been killed in the war, his wife was mangled during Tuesday's bombardment. He stands there alone, under the rain, on the bounds of Salamanca quarter. Raising up very straight in his black and plaited blouse, the water from the sky and tears washing his face, he blasphemes slowly, gravely, to revenge himself.

"What have I done to deserve that, sir?" he says to me.

And he looks at this crowd sat or lain under the rain and he does not understand them.

This crowd who bless the rain which makes them shiver.

For when the sun will reappear, the planes will also come back again.

The most frightful, strange and sinister thing that I have seen in Madrid is this: thousands of men, women and children who fear the return of the sun like the man condemned to death in his last night's cell.

Undated

Everything is quiet today on the front of Madrid. Rain, in a twelve hours' shower, has turned the battlefield into a bog where the attacks become impossible. All the depressions of the Casa del Campo are lakes and Manzanares itself, so thin, so puny, succeeds in resembling a true river.

This deluge might well suspend the thundering progress of war, but it cannot slacken the evacuation of the noncombatants. It continues with an accelerated rhythm, but with a perfect order. Fifteen thousand women and children leave Madrid every day, heaped upon trucks, on dowagers' limousines, on auto-cars of countryside weddings.

Women and children are by no means the only evacuated. Masterpieces also have set out on the way to exile. All the precious books of the National Library, the manuscripts, the incunabula, went out this morning with a children's convoy. On a lorry two little lads of seven sat on a case.

"What is within there?" I asked.

And they gave me this answer with haughtiness.

"The first edition of *Don Quixote.*"

Soon the Goyas and the Grecos, the Raphaels and the Zurbaráns will take their way to Valencia. If the siege still lasts for some weeks, there will not be in the city a single smile of women or children. The light of the masterpieces will shine under other skies.

Madrid will be but a warring city, gorged with fierce soldiers among ruined walls.

November 25th

While the soldiers were so killing each other by wholesale, the planes, later the cannons of the rebels continued in Madrid their work of destruction.

Every ten minutes or so, along fifteen hours, a shell of 75 or 155 has fallen on the centre of the town. At the end, nobody started at the explosion. They only grew restless when it made them wait. Man does not like to see his habits disturbed. I have seen people who muttered looking at their watch.

"There! 'It' is late!"

It is not bragging, but the apprehension rather that this accepted fear, this danger known had their place taken by other ones, worse.

And the worse comes of course with the great three-engined planes which everybody fears much more than the artillery. At 4:45 P.M. they have appeared over the city. Presently pursued by the government's squadrons, they have not flown away before throwing a dozen bombs between the Gran Vía and the Puerta del Sol. The college and the Church of Saint-Louis of the French have been once again hit. Like some buildings upon which the thunderbolt gave vent to its fury it will be very soon but a ruin, a heap of rubbish, a phantom of ruins.

I ignore the number of victims of this last bombardment.

But I have seen die one of those who were killed by it. It was a fine old "Limpiabotas," one of those bootblacks who wander through the city with a little box full of old brushes and odd blackings with which they impart a marvelous polish on the most worn down at the heel shoes. Although he had spent knelt down a half of his life, he was a haughty man who would have been able to shake his customers' hands without debasing. I had made his acquaintance a long time ago and more than once, when my shoes were blacked, he had honoured me with his conversation.

On Monday I had met him at the Gran Vía and he had said to me:

"They will kill us all, sir, if that goes on. Certainly me at least. I do not know where to take refuge when this falls. And I have forebodings."

He tossed a penny on his black hand.

"What are you doing?"

"I play at head or tail, to know where I am to go. If it is head, I'll go along the right footpath. If tail, I'll go along the left one."

This little game has led the poor old fellow to the Carmen Market at 4:50 P.M. But he has just arrived to receive a splinter of bomb in his head. I have passed by there five minutes later. He was still lying on the footpath, his box thrown down on the kennelstone, with its flagons and its brushes. He had a penny coin near his face. The penny-piece said "head": go on the right. The old limpia was on the left footpath.

Of course, this does not mean anything at all. But logic loses here all its rights. And I know several freethinkers who follow to the letter the order of the penny-piece.

These superstitions are pardonable when planes fly over your heads, laden with death.

November 28th

The military operations interrupted on all fronts for two days because of the bad weather have resumed tonight. A violent cannonade has shaken the banks of the Manzanares since two o'clock in the morning. And from both sides the infantry coming out from their marshes have already launched two attacks and counter-attacks in the University City.

In the cloudless sky a government's fighting squadron pursues six enemy planes which come to drop bombs on the centre.

Fine weather, blue sky . . . therefore women and children will be massacred today. . . .

Undated

General Franco suffered yesterday one of the worst failures he has met with since the beginning of the siege of Madrid. His desperate attacks have been repulsed on all fronts. And on all fronts the government troops taking the offensive have won ground.

For ten hours the rebels have launched attacks against Pozuelo-Aravana, against Las Rosas, in the University City, in the Moncloa sector. . . . None has been successful, in spite of the volume of the means employed and of the crowd of Moorish troops and legionaries.

At the end of the day the insurgent generals seem to run short of ammunition. This fact is not surprising, for in the Tagus sector the Uribarri column have succeeded in blowing up thirty-two wagon-loads of ammunition which were being conveyed to the Madrid front.

A tremendous blow has been dealt on the rebels with the reconquering of the Hospital Clínico. This huge building of red brick commanded with its bulk one half of the University City. From its windows the insurgents kept under the fire of their Mausers and machine-guns the lines of communication from the town to the trenches. Were I not afraid of wearying you by always referring to my personal experience (though little examples are sometimes indispensable in order to prove great things), I should tell you I have strong reasons for knowing the strategical importance of this cube of masonry. Having ventured the other day into the no man's land of University City with the men of a patrol, I was pursued for twenty minutes by a methodical rifleman. Impossible to escape. No matter where I went, the man saw me from his window and a bullet came to bury itself into the loam, nearby. It appeared that this untirable but luckless sniper had some pals who shared his game, for the men with me were submitted to the same treatment. As soon as we lifted the head, we heard a hiss and a little spurt of mud rose within our neighbourhood.

I should have said nothing of this little incident if it did not make understandable how the rebels from the Hospital Clínico were enabled to play, like a cat with mice, with the militiamen's life, mowing down the convoys of supplies, decimating the loyal troops in their drives, backing with close fire their own attacks.

Now it is finished. By dint of 155's the loyalists have begun by reducing the dangerous building to an enormous heap of bricks. Seen through the binoculars it looks like one of those shapeless Nineveh ruins which sink slowly into the uniformity of the desert. It was unbelievable that there were still some men alive in such a disaster. But it was true. When the dinamiteros and the governmental throwers of grenades advanced towards the ruins, flinging the thunderbolt with their distended arms, you could see little black silhouettes spring from the shapeless heap of bricks, running with all the strength of their legs in the direction of the enemy's lines. In two hours this enemy's position which for a week had endangered the defence of Madrid was transformed into a ruin where the governmental machine-gunners were driving in the trivet of their machines.

Everywhere a similar good fortune followed the loyal troops. In the Moncloa, in the very spot where raised the Palazette of the Duchess of Alba who was loved by Goya and whose beauty, from the splendour of the "Maja Desnuda" lights the centuries, the militiamen repulse an attack.

At the Iron gate they are clearing up the last houses occupied by the rebels and free the Corunna road. In the south they reconquer Villaverde where the Moors were strongly intrenched.

This morning the governmental attack widens. The militiamen advance on Casa Guemada and Garobitos.

In the sky the day is not less lucky for the government.

Twenty fighting planes suddenly appear while three enemy planes fly over the town. One of them falls blazing, comet of an incandescent red in the sunshine. The others flee.

Shortly before five o'clock, five rebel bombing machines escorted by 13 fighting planes appear to the east of Madrid. They have not yet reached the zenith of the town when 36 governmental fighting planes swoop upon them. The insurgents shun the combat and 500,000 persons gathered in the streets and on the roofs salute their flight with wild shouting.

At nightfall, a deep sadness falls in spite of all on the capital. The losses are numerous in the ranks of the Militia and of the International Brigade and, for the first time, the rebels made use of gas.

Who would not admire a population submitted to such dangers, menaced by such horrors, not knowing whether their reprieve will come or not, and who nevertheless keep smiling?

Madrid has not enough to eat. Madrid burns to warm herself the beams of her wrecked houses (it is not an image, it is true), but Madrid holds out and ever shall.

Undated

The insurgents have launched tonight new assaults against Madrid. From ten o'clock to one o'clock in the morning, we have heard a violent cannonade. The whole governmental artillery fired at the same time. It appears that the rebels try to gain a footing in the Rosales plateau. At the moment they have not succeeded yet.

This was the last message sent to Paris-Soir *by Louis Delaprée. For some time he had been aware that his dispatches were being tampered with by the editor, and only half of them were printed. He sent off a blast to the editor: "I thought you were my friend, and would spare me a useless task. For three weeks I have been getting up at 5 A.M. in order to get the news into the first edition. You made me work for the wastepaper basket. Thanks. I shall send you nothing more. It is not worth while. The massacre of a hundred Spanish children is less interesting than a Mrs. Simpson's sigh."*

On December 11th he drove to the airport and flew off to Paris. He never reached Paris. His plane was shot down in flames over Guadalajara.

Madrid survived the nightmare winter, and entered a nightmarish spring. John Dos Passos describes Madrid five months later:

The correspondents take their meals in the basement of the Hotel Gran Vía almost opposite the Telephone Building. You go in through the unlit lobby and through a sort of pantry and down some back stairs past the kitchen into a cavelike place that still has an air of pink lights and nightclub jippery about it. There at a long table sit the professional foreign correspondents and the young worldsaviours and the members of foreign radical delegations. At the small tables in the alcoves there tend to be militiamen and internationals on sprees and a sprinkling of young ladies of the between the sheets brigade. This particular night there's at a special table a group of British parliamentary bigwigs, including a duchess. It's been a big day for them, because General Franco's gunners have bagged more civilians than usual. Right outside the hotel, in fact under the eyes of the duchess, two peaceful madrileños were reduced to a sudden bloody mess. A splatter of brains had to be wiped off the glassless revolving doors of the hotel. But stuffed with horrors as they were, the British bigwigs had eaten supper. In fact they'd eaten up everything there was, so that when the American correspondents began to trickle in with nothing in their stomachs but whiskey and were fed each a sliver of rancid ham, there was a sudden explosion of the spirit of Seventy-Six. Why should a goddam lousy etcetera duchess eat three courses when a hardworking American newspaperman has to go hungry. A slightly punchdrunk little exbantamweight prizefighter, who was often in the joint wearing a militiaman's uniform and who had tended in the past to be chummy with the gringo contingent who were generous with their liquor, became our champion and muttered dark threats about closing the place up and having the cooks and waiters sent to the front, lousy profiteers hiding under the skirts of the C.N.T. who were all sons of loose women and saboteurs of the war and worse than Fascists, *mierda*. In the end the management produced a couple of longdead whitings and a plate of spinach which they'd probaby been planning to eat themselves, and the fires of revolt died down.

Still in Madrid the easiest and most sustaining thing to get, though it's high in price, is whiskey; so it's on that great national fooddrink that the boys at the other end of the wires tend to subsist. One of the boys who'd been there longest leaned across the table and said plaintively, "Now you won't go home and write about the drunken correspondents, will you?"

Outside the black stone city was grimly flooded with moonlight that cut each street into two oblique sections. Down the Gran Vía I could see the flashlight of a patrol and hear him demanding in low voices the password for the night of whoever they met on the sidewalk. From the west came a scattered hollow popping lightly perforating the horizon of quiet. Somewhere not very far away men with every nerve tense were crawling along the dark sides of walls, keeping their heads down in trenches, yanking their right arms back to sling a handgrenade at some creeping shadow opposite. And in all the black houses the children we'd seen playing in the streets were asleep, and the grownups were lying there thinking of lost friends and family and ruins and people they'd loved and hating the enemy and hunger and how to get a little more food tomorrow, feeling in the numbness of their blood, in spite of whatever scorn in the face of death, the low unending smoulder of apprehension of a city under siege. And I couldn't help feeling a certain awe, as I took off my clothes in my quiet clean room with electric light and running water and a bathtub and lay down on the bed to read a book, but instead stared at the ceiling and thought of the pleasantfaced middleaged chambermaid who'd cleaned it that morning and made the bed and put everything in order and who'd been coming regularly every day since the siege began just as she'd done it in the days of Don Alfonso, and wondered where she slept and what about her family and her kids and her man, and how perhaps tomorrow morning coming to work there'd be that hasty loudening shriek and the street full of dust and splintered stone and instead of coming to work the woman would be just a mashedout mess of blood and guts to be scooped into a new pine coffin and hurried away. And they'd slosh some water over the cobbles and the death of Madrid would go on.

The Volunteers

*ALMOST as soon as the war broke out, it became clear that it
would not be fought by Spaniards alone. The first foreigners to
take part in the war were Moorish troops flown into Spain on German
and Italian airplanes. There followed German and Italian advisers and
munitions agents. The Republic was therefore compelled to seek aid
abroad, and the long stream of volunteers and mercenaries serving the
Republic was already flowing into Spain during the last days of July.*

*Here is the account of a young aviator, Oloff de Wet, who was
among the first to fight in the air over Madrid:*

August 4th.

Madrid is a madhouse. Every man, woman and child has gone
crazy. They cannot have always been like this. The waiters wear
white overalls and pistols; they will not take "tips"; every man is his
fellow's equal. There are no taxis. It is dangerous to walk in the
streets, as all the commandeered cars are driven recklessly and at
great speed. I squeeze my way into the crowded trams but am never
able to get out at my destination. When the inside is filled to bursting,
and the whole air heavy with garlic, passengers festoon themselves
on the outside. Two hours ago I saw three people killed through this;
a tram going in the opposite direction crushed their bodies to pulp.
Nobody seemed to worry very much. Human life seems of little account here.

The Air Ministry is not immune from the madness that seems to
infect every place. I wonder if I shall ever catch it. I do not think so:
I am beginning to hate all the crowds of uncouth people drunk with
their new-found freedom, arrogant in their proletarian pomposity.
They remind me of nothing so much as ill-mannered children aping

their parents in a rude and unamusing manner. I have been here only two days, so I may not judge, but these are my thoughts at the moment; time may lessen my animosity, familiarity enable me to ignore the plastered propaganda posters of a policy for which I have no sympathy.

Still the fourth. My contract is settled with the Sub-Secretary for Air, Colonel Camacho; he clinched the deal with a whisky and soda. One copy in my pocket, the other sent to the Spanish Embassy in London, who are to pay my salary in advance. I shall do no flying till I hear from them. A hundred and eighty pounds a month, three hundred pounds for every enemy aircraft destroyed, all hotel bills found, two thousand pounds for my death or one thousand pounds for a permanent injury. It might all be worse.

September 5th.

I go out on my first patrol. The Nieuport 52 I am flying is heavy as lead. It is No. 6-27, I must remember she swings like hell in the take. I give full left rudder; it is useless, I have not checked enough. We leave the ground in a climbing turn to port. I thank God that I am on the left of the flight. I should have been on top of them otherwise.

The 600-h.p. Huispano engine still gives me plenty of "feel" on the "stick" as we climb above the orange groves. I am now back with the flight, hoping they did not notice the take-off. Five Nieuport scouts heading for the enemy lines at less than four hundred metres. Not a bad sight they must make.

The slight up-and-down movement of the individual aircraft gives us the appearance of being suspended by invisible strings. We are now climbing. Ahead, smoke is rising over the white haze. Is that a house fired by artillery? We are flattening out at last. What is the altitude? I cannot tell exactly, the altimeter needle is swinging across a third of the dial. The shadows stand out more than the shapes . . . ten thousand feet, no, twelve.

We are opening out to a looser formation; in this way it is more easy to keep a lookout. Throttle control becomes less sensitive with the widened gap between the machines. Are we over the enemy lines? God knows, I don't. The pilot next to me swings the nose of his aircraft to port, simultaneously letting off a burst from his two Vickers guns. The attention of our leader has been drawn to three black specks. With engines full open the whole flight is now headed in their direction. All is tension. The five machines are flying as one. The "clatter" of machine guns being warmed, I can hear distinctly above the roar of the motors. This is a great moment, one of the greatest moments in my life, I think.

The sky about is liquid blue, still as the sea and waiting. We roar on. The dots have turned into three biplanes, still too far away to name. We are closing on them rapidly, then they drop out of the sky as if all their levity is gone. The needle on the airspeed indicator swings to a standstill, as with the rest of the flight I dive in pursuit. It is idle. For one brief moment the sun glints on their bellies before they are swallowed in the ground haze. My machine shivers with sudden vibration, as, pulling out of the prolonged dive, we soar for a thousand feet in an effortless climb. A dull, uneventful flight ensues.

They tell me, back at the aerodrome, the machines we chased were German Heinkels, single-seater fighters which can easily outpace the Nieuport on the level; in the dive they cannot even be caught by the Fury. It seems we were lucky to get as near as we did. My shoulder is still heavy, aching from holding up that left wing. Do we always fly the same machine? Those Nieuports should be rerigged; all the three I have flown have been left-wing low. Flying with the port tank light would help, but long patrols must mean a full load. In future I shall close that right tank until the left is empty or that wing comes up. It is hell flying a machine that is fighting one all the time. . . .

I still have the excitement of this morning's chase. It must have been like that in the War. But this, a war—I cannot think of it as such. I always associate wars with others I rather admire: to be in it myself makes it at once commonplace. How can sudden death and destruction be ordinary? Cartwright's passing, was it that? God! no. But I am not he. I shall not die here. Must I always live detached from my surroundings? Is it heroic to be destroyed? I do not want to be destroyed, God knows, but better that than being blinded: the living death. . . .

September 25th.

Only a thousand feet above the thin ribbon of road leading to Barajas. There is nothing to be seen of any advancing columns. The country seems deserted. Two dark specks on the road . . . a peasant and his donkey. Tang, tang, tang. I feel rather than hear the bullets that crash through the metal covering of my starboard wing. The stick goes flabby in my hand; in my agitation I have pulled the machine up too steeply, and she is ready to stall. A fine state of affairs with the enemy close at hand somewhere. But where? Flattening out, I kick violently on the rudder bar. The air blows on one cheek and then the other as the Nieuport skids from side to side. Vainly I try to locate our attacker; was it my imagination? No—there, clearly, was the jagged tear in the wing surface.

The remainder of the flight, flying in ragged formation, are certainly not in pursuit of any enemy. I join them as they circle round, climbing, climbing. Why not continue straight? I do not know that the enemy have long since gone, that Locattelli is slowly spiralling over a certain spot. I have not noticed that we are only four. Were I to look over the side, I should see a black column of smoke rising in the still air.

They got Clifford—the five Heinkels that only Collins had glimpsed as they made away close to the ground. They came and were gone like the mysterious hand of God. At five thousand feet, we straightened out. It was four-thirty, we had been attacked ten minutes earlier, we had reached the Barajas road at four-twelve. It was not more than five minutes later that the holes had appeared in my wing. So it takes just ten minutes to drain about a hundred fifty litres of petrol from the tank of a Loire.

It was as we flattened out that Maurice left us—going down in a steep glide with a cold motor. It was a bad piece of ground we were over. It looked flat enough from high above; in reality it was all undulations and valleys. No place for a forced landing, but he had plenty of time to pick a spot—if there was one.

We flew in a wide circle. This is a bad trip. There he goes heading for that gap between the olive groves. He must be near the earth now. He should touch down any moment; there is no wind, he will be moving over the ground at all his sixty miles an hour when he hits. God! he has overshot the field . . . he will be into that village in a moment. No, he is over. Heights are deceptive. From above, he should most likely make that plowed field ahead of him over the dark dots that are trees. No, she is finished—the heart is out of her. Oh, slowly, so slowly she pivots round one wing tip, then the other, now, as a trapdoor closing, over onto her back, is still.

Anxiously we watch for the dark figure that, pray God, may still creep from beneath her. Several people are approaching from different directions—dim, distant dots moving like ants on the red earth. It is useless to stay longer. We head for Getafe. The disasters of our flight have preceded us. Maurice has escaped with two broken legs, is lying unconscious in the hospital, he should live. His petrol tank, as I suspected, had been holed by a bullet from one of the Heinkels.

September 27th.

High excitement in the commandant's office. The rebels have taken Barajas. They are pushing forward to the relief of the Alcázar. The three heavy bombers, Potez 54s, their Lorraine engines warming, stand ready, each loaded with nearly two thousand pounds of bombs. Six Breguets are rapidly being prepared. Everywhere there is activity. Nobody is very gay. We do not need to be told that we shall not all come back. This will be the biggest show I shall have been on. The Potez are to take off first, bomb the positions at Barajas, on their return the six Breguets are to repeat the operation. I am detailed for the second escort, with Loire No. 3-14 to fly in a mixed flight with five other fighters. We are to be ready to take off at 9:40. . . .

Heading towards Toledo, we fighters are flying in two flights of three machines. Our motors are throttled back to keep pace with the six Breguets a thousand feet beneath us. I wonder how old those Breguets can be. They must have just missed the Great War. How solid they look wallowing along under the power of their single motors, how like those pictures I have seen of the German Taubes with their swept-back wing tips, only the War-time bomber looked a much "cleaner job." Spaniards call the Breguet the "Guardian Angel." They say nobody ever gets killed in them.

It is 10:20—twenty minutes since we left Getafe. Away to the south I can still distinctly recognize the turrets of the Alcázar and beyond it a white bridge across the Tagus. We should be over the objective at any moment now. Hardly is the thought formed in my mind than, glancing over the side of the cockpit, I see the anti-aircraft barrage that is bursting unpleasantly near the Breguets. From high above, the explosions are vast daisies breaking into sudden bloom. I can see no aircraft. They will not have been expecting us back so soon, perhaps. On the return flight they will be there to punish us. The bombers have formed a fairy ring over the road junction. I suppose they know what they are dropping their "stuff" on. . . . I can see nothing—or is that a column coming up the road? . . .

White ribbons of smoke stream away from another salvo, bursting wide of the crossroad. . . . The bombers, unloaded, low to the ground, are heading for Getafe. . . . Now hanging forward in the webbing of my harness. Diving vertically on the road crowded with troops. Down, down, down. Motor racing to peak roar—a high, wild note. Far in front of me . . . red berets, lorries, trees, the khaki cloaks of the running men all coming to meet me. It is like blowing up a plate of sand, the grains scattering, leaving the road naked and white.

As a live thing in ecstacy the Dewoitine shivers to the touch of my hand on the trigger release. We plunge on, the skin tight on my forehead, my neck cold. Flecks of flame on the leading edge of the wind. Alone in God's heaven I hang in my small vibrating universe, self-girt. The flesh and bones of me quiver on the same short frequency while all my thoughts are wrapped in the blue, blue note of the exhaust. It is a great moment, an intense moment . . . an instant in a lifetime where man may find his own affinity in the male self-sufficiency of the pounding metal. Two and a half thousand revolutions a minute, the heartbeat of the steering mass of alloy close in front of me. The pulse of the metal organism. It is all good and strong and real. Every instant of the dive is lived. . . .

Gently back on the stick. The strap of my helmet whips my cheek. The aircraft shudders. I lose my breath as a last spasm sweeps the length of the machine. The world is moving round me . . . trees, houses, roads . . . village slip underneath the belly of my machine. The horizon falls like the edge of a blue blind suddenly drawn down, and I am climbing heavenwards. The day-bleached face of the moon peeps from beneath my wing. The sweet metallic flavor of blood is on my cheek as my nose bleeds. Once again we dive alternatively; the specks and dots of men scatter in the fields adjacent to the road.

Turning again for home, far away, the sun throws back from the Breguets.

Less than twenty minutes will see us over Getafe. The scene of our attack is already many miles behind. I wonder what can have become of the Heinkels and Fiats.

September 28th.

Toledo has fallen, the Alcázar has been relieved. Everybody is whispering it. I hope it is true. . . . I admire immensely those heroic defenders of the old fortress. There are many amongst even the most rabid who think as I.

September 29th.

I have come into Madrid for the night. I am tired of my quarters at Getafe. I want to see new faces and hear fresh voices. This morning Locattelli shot down a Junker. He attacked it flat from the front. All the crew were killed when it crashed. Everybody is drunk at the aerodrome. . . . Fiesta, fiesta. I suppose the rebels do the same when they shoot us down.

The Alcázar has been relieved; a young Hungarian artist confirmed the report. I heard the tragic story.

"For several days," he recounted, "I begged the civil governor to give me lorries to carry the El Grecos and Velázquez' to Madrid. But here, as you know, it is always *'Mañana . . . Momento! . . .'* Sunday morning—that is to say, yesterday—I learned that certain enemy units had penetrated into the town and held the points of Alcántara and San Martín. The governor was nowhere to be found. No lorries. I decided to come here to search for them; I left without even taking the time to dress properly"—he was wearing only a shirt and trousers —mud from head to foot. "Having no safe-conduct for leaving the town, I swam the Tagus; I wished from there to get on to the railway ten kilometers distant. The trains no longer come as far as the town. After that I had a journey of fifty kilometres. On arriving at Madrid I hurried to the search just as I was, dripping, muddy, my shoes without soles; but it was Sunday, everything was shut. I could find no one. Now it is too late."

He sagged in the chair, arms limp, his eyes filled with tears. Early in the month on a visit to Toledo, it was he who had shown me, in an aisle of the Church of Santo Tomé, El Greco's masterpiece, "The Burial of the Count d'Orgaz." I say he showed me the painting, but all I saw was the great pile of mattresses in which the canvas was tenderly swathed. This, with many other priceless paintings, had now fallen into the hands of the rebels. This young Hungarian painter had made his home in Toledo, had lived there for several years, become passionately attached to those works of the great masters. How well I can sympathize with him and appreciate his feelings on suffering such a desperate separation.

October 1st.

Flying at ten thousand feet under an overcast sky. The usual escort of the Breguets. Ten Heinkels punish us badly before we even reach the objective. The formation is forced back. Collins takes an explosive bullet in the left shoulder but gets his Nieuport back to Getafe. The doctor reports that he will be dead by morning. . . . I don't wonder. He was soaked in blood when they took him out of the cockpit. I remember how he lay on the stretcher—his jaw hanging loose, his mouth white, bloodless cheeks, ghastly gray through the smudges of oil; those staring, unseeing eyes in the white ovals where his goggles had been. What a pathetic, awful sight! God have mercy on the souls of the dead.

Still the first of October. I cannot sleep. Collins stares at me from the darkness. Why should he die like that? The four squares of moonlight on the floor beneath my window are good to look at. I in one square and he in the other: face to face. "There is beauty in an ideal yet," he says to me, "and the Republic is an ideal worth suffering for, and the liberty of these people worth a man's blood. God is the God of Freedom, not the God of Love. Man is the true God of Love." He is gone.

By the late autumn the amateurs of revolution were giving place on both sides to the professionals. Here Herbert Matthews describes his meeting with some of the military commanders and advisers sent by Stalin to aid in the defense of Madrid:

The best known in the early days, because he commanded the Column in the first few months of the siege, was Emil Kléber. He was the man of the hour then, and we all played him up sensationally—as he deserved. His headquarters were at the Prado in those days, and that was where I first met him. A big man, physically, nearly six feet tall, rather heavily built and with a heavy face, high cheekbones, broad nose, thick lips, bushy eyebrows. Like Mariotti's, it was a rather brutal face until he smiled. Moreover, there was a good-fellowship and modesty about him which the Italian general lacked.

Kléber is the genuine type of proletarian leader. He was born in

Austria; "Kléber" is doubtless his nom-de-révolution, for few of these men use their genuine names. During the World War he was drafted into the Austrian Army and found himself fighting as an officer against the Russians. He was "captured" and "escaped." I use the quotation marks because he smiled slyly and knowingly when he told me about it. That was when he became a Communist, I imagine. Later he went to Canada, where he joined the expeditionary force that was sent to Siberia. Needless to say, it did not suit his purpose in any sense to be fighting what amounted to a Japanese war of conquest, and he soon was found serving in those Russian forces which were fashioning what was then called the Far Eastern Republic.

By the time he left Siberia he was a soldier of experience and ability in a peculiar kind of warfare. Years of obscure struggle in Europe and America followed, during which he somehow acquired Canadian citizenship. Revolutionaries apparently have no trouble in getting any citizenship they please. One genial Russian officer assured me he had five perfectly valid passports, including an American one.

The next place Kléber made a mark was as leader of a Red army in China—56,000 men, all armed with rifles, having just twelve rounds of ammunition apiece. It was in Kiangsi, and Marshal Chiang Kai-shek, with 1,200,000 well-armed soldiers, had him virtually surrounded. Kléber took his men on a retreat back to Szechuan in eight months, during which they marched about 3,500 miles in a huge arc, defeating force after force which Chiang threw against them, maintaining order and discipline throughout, and ending up safe, coherent, and out of the Marshal's reach.

Something of an epic that was—and then he came to Spain. For some months he disappeared from circulation, and thereby hung many silly stories, mostly emanating from the insurgent ranks. As a matter of fact, the immediate cause of his quarrel with the Spanish authorities was obscure, but the main outlines have always been clear. The Government is going to win or lose this war on its own and with its own leaders and men. For political reasons of an imperative and obvious nature, they could not have their army led by a foreigner and one who took his orders from Moscow to boot. Although he shunned publicity, in the very nature of things Kléber got too much of it, and the impression abroad was bad. The upshot was his removal from command of the Madrid front and the offer of a minor post, which he rejected. Months of idleness followed and the name of Kléber was almost for-

gotten. By that very token it was time for him to come back, and he
was made commander of the Twelfth Brigade. However, in the Aragón offensive in August he did badly, was removed from command,
and has gone for good. He had played his part.

Kléber was a good example of one type of International commander
—the Communist leader under the orders of Moscow. There were
other more important ones—Russians—but they have always kept in
the background and none of us saw or knew anything in particular
about them. I understand, for instance, that it was De Gorieff (Van
Rosen is his correct name, I believe) who was the brains behind the
victory of Brihuega, but he has gone now. General Gall, who commanded the Fifteenth Division (now the Thirty-fifth, in which the
Americans fight), is another of Kléber's type—a Hungarian, who is
fighting, so to speak, for the Comintern rather than for Spain. The
general who commands the Thirty-fifth now is a Russian called
"Walter," whose record is exceptionally good.

A leader who is much more expressive of the spirit of the Internationals than any of these is Hans—just Hans, and nothing more.
Nobody knows his last name, and nobody asks, for he has relatives in
Germany and it would be unhealthy for them if the Nazis learned
exactly who Hans was. He is a divisional commander, too, who started
as the leader of the Thaelmann Battalion of anti-Fascist Germans. If
one had to pick out the crack unit of all the Internationals, at least
until recently, the choice would have to lie between them and the
Garibaldi Battalion of Italians. That is as it should be, considering
what Germany and Italy mean in this war.

Hans is thirty-eight or thirty-nine, married, tall, dark, heavy-set.
Before the World War he was a cadet in a military school, for he
comes of a good family. During the war he was an officer in the German Army, and he fought well. But what he saw then made him hate
nationalism, and he became a journalist for radical newspapers. In
the struggle against Hitler he was on the losing side and had to leave
Germany.

Thus far his case was that of thousands of refugees. However, he
was not content to accept his fate passively. During the Asturian
revolt here in 1934, Hans came to Spain to help the miners, who were
suppressed with a ferocity that provided one of the causes for the
present division in Spain. So when the Civil War started, Hans had no

hesitation. Leaving his wife and his job in France, he came here, as he says, "to defend liberty."

And then there was Lukacz, commander of the Twelfth Brigade, and now dead. He was a Hungarian whose real name was Matei Jalka. Once, out at the front, he assured me that he was a pacifist but (he said with a sigh and a smile) somehow he found it necessary again and again to fight for his beliefs. During the World War he was an officer in the Hungarian Hussars. Feeling that Communism held the possibility of bringing world peace, he joined the Soviets and found himself as divisional commander in the Red Army fighting against Kolchak. The Bolsheviks having won, he retired, like Candide, to cultivate his garden—until the Spanish conflict started, and he felt he had to fight again. When I asked why, he gave three reasons: because he hates Hitler and "this is Hitler's war"; because Franco is killing women and children; and because in spite of his Communism, he has democratic ideals.

One day in June as he was directing an unsuccessful operation against Huesca, a shell hit his moving car, and he was killed. In that same car was Gustav Regler, political commissar of the brigade and one of the most popular figures in the International Column. Regler comes of a Catholic family, and as a boy he was educated in a Catholic school. Intelligent and sensitive, he had a long internal struggle in his youth from which he emerged as a free-thinker. Like Lukacz and many of the Internationals, Regler is an author. One of his best-known books is about the Saar—*Under Crossfire*. Being anti-Nazi, he had to flee to France after the plebiscite. When the Civil War began he helped to raise the money whereby French workmen gave a group of trucks to the Spanish Government's cause, and he came here with them. Because he spoke French so well and was not too strong, he was made political commissar, but that did not remove him from danger. Of the four people in that car which was hit, three were killed, while Regler was so badly wounded his life was despaired of. Many blood transfusions pulled him through, and in less than a month he sat weakly in a chair at the Writer's Congress in Madrid addressing a moving and impassioned appeal against Fascism.

His fellow political commissar, Hans Beimler, also a German, was killed in action back in November. Beimler was a Bavarian, whom the Nazis put in the Dachau concentration camp. In some way he escaped, although his widow is still being kept hostage in Germany. He was the real leader of the German Communists here during his service, and although his job was political commissar of the Thaelmann Battalion, he could not resist the chance to take an active part in the fighting. The spirit that moved him was contagious. One day a group of Internationals had to make a charge that carried them around the dangerously exposed corner of a house. The first who went were shot down in their tracks and lay there dead. The others hung back in dismay. Beimler gathered them about him in the shelter of the house and spoke quietly for a few moments, spoke of ideals, of the things they had come to Spain for, of the uselessness of life for them in a world dominated by the forces for which the insurgents stood. A moment later, with Beimler among them, they swung around that corner and took the objective assigned to them. Shortly afterward he was killed, and his body was sent to Moscow for burial.

There are so many worth writing about! The Garibaldi Battalion fought so magnificently that its leader, at least, must be mentioned. He was Randolfo Pacciardi—one of the many who were intellectuals, but men of action at the same time. Pacciardi is a lawyer—handsome, cultured, less than middle-aged, with a World War record so fine that he was recommended for the highest award in the Italian Army—the Gold Medal. After the war he entered politics, not as a Communist or even as a radical, but as a Republican. The word "republican" did not mean that he wanted to make Italy into a republic, but it was used as an expression of liberalism and democracy. He formed a war veterans' organization of men sympathetic with his ideas. In a famous law case that Italo Balbo, now Governor-General of Libya, brought against a Socialist newspaper in Ferrara, Pacciardi successfully defended the newspaper.

It goes without saying that such a man became persona non grata when the Fascists took power, and one fine morning he fled to Switzerland an hour or so before the police came for him. As happened with so many of his associates, Switzerland did not welcome him either, and he ended in that haven of political refugees—Paris. There for years he successfully pursued the profession of journalism. He is married; he was earning a good living—and he left everything to fight for Spain, because he felt that it was just and right to do so. The Garibaldi Battalion is now dissolved and Pacciardi has gone, perhaps to return. He, too, has played his part. Each life is worth a book in itself, and there are thousands of such lives.

Until now I have not even mentioned any Americans, but recently I had a long talk with Hans Amlie, adjutant of the Washington Battalion, who was lying wounded in a room of the hotel-hospital. Amlie is a mining engineer from Montana—"a prospector," he calls himself, who has roamed far over our West, Mexico, South America. He is not a Communist, not a Socialist, knows and cares nothing about politics, except that he hates Fascism as much as any human being could hate it.

The "Ludlow Massacre" of striking miners occurred when he was twelve years old and it set an indelible stamp on his spirit. It made him a fighter for the underdog, and in his case the underdog was the miner. Although under age, he served through the World War as a sergeant of marines, and had a good record. Afterwards he studied mining engineering and found himself getting involved deeper and deeper in that struggle for the underdog.

"I've seen many a mine in my career," he told me, "where they sent men down to work where silicosis was inevitable. Two years' work, one year of dying, and no compensation—that was their career. I've always fought for them, and so I lost job after job, for the owners got to know me. And then this war started. It was perfectly natural for me to come to Spain. This is the only place in the world where people like me belong at the moment. Anyone who loves liberty and hates Fascism must come here!"

And then there was Oliver Law, a Texas Negro, and commander of the Lincoln Battalion after Martin Hourihan was promoted to regimental commander. In the same action that Hourihan got his wounds, although a few days later, Law was killed. A Negro commander of 150 white men who were proud to serve under him—does that not convey something of the spirit of the Internationals? Law was in some sense the typical Negro radical. Sensitive and rebellious against the fate of his people in the South, he naturally drifted into the movement. First, however, he received military training in the American Army, which he joined in Texas after the World War (he was only about thirty-three when he was killed).

His service completed, he went to Chicago, where he was when this war started. In the interim he had become a Communist and an important figure in Chicago's Negro world. A good businessman to boot, he owned a restaurant and other property, which he gave up to come to Spain. And here he died, leading his men in an attack. "We are here to show that Negroes know how to fight Fascists," he said one day of himself and others of his race in the American battalions.

Men came from all over Europe to fight in the University City, which had become the symbol of men's hopes of freedom from Fascist tyranny. One of the most sensitive accounts of the fighting was written by a young Englishman, John Sommerfield, who here describes a journey into the Philosophy building:

We moved up in the darkness, making a wide detour across country and through woods. Durruti's men were down on the Madrid front, and some were with us, and companies of Asturian miners with their dynamite, grand, tough, cheerful little men. The night was loud with bursting hand-grenades: the dynamite exploded with an odd, flat noise. In the distance a house burned fiercely, silhouetting the great cubical outlines of the university buildings, and throwing a dangerous light on our faces.

We saw the Philosophy building then, lit by reflected flames and moonlight, our first glimpse since we had left it to go down into the Casa del Campo; the light shone through shell-holes in the walls, from the windows the shattered sun-blinds hung drunkenly awry, a wrecked car sprawled in the drive, and there were great holes in the ground full of water.

We entered through the metal doors, that were pitted with bullet marks. Within it was completely dark, and we were lost, stumbling upon wreckage and broken glass, and guided by the sound of crunching feet we felt our way down a corridor, a door opened, and we entered.

In the big room a single candle burned, its dim wavering light dazzling to our eyes. Underfoot was a thick, soft carpet, heavy silk curtains half torn down sagged from the barricaded windows. Down the centre of the room ran a long table, of rich gleaming wood: bottles, broken glasses, plates, grape-stalks, cigar ends, were strewn upon it; chairs were overturned, cigar and cigarette ends scattered on the floor. For a moment we grasped the richness and the confusion, the startled disorder of the room, and then the candle was put out and we were lost in darkness again, waiting, hearing the sounds of firing outside. We slept a little, were roused, and went out.

It was almost dawn. Shells were falling now, and there was much shooting. We ran between buildings, and came to the huge red brick cubes of the Medical School. One by one we darted across the open space and charged up the steps of the main entrance.

Machine-guns stood by the doors, and there were sand-bag barricades. The tiled floor was thick with dirt and brick dust. We sat around and waited for orders. Fredo came in, his head done up in a bloody bandage, his face very pale and picturesquely good-looking. We gave him some aspirin, and he told us to wait for a while. We lay on sand-bags and sang. Everyone felt cheerful and we sang for half an hour, until they brought in some of the wounded. They brought a Frenchman from our section, on a stretcher, and laid him down and covered him with blankets; he was quite still, hardly breathing; the doctor said that he ought to be trephined, but they had not the means, and it was impossible to get him away. We sat and watched him die.

Then Fredo came back and picked out the good shots from amongst us, and sent us upstairs. Long corridors ran in echoing perspectives, dead lifts waited, at the end of passages were ruined rooms. We came to a high-up room with big windows; this was our position. A few hundred yards away was the Casa Velázquez, whose riddled baroque turrets still pointed at the raining sky. The Falangists were there, and we were to watch and snipe.

We found brooms and swept away the broken glass and rubble, barricaded the windows, arranged our gun positions and the order of watching. Every now and then bullets came in and ricochetted wildly between the walls.

Here we stayed, and settled down to a new routine. We explored the whole great building, finding many things of use in places from which men had fled surprised. I got myself a fine officer's tunic, very warm, and with big pockets; also a pair of good khaki trousers that were torn but could be easily mended, a new blanket, better than my old one. Also I found some bottles of decent wine, onions, garlic, a sack of rice, pencils, a cigarette case. Everyone searched, but Joe and I were the quickest and found the best things; we found oil and tools for the guns, and there were many other things that we would have liked but could not take with us. Men had been working on the building when the fighting began, many rooms had not yet been completed, and tools and materials were scattered everywhere.

This decay and ruin had not the pleasant mournfulness of old buildings; this destruction, this crumbling, this wreckage of new unfinished places had a strange, unnatural sadness of its own. Everywhere, replacing the gentle dust of slow decay, was a coarse, brittle rubble of broken glass and plaster and brick that lay over everything.

The Civil War dealt ruthlessly with its volunteers. Here Peter Kemp, an Irishman fighting for Franco, describes how he acted as the unwilling executioner of an Irishman fighting for the Republic. He also provides a little-known explanation for the death of the poet, Federico García Lorca:

On January 2nd a new alférez, called Campos, came to my company. Being senior to me he took over my platoon and I was put in command of the two 81 mm. mortars. It was a blow to me because I liked and thought I understood my men. They seemed to think so too, for a party of them, under a corporal, came to see me and begged me to ask the Captain to retain me in command. I was fool enough to pass this on to Almajach, who said coldly: "Of course they want you. They can get away with more under you than they could under a Spanish officer."

Campos was a tall, flabby young man, a little stupid and morose. He told me that he had been one of the original members of the Falange in Granada, and that he had taken part in the firing squad that executed the poet García Lorca. I prefer to believe him a liar. The Nationalists, including the Falange, strongly denied any responsibility for Lorca's death, attributing it to the vengeance of his private enemies, of which he had a large number; certainly he had many good friends on the Nationalist side who would have saved him if they could. His murder was a crime that robbed the world of one of its greatest living lyric poets; the mystery of it has never been satisfactorily explained. I say this with all respect to Mr. Gerald Brenan, who claims to have fixed the responsibility on the *Guardia Civil*. No two versions of the tragedy coincide. Campos's account was not circumstantial enough to convince even me at the time; he was careful not to mention it in front of Alonso de Castañeda. The reason he alleged for the execution—that Lorca was a Communist, who was to have led a column against Granada—is too absurd to be worth consideration. In his lines on the death of his friend, Sánchez Mejías, it seems, lies Lorca's own epitaph:

> *Díle a la luna que venga,*
> *Que no quiero ver la sangre*
> *De Ignacio sobre la arena.*[1]

A day or two after the appearance of Campos a Subteniente arrived to join the 56th Company. This rank corresponds roughly though not precisely, to that of Warrant Officer Class I in the British Army; the rank, suppressed in the Regular Army, persisted in the Legion. This particular creature was a cocky, officious little man with a shiny red face and pert expression, a squeaky, angry voice and the appearance and manners of a monkey. He started to throw his weight about from the first moment, abusing the N.C.O.s and laying into the men with his *fusta* on the slightest pretext. It was impossible for us to control him, for Almajach approved of him, or at least of his methods. With the officers his manner varied between impertinence to us ensigns and a sickening obsequiousness towards the Captain. Day and night the hours were made hideous by his squawks of complaint or abuse.

At last we received orders to move, and on January 10th we left Berlanga in a long column of lorries. To our disappointment our destination proved to be, not Teruel, but another part of the static Guadalajara front—the ruined and virtually deserted village of Almadrones. Situated just off the main Madrid-Zaragoza road, about 65 miles north-east of Madrid, it had suffered severely from bombardment during the Guadalajara battle of the previous March. Few of the houses were undamaged, and the only inhabitants were a handful of miserable, underfed peasants who wandered disconsolately through the dirty streets. We lingered here a week, then set off on foot with our

---

[1] Tell the moon it's time to rise,
I do not want to see his blood
Where spilt upon the sand it lies.
(Translation—Roy Campbell)

mules and all our equipment on a twenty-mile march eastwards. It was a hard march, across difficult country, but the weather was bright and cold and the men were in excellent spirits, singing lewd songs from the different regions of Spain when neither the Padre nor the Major were around, both of whom disapproved of communal bawdry. In the evening we came to the mountain hamlet of Torrecuadrada, about two miles from the front line.

The inhabitants of this region were the poorest I ever saw in Spain, the country the most desolate. It is to the credit of the Falange relief organization, *Auxilio Social,* that as soon as the war was over it directed a great deal of its effort towards improving conditions here. Every morning and evening at meal times the children of the village would gather round our field kitchens, each carrying a little jar or bowl, which the cooks would fill with meat, fish, vegetables and bread. After two days the villagers asked us to stop giving their children meat and fish, which they had never tasted before and which upset their stomachs. Even bread was a luxury to which they were unaccustomed, their normal—indeed their unvarying—diet consisting of a mess of beans or *garbanzos* (chick-peas). The houses were hovels, the street mean, filthy and dangerously pitted. But the people, though underfed and miserably clothed, were kind and warm-hearted and did all they could to make us welcome and comfortable.

After three days we left Torrecuadrada for the front, to effect what the communiqués called "a rectification of the line." This meant occupying and fortifying a range of hills overlooking the valley of the Tajuña. The enemy, evidently fearing an attack in strength, had withdrawn beyond the river, and so we were able to occupy the ground without loss. Noriega had gone on leave, and I had taken over his platoon of machine-guns. The work of fortification was extremely arduous, for the ground was hard—in some places it was rock—so that our picks and shovels made little impression. At the end of five days the men's hands were covered with blisters and sores. Much of the work was in view of the enemy and had to be done at night. There was no shelter; we had to snatch what sleep we could lying in the open, each wrapped in his *capote* and blanket, in a temperature well below zero. Luckily the weather was fine. The men worked with a will, their high spirits seemingly unaffected by cold, fatigue or the pain of their hands. My platoon was attached to Captain Cancela and the 53rd Company, an arrangement that gave me great pleasure, for he and his officers were such a gay and friendly crowd that it was impossible not to be happy in their company. . . .

While we were enjoying our rest on the 13th, other forces were mopping up the numerous large pockets of the enemy isolated by the last few days' advance. Although doubtless necessary—and certainly welcome to us—this delay gave the enemy time to reorganize his defence and give us a nasty shock a few days later.

The following day remains in my memory for one of the most horrible incidents in my experience.

The horror of it is still with me as I write; nor, I fear, will it ever leave me. I can scarcely bear to write of it now. At noon next day we were still resting on our cliff-top when I was ordered to report to Cancela. I found him talking with some legionaries who had brought in a deserter from the International Brigades—an Irishman from Belfast; he had given himself up to one of our patrols down by the river. Cancela wanted me to interrogate him. The man explained that he had been a seamen on a British ship trading to Valencia, where he had got very drunk one night, missed his ship and been picked up by the police. The next thing he knew, he was in Albacete, impressed into the International Brigades. He knew that if he tried to escape in Republican Spain he would certainly be retaken and shot; and so he had bided his time until he reached the front, when he had taken the first opportunity to desert. He had been wandering around for two days before he found our patrol.

I was not absolutely sure that he was telling the truth; but I knew that if I seemed to doubt his story he would be shot, and I was resolved to do everything in my power to save his life. Translating his account to Cancela, I urged that this was indeed a special case; the man was a deserter, not a prisoner, and we should be unwise as well as unjust to shoot him. Moved either by my arguments, or by consideration for my feelings, Cancela agreed to spare him, subject to de Mora's consent; I had better go and see de Mora at once while Cancela would see that the deserter had something to eat. De Mora was sympathetic. "You seem to have a good case," he said. "Unfortunately my orders from Colonel Peñarredonda are to shoot all foreigners. If you can get his consent I'll be delighted to let the man off. You'll find the Colonel over there, on the highest of those hills. Take the prisoner with you, in case there are any questions, and your two runners as escort."

It was an exhausting walk of nearly a mile with the midday sun blazing on our backs.

"Does it get any hotter in this country?" the deserter asked as we panted up the steep sides of a ravine, the sweat pouring down our faces and backs.

"You haven't seen the half of it yet. Wait another three months," I answered, wondering grimly whether I should be able to win him even another three hours of life.

I found Colonel Peñarredonda sitting cross-legged with a plate of fried eggs on his knee. He greeted me amiably enough as I stepped forward and saluted; I had taken care to leave the prisoner well out of earshot. I repeated his story, adding my own plea at the end, as I had with Cancela and de Mora. "I have the fellow here, sir," I concluded, "in case you wish to ask him any questions." The Colonel did not look up from his plate: "No, Peter," he said casually, his mouth full of egg, "I don't want to ask him anything. Just take him away and shoot him."

I was so astonished that my mouth dropped open; my heart seemed to stop beating. Peñarredonda looked up, his eyes full of hatred:

"Get out!" he snarled. "You heard what I said." As I withdrew he shouted after me: "I warn you, I intend to see that this order is carried out."

Motioning the prisoner and escort to follow, I started down the hill; I would not walk with them, for I knew that he would question me and I could not bring myself to speak. I decided not to tell him until the last possible moment, so that at least he might be spared the agony of waiting. I even thought of telling him to try to make a break for it while I distracted the escorts' attention; then I remembered Peñarredonda's parting words and, looking back, saw a pair of legionaries following us at a distance. I was so numb with misery and anger that I didn't notice where I was going until I found myself in front of de Mora once more. When I told him the news he bit his lip:

"Then I'm afraid there's nothing we can do," he said gently. "You had better carry out the execution yourself. Someone has got to do it, and it will be easier for him to have a fellow-countryman around. After all, he knows that you have tried to save him. Try to get it over quickly."

It was almost more than I could bear to face the prisoner, where he stood between my two runners. As I approached they dropped back a few paces, leaving us alone; they were good men and understood what I was feeling. I forced myself to look at him. I am sure he knew what I was going to say.

"I've got to shoot you." A barely audible "Oh my God!" escaped him.

Briefly I told him how I had tried to save him. I asked him if he wanted a priest, or a few minutes by himself, and if there were any messages he wanted me to deliver.

"Nothing," he whispered, "please make it quick."

"That I can promise you. Turn round and start walking straight ahead."

He held out his hand and looked me in the eyes, saying only: "Thank you."

"God bless you!" I murmured.

As he turned his back and walked away I said to my two runners: "I beg you to aim true. He must not feel anything." They nodded, and raised their rifles. I looked away. The two shots exploded simultaneously.

"On our honour, sir," the senior of the two said to me, "he could not have felt a thing."

I went to examine the body. There was no doubt that death had been instantaneous. When we had buried him I reported to Cancela, who said:

"The Comandante has asked me to give you a message: he wishes you to know that he deeply regrets the shooting of that Englishman; that he considers it a crime, and that the responsibility for it must rest for ever upon the conscience of *that*"—he spat the word— "gentleman! You know, he went so far as to send a pair of legionaries after you to shoot you if you did not immediately carry out his order? That is something we shall none of us forget."

The Winter War

DURING the first winter of the war the opposing forces were very nearly equal. While the Germans and Italians sent Junkers and Savoia-Marchettis to aid the Nationalists, the Russians sent small, sleek, snub-nosed chatos *to aid the Republicans. The forces of the Nationalists were stiffened by "volunteers" from Germany, Italy and Ireland, but they were balanced by the International Brigade which made up for their lack of numbers by their daring and enthusiasm. Thus balanced, the armies grappled on seven or eight different fronts, but few advances were made.*

Here and there a small battle would flare up, or a column would blunder into another column. Sorties were made, and on the high plateau where Don Quixote fought the windmills, snipers fired across the lines and men died in their icy dugouts. Significant battles were fought along the Corunna Road and on the banks of the Jarama River near Madrid, but they ended in stalemate. All that winter they were testing their strength in the nightmarish cold weather.

What it was like to fight through that winter has been told by George Orwell, who found himself more by accident than design in a brigade of Catalan Trotskyists:

In trench warfare five things are important: firewood, food, tobacco, candles and the enemy. In winter on the Zaragoza front they were important in that order, with the enemy a bad last. Except at night, when a surprise-attack was always conceivable, nobody bothered about the enemy. They were simply remote black insects whom one occasionally saw hopping to and fro. The real preoccupation of both armies was trying to keep warm.

I ought to say in passing that all the time I was in Spain I saw very

169

little fighting. I was on the Aragón front from January to May, and between January and late March little or nothing happened on that front, except at Teruel. In March there was heavy fighting round Huesca, but I personally played only a minor part in it. Later, in June, there was the disastrous attack on Huesca in which several thousand men were killed in a single day, but I had been wounded and disabled before that happened. The things that one normally thinks of as the horrors of war seldom happened to me. No airplane ever dropped a bomb anywhere near me, I do not think a shell ever exploded within fifty yards of me, and I was only in hand-to-hand fighting once (once is once too often, I may say). Of course I was often under heavy machine-gun fire, but usually at longish ranges. Even at Huesca you were generally safe enough if you took reasonable precautions.

Up here, in the hills round Zaragoza, it was simply the mingled boredom and discomfort of stationary warfare. A life as uneventful as a city clerk's, and almost as regular. Sentry-go, patrols, digging; digging, patrols, sentry-go. On every hill-top, Fascist or Loyalist, a knot of ragged, dirty men shivering round their flag and trying to keep warm. And all day and night the meaningless bullets wandering across the empty valleys and only by some rare improbable chance getting home on a human body.

Often I used to gaze round the wintry landscape and marvel at the futility of it all. The inconclusiveness of such a kind of war! Earlier, about October, there had been savage fighting for all these hills; then, because the lack of men and arms, especially artillery, made any large-scale operation impossible, each army had dug itself in and settled down on the hill-tops it had won. Over to the right there was a small outpost, also P.O.U.M., and on the spur to our left, at seven o'clock to us, a P.S.U.C. position faced a taller spur with several small Fascist posts dotted on its peaks. The so-called line zigzagged to and fro in a pattern that would have been quite unintelligible if every position had not flown a flag. The P.O.U.M. and P.S.U.C. flags were red, those of the Anarchists red and black; the Fascists generally flew the monarchist flag (red-yellow-red), but occasionally they flew the flag of the Republic (red-yellow-purple). The scenery was stupendous, if you could forget that every mountain-top was occupied by troops and was therefore littered with tin cans and crusted with dung. To the right of us the sierra bent south-eastwards and made way for the wide, veined valley that stretched across to Huesca. In the middle of the plain a few tiny cubes sprawled like a throw of dice; this was the town of Robres, which was in Loyalist possession. Often in the mornings the valley was hidden under seas of cloud, out of which the hills rose flat and blue, giving the landscape a strange resemblance to a photographic negative. Beyond Huesca there were more hills of the same formation as our own, streaked with a pattern of snow which altered day by day. In the far distance the monstrous peaks of the Pyrenees, where the snow never melts, seemed to float upon nothing. Even down in the plain everything looked dead and bare. The hills opposite us were grey and wrinkled like the skins of elephants. Almost always the sky was empty of birds. I do not think I have ever seen a country where there were so few birds. The only birds one saw at any time were a kind of magpie, and the coveys of partridges that startled one at night with their sudden whirring, and, very rarely, the flights of eagles that drifted slowly over, generally followed by rifle-shots which they did not deign to notice.

At night and in misty weather patrols were sent out in the valley between ourselves and the Fascists. The job was not popular, it was too cold and too easy to get lost, and I soon found that I could get leave to go out on patrol as often as I wished. In the huge jagged ravines there were no paths or tracks of any kind; you could only find your way about by making successive journeys and noting fresh landmarks each time. As the bullet flies, the nearest Fascist post was seven hundred metres from our own, but it was a mile and a half by the only practicable route. It was rather fun wandering about the dark valleys with the stray bullets flying high overhead like redshanks whistling. Better than nighttime were the heavy mists, which often lasted all day and which had a habit of clinging round the hill-tops and leaving the valleys clear. When you were anywhere near the Fascist lines you had to creep at a snail's pace; it was very difficult to move quietly on those hill-sides, among the crackling shrubs and tinkling limestones. It was only at the third or fourth attempt that I managed to find my way to the Fascist lines. The mist was very thick, and I crept up to the barbed wire to listen. I could hear the Fascists talking and singing inside. Then to my alarm I heard several of them coming down the hill towards me. I cowered behind a bush that suddenly seemed very small, and tried to cock my rifle without noise.

However, they branched off and did not come within sight of me. Behind the bush where I was hiding I came upon various relics of the earlier fighting—a pile of empty cartridge-cases, a leather cap with a bullet-hole in it, and a red flag, obviously one of our own. I took it back to the position, where it was unsentimentally torn up for cleaning-rags. I had been a corporal, or *cabo,* as it was called, as soon as we reached the front, and was in command of a guard of twelve men. It was no sinecure, especially at first. The *centuria* was an untrained mob composed mostly of boys in their teens. Here and there in the militia you came across children as young as eleven or twelve, usually refugees from Fascist territory who had been enlisted as militiamen as the easiest way of providing for them. As a rule they were employed on light work in the rear, but sometimes they managed to worm their way to the front-line, where they were a public menace. I remember one little brute throwing a hand-grenade into the dug-out fire "for a joke." At Monte Pocero I do not think there was anyone younger than fifteen, but the average age must have been well under twenty. Boys of this age ought never to be used in the front line, because they cannot stand the lack of sleep which is inseparable from trench warfare. At the beginning it was almost impossible to keep our position properly guarded at night. The wretched children of my section could only be roused by dragging them out of their dug-outs feet foremost, and as soon as your back was turned they left their posts and slipped into shelter; or they would even, in spite of the frightful cold, lean up against the wall of the trench and fall fast asleep. Luckily the enemy was very unenterprising. There were nights when it seemed to me that our position could be stormed by twenty Boy Scouts armed with air-guns, or twenty Girl Guides armed with battledores, for that matter.

At this time and until much later the Catalan militias were still on the same basis as they had been at the beginning of the war. In the early days of Franco's revolt the militias had been hurriedly raised by the various trade unions and political parties; each was essentially a political organization, owing allegiance to its party as much as to the central Government. When the Popular Army, which was a "non-political" army organized on more or less ordinary lines, was raised at the beginning of 1937, the party militias were theoretically incorporated in it. But for a long time the only changes that occurred were on paper; the new Popular Army troops did not reach the Aragón front in any numbers till June, and until that time the militia-system remained unchanged. The essential point of the system was social equality between officers and men. Everyone from general to private drew the same pay, ate the same food, wore the same clothes, and mingled on terms of complete equality. If you wanted to slap the general commanding the division on the back and ask him for a cigarette, you could do so, and no one thought it curious. In theory at any rate each militia was a democracy and not a heirarchy. It was understood that orders had to be obeyed, but it was also understood that when you gave an order you gave it as comrade to comrade and not as superior to inferior. There were officers and N.C.O.'s, but there was no military rank in the ordinary sense; no titles, no badges, no heel-clicking and saluting. They had attempted to produce within the militias a sort of temporary working model of the classless society. Of course there was not perfect equality, but there was a nearer approach to it than I had ever seen or than I would have thought conceivable in time of war.

But I admit that at first sight the state of affairs at the front horrified me. How on earth could the war be won by an army of this type? It was what everyone was saying at the time, and though it was true it was also unreasonable. For in the circumstances the militias could not have been much better than they were. A modern mechanized army does not spring up out of the ground, and if the Government had waited until it had trained troops at its disposal, Franco would never have been resisted. Later it became the fashion to decry the militias, and therefore to pretend that the faults which were due to lack of training and weapons were the result of the equalitarian system. Actually, a newly raised draft of militia was an undisciplined mob not because the officers called the privates "Comrade" but because raw troops are always an undisciplined mob. In practice the democratic "revolutionary" type of discipline is more reliable than might be expected. In a workers' army discipline is theoretically voluntary. It is based on class-loyalty, whereas the discipline of a bourgeois conscript army is based ultimately on fear. (The Popular Army that replaced the militias was midway between the two types.) In the militias the bullying and abuse that go on in an ordinary army would never have been tolerated for a moment. The normal military punishments existed, but they were only invoked for very serious offences. When a man refused to obey an order you did not immediately get him punished; you first appealed to him in the name of comradeship. Cynical people with no experience of handling men will say instantly that this will never "work," but as a matter of fact it does "work" in the long run. The discipline of even the worst drafts of militia visibly improved as time went on. In January the job of keeping a dozen raw recruits up to the mark almost turned my hair grey. In May for a short while I was acting-lieutenant in command of about thirty men, English and Spanish. We had all been under fire for months, and I never had the slightest difficulty in getting an order obeyed or in getting men to volunteer for a dangerous job. "Revolutionary" discipline depends on political consciousness—and on understanding of *why* orders must be obeyed; it takes time to diffuse this, but it also takes time to drill a man into an automaton on the barrack-square. The journalists who sneered at the militia-system seldom remembered that the militias had to hold the line while the Popular Army was training in the rear. And it is a tribute to the strength of "revolutionary" discipline that the militias stayed in the field at all. For until about June 1937 there was nothing to keep them there, except class loyalty. Individual deserters could be shot—were shot, occasionally—but if a thousand men had decided to walk out of the line altogether there was no force to stop them. A conscript army in the same circumstances—with its battle-police removed—would have melted away. Yet the militias held the line, though God knows they won very few victories, and even individual desertions were not common. In four or five months in the P.O.U.M. militia I only heard of four men deserting, and two of those were fairly certainly spies who had enlisted to obtain information. At the beginning the apparent chaos, the general lack of training, the fact that you often had to argue for five minutes before you could get an order obeyed, appalled and infuriated me. I had British Army ideas, and certainly the Spanish militias were very unlike the British Army. But considering the circumstances they were better troops than one had any right to expect.

Meanwhile firewood—always firewood. Throughout that period there is probably no entry in my diary that does not mention firewood, or rather the lack of it. We were between two and three thousand feet above sea-level, it was mid-winter and the cold was unspeakable. The temperature was not exceptionally low, on many nights it did not even freeze, and the wintry sun often shone for an hour in the middle of the day; but even if it was not really cold, I assure you that it seemed so. Sometimes there were shrieking winds that tore your cap off and twisted your hair in all directions, sometimes there were mists that poured into the trench like a liquid and seemed to penetrate your bones; frequently it rained, and even a quarter of an hour's rain was enough to make conditions intolerable. The thin skin of earth over the limestone turned promptly into a slippery grease, and as you were always walking on a slope it was impossible to keep your footing. On dark nights I have often fallen half a dozen times in twenty yards; and this was dangerous, because it meant that the lock of one's rifle became jammed with mud. For days together clothes, boots, blankets, and rifles were more or less coated with mud. I had brought as many thick clothes as I could carry, but many of the men were terribly underclad. For the whole garrison, about a hundred men, there were only twelve greatcoats, which had to be handed from sentry to sentry, and most of the men had only one blanket. One icy night I made a list in my diary of the clothes I was wearing. It is of some interest as showing the amount of clothes the human body can carry. I was wearing a thick vest and pants, a flannel shirt, two pullovers, a woollen jacket, a pigskin jacket, corduroy breeches, puttees, thick socks, boots, a stout trench-coat, a muffler, lined leather gloves, and a woollen cap. Nevertheless I was shivering like a jelly. But I admit I am unusually sensitive to cold.

Firewood was the one thing that really mattered. The point about the firewood was that there was practically no firewood to be had. Our miserable mountain had not even at its best much vegetation, and for months it had been ranged over by freezing militiamen, with the result that everything thicker than one's finger had long since been burnt. When we were not eating, sleeping, on guard or on fatigue-duty we were in the valley behind the position, scrounging for fuel. All my memories of that time are memories of scrambling up and down the almost perpendicular slopes, over the jagged limestone that knocked one's boots to pieces, pouncing eagerly on tiny twigs of wood. Three people for a couple of hours could collect enough fuel to keep the dug-out fire alight for about an hour. The eagerness of our search for firewood turned us all into botanists. We classified according to their burning properties every plant that grew on the mountainside; the various heaths and grasses that were good to start a fire with but burnt out in a few minutes, the wild rosemary and the tiny whin bushes that could burn when the fire was well alight, the stunted oak tree, smaller than a gooseberry bush, that was practically unburnable. There was a kind of dried-up reed that was very good for starting fires with, but these grew only on the hill-top to the left of the position, and you had to go under fire to get them. If the Fascist machine-gunners saw you they gave you a drum of ammunition all to yourself. Generally their aim was high and the bullets sang overhead like birds, but sometimes they crackled and chipped the limestone uncomfortably close, whereupon you flung yourself on your face. You went on gathering reeds, however; nothing mattered in comparison with firewood.

Beside the cold the other discomforts seemed petty. Of course all of us were permanently dirty. Our water, like our food, came on mule-back from Alcubierre, and each man's share worked out at about a quart a day. It was beastly water, hardly more transparent than milk. Theoretically it was for drinking only, but I always stole a pannikinful for washing in the mornings. I used to wash one day and shave the next; there was never enough water for both. The position stank abominably, and outside the little enclosure of the barricade there was excrement everywhere. Some of the militiamen habitually defecated in the trench, a disgusting thing when one had to walk round it in the darkness. But the dirt never worried me. Dirt is a thing people make too much fuss about. It is astonishing how quickly you get used to doing without a handkerchief and to eating out of the tin pannikin in which you also wash. Nor was sleeping in one's clothes any hardship after a day or two. It was of course impossible to take one's clothes and especially one's boots off at night; one had to be ready to turn out instantly in case of an attack. In eighty nights I only took my clothes off three times, though I did occasionally manage to get them off in the daytime. It was too cold for lice as yet, but rats and mice abounded. It is often said that you don't find rats and mice in the same place, but you do when there is enough food for them.

In other ways we were not badly off. The food was good enough and there was plenty of wine. Cigarettes were still being issued at the rate of a packet a day, matches were issued every other day, and there was even an issue of candles. They were very thin candles, like those on a Christmas cake, and were popularly supposed to have been looted from churches. Every dug-out was issued daily with three inches of candle, which would burn for about twenty minutes. At that time it was still possible to buy candles, and I had brought several pounds of them with me. Later on the famine of matches and candles made life a misery. You do not realize the importance of these things until you lack them. In a night-alarm, for instance, when everyone in the dug-out is scrambling for his rifle and treading on everybody else's face, being able to strike a light may make the difference between life and death. Every militiaman possessed a tinder-lighter and several yards of yellow wick. Next to his rifle it was his most important possession. The tinder-lighters had the great advantage that they could be struck in a wind, but they would only smoulder, so that they were no use for lighting a fire. When the match famine was at its worst our only way of producing a flame was to pull the bullet out of a cartridge and touch the cordite off with a tinder-lighter.

It was an extraordinary life that we were living—an extraordinary way to be at war, if you could call it war. The whole militia chafed against the inaction and clamoured constantly to know why we were not allowed to attack. But it was perfectly obvious that there would be no battle yet for a long while, unless the enemy started it. Georges Kopp, on his periodical tours of inspection, was quite frank with us. "This is not a war," he used to say, "it is a comic opera with an occasional death."

But the Spanish Civil War was not always, or even very often, a comic opera. In the Madrid sector each army was looking relentlessly for weaknesses in the other. The Republicans believed that they had found such a weak spot in the neighborhood of Guadalajara, fifty miles from Madrid, where the enemy lines were held with a mixed force of Moroccans, Carlists, legionaries and Italian conscripts fresh from the easy conquest of Málaga. The Nationalist army numbered about 50,000, and of these the greater number were Italians.

Against this force General Miaja threw many of the seasoned troops who had fought in the Casa del Campo. The commanders bore names which were already famous in Spain—Modesto, Lister, "El Campesino," "Hans," Lukacz. The Anarchists and Communists fought side by side. The weather was dreadful, with fog, sleet, snow, and bitterly cold winds. Sometimes through the fog it was impossible to see the snowy heights of the Guadarrama mountains.

Here Gustav Regler, a novelist and refugee from Nazi Germany, attached to the Garibaldi Battalion consisting of refugees from Musso-

lini's Italy, describes the uses of propaganda during the early part of the battle.

We pulled up at kilometre-stone 74. Torija, the mountain village, lay behind us, and before us two roads from the east came together. One came from Sigüenza, and the other curved over the plateau towards Brihuega. The enemy was in both places. He was advancing along both roads. What had been done to stop him?

I gathered that all the field-kitchens were out of firewood, that the men of the International Brigade were at their posts, but that the Spaniards were holding a debate, and that no field-telephone had been laid.

There was nothing very new in this. All our battles had started in the same fashion—in chaos. We were all amateurs, Russians, Spaniards and "internationals" alike. But this battle was more vital than any. Here we were up against the troops of the Duce and the Führer. There were ticklish political considerations, and the overriding consideration, which was the reason why my title was that of commissar and not commander.

An African from the Garibaldi Battalion came up to me. He was a man I knew, an Abyssinian whose father had been hanged by Mussolini's soldiers. He greeted me and said, drawing his hand across his throat, "*Mío giorno*—my day." He had vanished in the direction of Brihuega before I quite grasped what he meant.

But his gesture frightened me. This was exactly what must *not* happen! It was here that ideology cut across purely military considerations. This was a battle that had to be decided as between officers and men, between the Duce and his troops.

The object was not to cut their throats but to win them over. That was what we were here for. That was what I had come for—to point out the new frontiers and abolish the old. The revolution in ideas. The true civil war in all its tremendous novelty—to bring about the disintegration of the enemy, to unmask the lying propaganda. To restore humanity in the midst of murder.

I telephoned Madrid from the half-demolished staff office. The Italian commissars were already at work and would be sending a motor cyclist in an hour with a proof of a leaflet for my approval. I was so excited that I could scarcely control myself. I had waited so long for this moment! "Approval?" I cried. "Don't wait for that! Consider that you've got it. Run them off at once and send me a supply. *Imprimatur, imprimatur, imprimatur!*"

I repeated the clerical word, sanctioning publication, with especial delight.

And then began the drama of the leaflets. For days on end I struggled through all its human and sad phases. I remember that for nine days I scarcely slept.

Snow fell upon the roads, upon the fortified castle of Ibarra, before which our French and Italians lay, and upon our right wing, where the Poles were working their way forward in a series of short, rapid advances. Machine-guns were installed under the bushes, at the park-gates and the holes in the walls, but they still kept silent.

It was for the loudspeakers to speak first, to proclaim their heart-warming message through the cold air. I looked up at the black gaping mouths in the white-clad trees. The first was already speaking. I stood directly beneath it, a hundred yards from Ibarra Castle, listening to the men of Garibaldi calling to the men of Il Duce:

"Italian brothers! Marshal Graziani, whom you call the Libyan hyena, and whom the Ethiopians christened 'General Yperite,' has been overtaken by their revenge. He was seriously wounded in an attempt to assassinate him. You too, if you stay where you are, will be in danger. The hatred of Spain will sweep over you! Italian brothers, the Spanish people are fighting for their freedom. Desert the ranks of their enemies! Come over to us! We will welcome you as comrades-in-arms, we, the men of the Garibaldi Battalion."

A bullet burst against the wall where I was standing with the French, waiting to see what effect this would have.

"Not a bad full-stop!" said Boursier, their youthful commander. He said it so grimly that I suspected something.

"What was so special about it?" I asked.

"It was a dum-dum. They cut the nose off the bullet and—"

"I know what a dum-dum bullet is."

"And what are we supposed to do? Answer them with love-letters?"

"Ta gueule!"—but he must have realized from the sharpness of my voice that he had scored a point. But had he? The Garibaldi men did not give up so easily. The loudspeaker cleared its throat, and quoted from a speech by Pacciardi, their commander, who had been in Paris,

buying arms, but had been ordered to return the previous night, since this was the moment he had been awaiting for years.

"In the mud of the trenches, amid the thunder of the guns, an ideal of peace smiles upon us . . ."

The Italians around me wept, but they were happy tears. Their exile was ended! They could talk now with a very different voice. There was no longer any police to humiliate them, no scurrilous reports to distress them. They were fighting on level terms, no longer like a fox pretending that the grapes were green. The self-imposed silence of the Paris cafés was lifted; they could answer back, say what they really thought, prove that they were in earnest with their humanitarian ideals. The struggle was extending its frontiers, which hitherto had been directed against the police, the torture-chamber and starvation. Now the new demigods were being challenged, the Imperium Romanum and the Third Reich. This was the new frontier, before the dilapidated castle of a Spanish grandee, and the loud-speakers proved it.

"You gave us this chance!" said the Italian, Barontini, to Augusto, the tall, universally popular Spanish captain. Augusto smiled. "The honor is mine," he said modestly and looked over the sights of his machine-gun towards the castle from which presently an answer would come. But when, oh, when? *Quién sabe?* Augusto had no faith in leaflets.

"If they were all like you, Augusto," said the Pole Janek, "there would be no need for us 'internationals.' "

Augusto smiled again and signalled to the left wing of his company. His young men dashed forward twenty yards, advancing with him towards the chapel. The machine-gun opened up, but they were already flattened to the ground.

Another report came from the Italians. "Augusto is thirty yards from the chapel. It is time to frighten the Fascists again. Loud-speakers!"

The loudspeakers sang the Italian song, *"Fratelli nostri . . ."* Augusto got within ten yards of the castle. Which would win, reason or courage?

The bullet got Augusto as he was making his final sprint to the doorway. He clutched his heart, opened his mouth, then fell on his face in the snow.

His fellow-countrymen fell silent when the news went round. Some of his own men carried the body back, and the whole company went with the bearers, weeping; they did not ask who would take his place. Had not the world stood still?

I met them with the dead man on the road to Trijueque. Augusto seemed even taller under the sheet that covered him. I had often looked at him when I was giving him instruction. Now I bent down, uncovered his face and kissed his forehead, on which the melting snow lay. The bearers wept.

"Murdered by an Italian!" one of them cried.

"*Caído*—fallen in battle," I corrected him.

Mortar and machine-gun fire was now coming from the castle, and the boom of tank guns. The battle was again in full swing, and the loudspeakers were silent as though ashamed. The first day of ideological warfare had ended in defeat.

But I did not give up. The next day I took the yellow leaflets along to the Poles who were working their way forward through the rocky ridges. Commissar Henri translated them while we crouched on the rim of the Brihuega valley. The men protested violently, and Henri translated their remarks for my benefit. "Why had no one dropped any bombs on Mussolini? If the Italians on the other side are so ready to desert, why aren't they shooting their officers? We aren't the Salvation Army!"

The men who protested were all Communists. Finally, not knowing what else to do, I adopted Gallo's technique and said that the distribution of the leaflets was a Party order.

That night they took them over to the enemy lines.

I did the same with the Italians. We wrapped the leaflets round stones. "Scissors cut paper, stones sharpen scissors, paper wraps stones . . ."—the old children's game. We flung our messages of peace into the trenches where Mussolini's soldiers lay sleeping, and then crept back. That second night was a victory.

I said so to Augusto when we buried him on the morning of the third day.

And on the third day some of our Italians rebelled. They had not come here for this sort of thing. They wanted to be revenged for the shame of exile, the years in foreign cities where there was no Corso and the people talked ugly languages, and where one could only dispute with other *émigrés* and not with one's own kind. Verona, Perugia, Florence, Rome . . . they wanted to be revenged for the life of which Mussolini had robbed them—and now, there were his officers, within reach! Well, blow them to bits with mortar-fire! Let's have more guns, to teach them what we really mean! Leaflets? You must be mad! The sort of thing only a highbrow would think of (they had just discovered that I was a writer)! Why don't we attack Brihuega with knives between our teeth? They captured Luigi today, the light-hearted Luigi—God knows what they'll do with him in Brihuega!

It was hard, I must admit, to stand up against this. But again the Communists helped me.

They announced that the enemy was on the verge of surrendering; and in fact the fire from Ibarra died down that afternoon. The loud-speakers got the upper hand. *"Fratelli nostri . . ."* Our speakers put more emotion into their voices. We were all full of hope until, in the course of the rainy evening, a patrol found Luigi. He lay in a furrow near a tent that had been hastily abandoned by the enemy. His wrists bore the marks of torture, and all the teeth had been battered out of his head. He was scarcely recognizable, but the Garibaldi men knew him. They did not weep.

But if I had gone to them with more leaflets on that third night, while they were talking about Luigi in the fox-holes of Brihuega, under the walls of Ibarra, amid the furrows of the fields and in the caves of Fuentes village, I might have been met with such contumely as no commissar can encounter without being punished for it. Perhaps they would have thrown grenades at me.

So I bided my time and helped to bury Luigi.

Then a red flag waved from one of the windows of Ibarra. When it was noticed we all held our breath. And when shortly afterwards a number of blackshirts emerged from the castle and came towards a tank hidden amid the bushes, the young Spaniards sprang to their feet like delighted children, swarmed round the deserters, overwhelmed them with greetings and offered them cigarettes.

It was nothing but a trick! Suddenly the machine-guns opened up again and swept the field of reconciliation clear. But half an hour later I saw a hand at the same window groping for the red flag. I turned my field-glasses on it just in time to see it quivering in a death-agony. An officer had punished the presumably genuine gesture of some dispirited soldier with a bullet in the neck. But the sight of that quivering hand gave me strength to continue the "battle within a battle."

More loudspeakers were brought into action. Our Italians drafted fresh texts. Loudspeaker vans were brought from Madrid as close as possible to the front. Actors spoke to the soldiers of the Duce, appealing to their pride, invoking their home-sickness, and, as though talking to children, reminding them of the danger in which they stood. *"Ritornate alle vostre case, non dovete morire*—go home, you must not die!"

That night the Fascist commander departed from the castle, accompanied by the officers who were party members but leaving behind a number of career-officers and sergeants to keep the demoralized troops in hand. As he vanished into the night he may have heard the voice of Garibaldi crying: "They promised you the earth, but they are giving you death."

The snow fell, covering the bodies of their dead and ours with its merciful white shroud.

The next day the commissars won. I had the "Internationale" played. It might shock the Catholics on the other side, and harden the hearts of the Fascists, but it seemed to me that after so much talking we needed music, the message without words, and that it must be a chorus that would swell and warm the heart like a symphony. It seemed to me now, as it poured out over the countryside from the hidden loudspeaker van, that the song, that had filled me with terror in Russia, had again acquired the purity of superhuman striving.

The Poles no sooner heard the song than they fixed bayonets and pressed forward to the walls high above Brihuega. They did not want to arrive too late.

Barontini, the Italian commissar, whose companies were having to stand up to the fire of the Fascist artillery, was cursing when I scrambled down into his quivering dug-out. Shells were bursting all round, and the notes of the hymn reached us on gusts of wind.

"Theatre!" growled Barontini. "Mass-murder of volunteers with musical accompaniment!" He snorted in disgust. "Another headquarters notion!"

"What do you mean by headquarters?" I asked. "I'm *here!*"

He was silent. A shell exploded above and a heavy man came sliding down the steps. It was the Abyssinian. "Cut their throats!" he said and started to climb up again, but I gripped his arm. "Not to touch the wounded, do you hear? All comrades, understand? All Abyssinians, do you hear?" I felt that the last words had impressed him.

He did not wait for the shell-splinters to stop falling, but vanished into the hell above.

An hour later Ibarra surrendered. Mussolini's soldiers came hesitatingly towards us, but this time there was no deception; they all had their hands above their heads. They were rapidly searched for weapons by the commissars and then allowed to put them down.

They came in hordes to our headquarters. We did not count them. Lukacz beamed and then pointed to the men of the Garibaldi Battalion, who were looking almost shyly at the prisoners.

"It's almost as though they were ashamed," said Lukacz.

It was, I thought, symptomatic of the confusion of our century. Then the Abyssinian pushed his way through the crowd leading two Italians, their wrists tied with cord. He came up to me and saluted with a broad smile, and the men all around laughed, happy in their triumph. Even the prisoners were laughing.

"Well done!" I said, and embraced him. "And now take the rope off them."

It was our most significant victory.

❁

With the first successful attacks in the Guadalajara sector, the Republican forces gained confidence in themselves. They were heavily outgunned and outnumbered, their supply situation was precarious, and they had difficulties of communication, but for the first time they were able to overrun the enemy. It was the first major defeat suffered by Fascist forces anywhere. Herbert Matthews, the correspondent of The New York Times, *compared it to the defeat of Napoleon at Bailén in southern Spain, which later historians came to regard as the turning point of his triumphant career.*

Here is Herbert Matthews' account of the rout of the Italians:

Trijueque lies a few hundred yards off the northern side of the road, dominating a marvelous panorama out to the snow-capped Guadarramas. We drove our car quickly behind a house, but not so quickly as to escape detection. There I saw one of the unhappiest sights (for me) of this whole war—two pathetic heaps of Italian bodies, piled haphazardly into farmers' carts like so many old rags. "Sic transit" indeed, for I could not help thinking of the first pile of Italian dead I saw in Ethiopia, at the foot of Amba Aradam, on the eve of a great victory.

By the time we reached the main square of the little town, which was by then utterly wrecked, we heard the first boom of a 3-inch gun, instantly followed by the whistle and shriek of the approaching shell. That first one struck on the opposite side of the plaza from where we were standing. And what a picture of desolation that square was! Houses crushed to the ground or riddled by shells; the church steeple had been thrown down and its large iron bell lay on one side on the ground.

More shells were coming over at half-minute intervals. Each time we would throw ourselves down or crouch against the wall of some house. The third or fourth shell hit the corner of the plaza where we had been standing, and as we moved out toward our car the shells seemed to follow us, showing that the gunners probably had us under direct observation.

Then someone shouted, "Planes overhead!" There they were, six Loyalist bombers, going down toward Brihuega. That morning, the officer told us, twenty-five heavy bombers had unloaded 760 bombs around Brihuega, while thirty chasers machine-gunned the lines in the same sector.

It was time to go, for there was nothing more to be seen in that ruined and deserted town which we left to those two heaps of Italian dead.

It was at this point that the Defense Junta and its Russian advisers made one the most brilliant decisions of the war. The temptation obviously was to push their advantage while the Italians were still demoralized and the two fresh divisions were being sent into the lines. They could have been driven back, the lines restored more or less to their original positions, and the way to Guadalajara as irrevocably blocked as the Jarama River was. On the other hand, those fresh divisions were something to reckon with, and the troops used by the Government had had an exhausting week. Moreover, their numbers were not large. By waiting for reinforcements they gave the Italians time for a breathing spell and to dig in and fortify their lines, but at the same time an opportunity was presented to win that rarest of all things in history—a decisive victory on the field of battle.

The decision was to wait and then launch a daring attack with four brigades, two on each side of the Brihuega road, while a fifth brigade defended the left flank.

During the next four days, whenever weather permitted, the Loyal air force was over the Italian lines, bombing and strafing. On Tuesday, the 16th, no less than 880 bombs were dropped on the Italian positions, including two bombs of 250 kilos, ten of 100, and twenty of 50 kilos. That was without counting the strafing by machine guns.

Thursday, the 18th, was the anniversary of the Paris Commune, and that was the morning the order for the attack was given. Twenty minutes before the start eighty planes bombed and strafed heavily and, although it could not be known at the time, that had the Italians virtually beaten before the battle began, for they began to evacuate Brihuega under the merciless barrage, which was seconded by a heavy and equally precise artillery curtain.

The enemy made one half-hearted riposte before giving up. It consisted in a flanking attack against the Loyalists' right wing on the side of the Brihuega road. For a short while the Government troops were held back, but by cool and steady rifle and machine-gun fire they first stopped the thrust, and then, in counterattacks by the Thaelmann and Edgar André Battalions of the Eleventh Brigade, broke the Italian line. Small groups of Fascists, sheltered hopelessly behind heaps of stones, fought a valiant rearguard action with machine guns, and died fighting at their posts. It gave a little respite, which was sorely needed, for there was grave danger of a part of the Italian force being trapped in the town. But the road to Brihuega was free!

The town is in a hollow, surrounded by hills that reach almost to its edge. Five roads lead into it, one from Torija on the west, one from Budia on the southeast, one that goes due north to the Aragón highway and still another that strikes off northeast to the same highway, while a secondary, dirt road went southwest to join an important road going to Guadalajara. By the time the Brihuega road was cleared the

Loyalists were in possession of all those spokes of the wheel except the one running northeast to the Aragón highway. That was the Italians' back door, and a Spanish battalion had orders to close it.

They hung back and arrived too late. In that respect only did the Government's strategy fail of fulfillment. For the rest it was a walk-over. The four brigades poured down into Brihuega—Spaniards and Internationals shoulder to shoulder. The honor of first entering the town itself was given to the Spanish battalions commanded by El Campesino. The last nest of Fascist resistance was in a house off the edge of the town called the "Casa de Cobo," which was taken by a patrol of the Paris Commune Battalion.

Late that night, in Madrid, we were handed this historic communiqué:

"Brihuega and the heights which dominate it have been taken. Two hundred Italian prisoners were captured. The body of an Italian lieutenant-colonel has been found. Six cannons, a number of machine guns and sub-machine guns, three trucks with munitions, and sixty other trucks were also taken."

Not what might be called a literary masterpiece—but for all that it means in modern history, you will search long before finding a more pregnant collection of words.

The news broke so late and in such non-committal fashion that there was nothing for it but to send a hasty new lead to my previous story. None of us knew the full significance of what had happened for we could not know that the Italians had not only been driven from another town, but were routed. Above all, we could not know the decisive character of the defeat. That was the important thing—that the defeat was decisive, that the stream of history had been deflected into new channels, that a change had taken place, not only in the war, but in the world.

It was considered so unimportant in New York that none of the newspapers, so far as I know, front-paged the story. As news started pouring into Madrid the next day we began to get some inkling of the true state of affairs, but despite our efforts it was impossible to dig up the cars and gasoline to make the long trip out there on that day. Henry Gorrell, of the United Press, and I managed to find an Anarchist captain who was going out the next morning and promised to take us along, and with that we had to be content.

Meanwhile, the last phase of the battle was initiated with an order to the troops to advance all along the front, using the Aragón highway as the axis. This was done by three battalions of the Lister Brigade and units of Hans's Eleventh Brigade. In five hours, singing the "International," the "Marseillaise," the "Hymn of Riego" as they went along, the Loyalists advanced six miles, taking Gajanejos on Kilometer 90.

Of all the things we wondered about that night (and thoughtful Spaniards must have been doing the same) the most persistent question was: "What will Mussolini do now?" By then there could be no minimizing the loss of prestige which the events of that week entailed for the Italian Army. By one of the choicer ironies of fate, it so happened that in going through five cases of documents captured in Brihuega a message from Il Duce to General Mancini of the Italian force was found and copies distributed to the press that night, as well as read over the radio, by the Information Department of the Spanish Army. Mancini had ordered the distribution of copies to all commands and all troops on the Guadalajara front, which was done in a memorandum signed by First Adjutant Major Luigi Bernardi.

The message read as follows:

"On board the *Pola,* on my way to Libya, I have received your dispatches in connection with the great battle which is going on in the direction of Guadalajara. I am following the incidents of the battle with unshakable confidence because I am sure that the impetus and daring of our Legionaries will break the enemy's resistance. To crush the International forces will be a great success, including the political aspect. Tell the Legionaries that I follow their action hourly and that their efforts will be crowned with victory."

The message, which was signed "Mussolini," was dated March 13, the day that the Internationals recaptured Trijueque, and it was distributed to the troops on March 16, two days before the fall of Brihuega.

The next day was one of the most memorable of my life. The realization of what had happened was gradual but before mid-afternoon I was overwhelmed by what I had seen. We entered Brihuega at about two o'clock, marveling to find it so little damaged. The air communiqués had foolishly kept announcing the terrific bombardment of the town so that we expected to find it ground to dust. Actually, the pilots had received orders not to bomb the town itself, but the Italian positions around the town. There were shell holes in some of the houses, but that was all.

The civilian population never had had time to evacuate it. When the Italians entered, they just fled to their cellars. Some were routed out, some came out of their own free will, while others stayed down there, not daring to make their presence known. One woman told Gorrell and me that she had taken her baby and stayed in the cellar of her house for eight days, never seeing an Italian and only emerging when the Loyalists retook the town. Forty of the inhabitants, men, women, and youths, had been imprisoned and were under sentence to be shot. Seven, in fact, had been executed, but before the other sentences could be carried out the Government troops entered.

Two sisters, eighty-two and eighty-six years old, had stuck it out with the rest, and were now happily pottering around their house. We walked around assessing the damages and talking to people. All of them assured us that the invading troops had been Italian, with the exception of a few interpreters and liaison officers. One of the churches had been employed as a stable, and militiamen were busy collecting dozens of fine, new mule-saddles that had been left behind. The post office was completely sacked. On a wall opposite one of the churches was painted *"Viva Mussolini! Arriba España!"* Farther up the same street, on another house, the inscription *"Viva el Generalissimo Franco!"* had been scrawled.

We soon drove on toward Budia, through terrain that a few days before had been full of Italians. A small part of the captured war material had been piled in there—cannons, mortars, machine guns, hand-grenades, rifles, and other things. Under ordinary circumstances it could have been considered a large haul, but the Loyalists had taken so much that what we saw was unimportant. However, before lunching we went over the material carefully, verifying from the markings and names that it was all Italian.

The officers we ate with were almost delirious with joy. A word of caution would have been considered treason. For them, and everyone we saw that day, the turning point in the war had come and all battles and all weeks in the future were to be just like Brihuega. The overconfidence engendered in those days was to cost the Loyalists heavy. The evidence was all there for them, in front of their eyes, but they had missed its significance. What they had defeated was an Italian force, not a Spanish insurgent army. The loss and the shame was Italy's, not Franco's, and I fully believe the stories told of rejoicings in Salamanca, accompanied by banquets, at the defeat of the hated foreigners. The victory was not national but international: the anti-Fascists had defeated the Fascists—that was the chief significance of Brihuega.

While still in Budia, planes had been flying over us in the direction of Brihuega—rebel reconnaissance machines, as they turned out to be. We drove back toward Brihuega and had reached the last height over the town, where we would have arrived in a few minutes, when we spotted seven Junker tri-motors flying over the valley on our right. They had almost reached Brihuega, and as we stopped our car to watch them, they unaccountably swung around and turned back. For a moment it was puzzling, and then we saw the reason. A Loyalist squadron had arrived and right in front of us, over Brihuega, were engaged in a spectacular fight with three other Junkers and an inde-terminate number of Fiat combat planes.

A correspondent's dream had come true! Here, right in front of our eyes, was a big aerial battle! Surely, this world of ours can offer few more thrilling sights. As a matter of fact, it was the purest of accidents. The Loyalist squadron was on a bombing mission of its own and was caught just as much by surprise as the rebels.

There could have been no less than forty planes gyrating there, without counting the seven which were fleeing. Out of the loops and darts and whirls that the fighters were making, like so many birds, an orderly movement began to emerge as the insurgent planes sought to fly back to their lines, tormented by the snubnosed "Chatos" and monoplane chasers of the Loyalists. Slowly the bombers worked free behind the screen of Fiats, which kept the Government planes occu-pied. There were such daring twists and turns as would have taken the breath away from any crowd watching stunt fliers in peaceable America. More than once a plane seemed to go into a spin, only to pull up at the last minute. A Fiat made a daring "falling leaf," and when we thought it must crash into the hill opposite to us, it zoomed upward almost perpendicularly. One dropped down nose first on the other side of the hill, out of sight, and later we learned it had crashed. Another Fiat shot out from the crowd with a biplane chaser on its tail. A half-hour later, at the front lines, a commander told us the pilot had bailed out near Yela, coming down in Government lines where he was taken prisoner, while his machine crashed and was destroyed. The pilot who shot him down was an American named Baumler. Dahl also took part in that battle.

In fifteen minutes it was all over, and the Loyalists soared triumphantly around Brihuega while the insurgent planes disappeared in the distance.

Yet those first three Junkers, as we quickly learned, had managed to give Brihuega a fearful bombing just before the Loyalist planes arrived. Now, indeed, Brihuega was a horrible sight! At least twenty large bombs had been dropped within a few square blocks right in the center of the town. The main street was a shambles of rocks, gaping holes, wooden beams, and bricks. A dozen houses were nothing but an incoherent mass of stones and wood in which soldiers were feverishly digging for bodies. Two stretchers came by with inert bodies mercifully covered with blankets. Then came three stretchers with wounded. On one of them lay a man whose eyes had been blown out. Absorbent cotton was stuffed into the sockets to stop the bleeding. And then still other stretchers were carried by. A woman ran screaming through the streets in a terror that could not be assuaged, despite the return of safety.

We made for the house in which we had seen the two old sisters. There was one of them, sitting pale and ghastly looking on a chair while a neighbor bound her bleeding head. "How is your sister?" we asked. "She is dead," the old woman answered dully.

Down the main street, at a house which I had admired a few hours earlier, for it had not been touched, a pale-faced woman, her head white with fallen plaster, begged me in a voice panting with terror to help her move the few things she had left, down to her sister's a block away. As we walked she kept repeating interminably: "For eleven days it has been hell!"

There was nothing more we could do in Brihuega, so we drove on. A dead mule had to be dragged from the street at one place to let us pass. Next to him, against the curb, a badly wounded horse stood trembling and waiting patiently for someone to put him out of his misery.

All that had happened within a space of two minutes!

Instead of returning to Torija at once, we went north, following the line of retreat of the Italians. It was on that side trip of five or six miles that I got a truer idea of the amount of material which had been abandoned, and satisfied myself beyond the shadow of a doubt that the retreat had been turned into a rout. There was only one explanation for what I saw that day—panic. The Italians had thrown their rifles away, their gas masks, their knapsacks. They left cannons of various sizes, mortars, more than a hundred machine guns, hand-grenades by the thousands and thousands, trucks, bicycles, tractors, food, clothes, tents, tools, field radio and telephone sets. It took the Loyalists five days to collect that material. Two whole munitions depots, established by the Italians in expectation of further advances, were captured. The list could be continued indefinitely, but it would serve no purpose except to establish further the contention that it was not a retreat but a collective panic.

All day, at every place we stopped and no matter whom we talked to or what we saw, there was only one label—Italian. The dead bodies, the prisoners, the material of every kind, the men who had occupied Brihuega and then fled, were Italian and nothing but Italian.

About a mile out of Brihuega on that road running north there was a depot of at least 300 cases of cartridges, each containing 2,000 bullets. And all along the road on both sides we saw more full cases—surely 200 more—which would give a total of a million cartridges abandoned in that stretch alone, while the officers with us claimed they had knowledge of another million in all found elsewhere. On three occasions I descended from the car to read the labels on the boxes and make sure that the material was Italian. There were dead along that road, many abandoned trucks, heaps of 75-millimeter shells, about half a dozen field pieces.

And so it went until we reached the front lines just short of Yela. That town had been occupied a half hour before without a shot being fired. The Commander came over to talk to us. Under his arm he had a pile of documents which he showed us. They were all Italian—passports, carnets, private letters, official documents—taken from four prisoners who were found hiding in Yela.

The Commander told us about a terrific bombardment carried out during the morning by some eighty Government planes on the Aragón highway beyond Algora, where a train of about a thousand trucks carrying soldiers and material was surprised. Six hundred and fifty bombs were dropped on them, and then the combat planes swooped down, machine-gunning the soldiers.

Nobody knew where the main body of Italians could be. The Commander's guess (which proved true) was that they had fled to the high town of Bujalaro, north of the Aragón road. It is true that a few miles beyond we were stopped by guards and warned that if we proceeded farther we would come under cannon fire, but that merely meant that the Italians were covering their retreat with artillery. At that point we were even with Kilometer 92.

Back in Brihuega for the last time we were just turning on to the main road when a group of women and children and an old man ran screaming toward us, holding out their hands imploringly. On stopping, a woman with a baby in her arms begged us weeping to take them back to Guadalajara. Their house had been destroyed in the bombing and they all had barely escaped with their lives by running into a neighbor's cellar a moment before the disaster. We somehow managed to squeeze six into our car while another automobile took the remaining two.

The children were whimpering when we started, but soon calmed down and it was from one of them, a lad of seven, that I heard the only sane remark of that whole astonishing day.

"What do you think of all this?" I asked.

"Muy bueno," he answered happily. "The bombs destroyed our school!"

Guernika

GUERNIKA *was not the first town to be destroyed by German bombers during the Spanish Civil War. Already other small towns in the Basque provinces had been heavily bombed. But the destruction of Guernika came at a time when the democracies still hoped that in some way the Non-Intervention Agreements could be enforced, and that the war could be localized. Guernika was proof that Franco would go to any extreme to gain a victory over Spain.*

Guernika was the sacred town of the Basques. There, under an oak tree, the ancient lawmakers proclaimed the laws and held their parliament. For at least eight hundred years it was a place of pilgrimage. For the Basques this small market town standing in the shelter of the pinewood hills was a shrine. Early in the evening of April 26, 1937, the Germans bombed the town. It was market day. The stalls were set up in the town square. Wave after wave of bombers flew over the town, bombed it, and machine-gunned the people fleeing into the hills.

Father Alberto de Onaindía, a young Basque priest, watched the bombing:

Late in the afternoon of April 26 I was going by car to rescue my mother and my sisters, then living in Marquina, a town about to fall into the hands of Franco. It was one of those magnificently clear days, the sky soft and serene. We reached the outskirts of Guernika just before five o'clock. The streets were busy with the traffic of market-day. Suddenly we heard the siren, and trembled. People were running about in all directions, abandoning everything they possessed, some hurrying into the shelters, others running into the hills. Soon an enemy airplane appeared over Guernika. A peasant was passing by. "It's nothing, only one of the 'white' ones," he said. "He'll drop a few bombs, and then he'll go away." The Basques had learned to distinguish between the twin-engined "whites" and the three-engined "blacks." The "white" airplane made a reconnaissance over the town, and when he was directly over the center he dropped three bombs. Immediately afterwards we saw a squadron of seven planes, followed a little later by six more, and this in turn by a third squadron of five more. All of them were Junkers. Meanwhile Guernika was seized with a terrible panic.

I left the car by the side of the road and took refuge with five milicianos in a sewer. The water came up to our ankles. From our hiding place we could see everything that happened without being seen. The airplanes came low, flying at two hundred meters. As soon as we could leave our shelter, we ran into the woods, hoping to put a safe distance between us and the enemy. But the airmen saw us and went after us. The leaves hid us. As they did not know exactly where we were, they aimed their machine-guns in the direction they thought we were traveling. We heard the bullets ripping through branches, and the sinister sound of splintering wood. The milicianos and I followed the flight patterns of the airplanes; and we made a crazy journey through the trees, trying to avoid them. Meanwhile women, children and old men were falling in heaps, like flies, and everywhere we saw lakes of blood.

I saw an old peasant standing alone in a field: a machine-gun bullet killed him. For more than an hour these eighteen planes, never more than a few hundred meters in altitude, dropped bomb after bomb on Guernika. The sound of the explosions and of the crumbling houses cannot be imagined. Always they traced on the air the same tragic flight pattern, as they flew over all the streets of Guernika. Bombs fell by thousands. Later we saw the bomb craters. Some were sixteen meters in diameter and eight meters deep.

The airplanes left around seven o'clock, and then there came another wave of them, this time flying at an immense altitude. They were dropping incendiary bombs on our martyred city. The new bombardment lasted thirty-five minutes, sufficient to transform the town into an enormous furnace. Even then I realized the terrible purpose of this new act of vandalism. They were dropping incendiary bombs to try to convince the world that the Basques had fired their own city.

The destruction of Guernika went on altogether for two hours and forty-five minutes. When the bombing was over, the people left their shelters. I saw no one crying. Stupor was written on all their faces. Eyes fixed on Guernika, we were completely incapable of believing what we saw.

Towards dusk we could see no more than five hundred meters. Everywhere there were flames and thick black smoke. Around me people were praying, and some stretched out their arms in the form of a cross, imploring mercy from Heaven.

Soon firemen arrived from Bilbao and started to work on some of the buildings which had not been bombed. We heard that the glow of the flames had been seen from Lequeitio, twenty-two kilometers away. Not even the people who went into the refuges were saved; nor the sick and wounded in the hospitals. Guernika had no anti-aircraft guns, no batteries of any kind; nor were there any machine-guns.

During the first hours of the night it was a most horrifying spectacle: men, women and children were wandering through the woods in search of their loved ones. In most cases they found only their bullet-riddled bodies.

The buildings near the Tree of Guernika, which stands on a small hill, were unharmed, but the City Hall with its valuable archives and documents was completely destroyed.

When it grew dark the flames of Guernika were reaching to the sky, and the clouds took on the color of blood, and our faces too shone with the color of blood.

Father de Onaindía went on to nearby Marquina that night to rescue his mother and sisters. He returned to Guernika a few hours later. About midnight, when he was passing through the town, the flames were being fanned by a high wind and a huge cloud of smoke hung over the town. The people of Guernika were digging out their dead. Through the night, and all the next day and the two following days, the town continued to burn.

From Seville the tipsy general, Queipo de Llano, broadcast the information that Basque Reds had set fire to the town to compromise Franco. Few believed him, though the claim was constantly reiterated in the following days by the Nationalist press. Those who knew the

*character of the Basques found it difficult to believe that Basque sol-
diers had gone about digging bomb craters and pouring gasoline on
the walls to give the impression of a bombing raid. The evidence of
captured German airmen—one of them had the word* Garnika *clearly
written in his diary under the date April 26, 1937—and the scattered
bomb fragments with clearly recognizable German inscriptions,
pointed to a deliberate and cold-blooded exercise in the art of destruction committed by the Condor Legion. Soon Picasso would be
sketching out the first designs for his monumental painting, which he
called simply, "Guernika."*

*About two o'clock in the morning of April 27th, a detachment
of Basque troops sent from Bilbao to relieve a forward position in
the hills passed through Guernika. Among them was young Sergeant
Aristarco Yoldi, belonging to the Maebe Brigade, who had taken
part in nearly all the campaigns in Basque territory. A skilled mechanic, short and wiry, with a passion for dangerous adventures, he
had heard rumors of the attack on Guernika during the journey, but
he was not prepared to see the whole town in flames. Here he describes the burning town a few hours after Father de Onaindía left it:*

We came up in lorries, but when we came to Guernika we knew we
would have to abandon them. We could not take the lorries through
the flames. We jumped out and made our way through the town as
well as we could, dodging the flames.

The flames were everywhere. The whole town was burning. Army
ambulances were coming up from Bilbao. Men and women were still
digging out the bodies. Around the main square every other building
had collapsed. The church had been bombed, but the façade was still
standing. The convent was destroyed, but there were nuns everywhere, working to help the wounded. Strangely, the tree of Guernika,
which is a little way behind the church, was still standing. The tree
is in a stone courtyard, with stone benches arranged around it, but the
whole courtyard had been spared.

Except for the roaring of the flames, there was no sound. No one
spoke, and even the oxen, wandering aimlessly around the town, were
silent. Everyone was stunned.

I knew Guernika well, but it was unrecognizable. It is a small town
of red roofs and whitewashed walls, very clean. On market days peo-

ple come from miles around to trade donkeys and cows and dairy produce. Market days were happy days. People sat around and bargained and drank wine and sang. There was no singing. There were dead animals burning in the street. They were digging into the rubble, and removing the charred bodies in oxcarts and taking them to the cemetery. The clouds were low. The sky seemed to be full of livid flames, for the clouds reflected the burning town.

We passed quickly through Guernika and made our way to the front. We marched for about a mile, and then looked back. We could see Guernika burning, and we heard the roaring of the flames, but there was not a single human voice anywhere to be heard.

Then in silence we went up to the hills.

Most of the fighting in the Basque provinces took place in the hills. Franco was determined to punish the Basques for coming out on the side of the Republic, and his soldiers showed peculiar animosity to the Basque priests they captured. The Basques were fighting desperately for national survival, for their own quiet form of Catholicism, and for their ancient language and customs. Germans, Italians, Moors and Legionaries were hurled against their small, ill-equipped armies clinging stubbornly to the foothills. It was a savage and little-known war, for there were few foreign correspondents with the Basque forces.

All the advantages of geography and superior equipment fell to the side of Franco. The Basques themselves were tragically divided, for while the two coastal provinces declared for the Republic, the inland provinces declared for Franco. The hatred between Navarre and Vizcaya was deeply rooted. The Requetés, recognized by their red berets and their passionate cry of "Viva Cristo-Rey," were taking revenge for their defeats during the Carlist wars of a century before, and all those other political defeats which in earlier centuries had reduced the power of Navarre (Nabara). Once Navarre and Castille ruled Spain between them, but those days had long since passed.

Until his death in an airplane crash, General Mola commanded the Nationalist forces in the Basque provinces. "I have decided to terminate rapidly the war in the north," he wrote. "If they do not surrender immediately, I will raze all Vizcaya to the ground, beginning with the industries of war." It was not an empty threat.

The Basques of the lowland were as deeply religious as the Basques of the high plateau. Priests fought against priests, sons against fathers, brothers against brothers. Sometimes the lowland Basques were able to hold back the enemy, but never for long. With the frontier closed, and little aid coming from abroad, they found themselves squeezed in a vise, fighting a losing war.

Sergeant Yoldi describes the bitter fighting in the hills:

We went on fighting because there was nothing else to do, and because we believed in ourselves, and because we lived on hopes of help coming from abroad. We could fight well against the Moors, the Italians, and the Legionaries, for we knew the mountain trails better than they did. The Requetés were our worst enemies; they spoke our language, and they knew the trails as well as we did. They could infiltrate into our lines. Also, they were fanatical fighters.

We fought best at night. We would dig into the hills, and send out scouting parties to find the weak points of the enemy, and push them back. By night we advanced, but during the day, without supporting artillery, airplanes and tanks, we were often forced back. Yet we could not afford to retreat, because there was so little ground to retreat to. During the day all the advantages belonged to the enemy. By late afternoon we were always looking at our watches and calculating how long it would be before sunset. The nights were ours.

We were a strange army composed of students, mechanics and peasants, led by a handful of regular officers. We wore navy blue coveralls, and we used whatever weapons were handy—French rifles, which were last used during the Franco-German War of 1870, and the most up-to-date rifles from Czechoslovakia. France refused to give us arms, and our chief supply of weapons came from Mexico. In Bilbao we had built five ships for the Mexican Government. When we were in trouble, they sent back the ships loaded with rifles and machine guns, running the blockade. We also had homemade dynamite bombs—three sticks of dynamite in a tomato can with a sixteen-second fuse. We lit the fuse with a cigarette.

We fought up and down the hills, and the strange thing was that the enemy always knew where we were. Every evening, when we turned on the radio, we would hear Queipo de Llano, drunk or pretending to be drunk, clinking his glass against the microphone, and announcing our exact positions. We had our Fifth Column like everyone else. It was unnerving, but it was something you had to live with all through the war.

In March 1937 we were up in the mountains, digging in and trying to prevent General Mola from coming across the plains on the other side of the mountains. There were three great mountains called Maroto, Albertía and Jacinto, and we knew that if we lost them the enemy would be able to plant their heavy guns on the mountain-tops and command all the lowlands. We had our observation posts on the mountain-tops, and our own guns were on the slopes below. Our guns were small, but they made a good deal of noise.

There was thick snow on the ground. Everywhere you looked, there was snow. We wore white capes, and we dug slit-trenches in the earth, and so did the enemy. We were white ghosts moving about in the snow. We used to tie sticks of dynamite to hand grenades—it's a fearful weapon, and the Requetés never learned to use it, or perhaps they didn't dare to. With this weapon we were sometimes able to kill everyone in an enemy trench. We knew how to hurl these grenades accurately: we were good pelota players.

The enemy knew we had men on the slopes of the mountains, and they kept sending shells over. They had airplanes and could spot our positions. The shells came over regularly at eleven o'clock in the morning, and some of them were buried harmlessly in the undergrowth and others slid over the snow or dug through the earth and slithered underground before they exploded. It was uncanny, but everything on the mountains was uncanny. The Requetés had a fondness for dum-dum bullets, which cause wounds that can never heal. Dum-dum bullets explode into fragments whenever they hit anything: a leaf will make them explode. And when they fall in the snow they make little ghostly blue and red flames, and there is no noise. Only the little ghostly puffs of flame in the snow.

We held the mountain-tops as long as we could, but they brought up heavier and heavier guns, and we were forced back on the slopes thickly covered with oak trees. The snow gave place to rain and heavy fogs shrouding the mountains. We fought through the rain and the fog. We hardly knew whether the enemy was in front of us or behind us.

Between the mountains and the foothills there is a place called Crucetas, the crossroads, where the road from Ochandiano branches off, one branch going to Villarreal, the other to Aramayona. There is no town at Crucetas, only the rolling grass and the two roads vanishing into the distance. We had orders to defend Crucetas, and some of the bitterest fighting of the war in the North took place there. The left flank was composed of young soldiers who had never been in battle before. The Requetés swooped down from the hills and massacred them. I went over to see why they were not supporting us, and found none of them left alive. It was early morning and the rain was falling. For the rest of the day the stretcher-bearers were busy picking up the bodies and taking them down the hill to Ochandiano. Many of the stretcher-bearers were killed. Perhaps we should not have gathered up the bodies, but it is an article of faith among the Basques to bury the dead. We did not dare to leave them in the open.

The enemy captured Crucetas and hurled us back, but we recaptured it. We lost it three times and regained it three times. Crucetas was open country and there was nowhere to hide. Once I lay down beside a tree trunk, thinking I was safe there, until I discovered the tree was hollow and a bullet would have gone through it like paper. At last the rain stopped, the sun came up, and the enemy could see all our positions. The airplanes came over, and soon the heavy guns were being aimed at us again. The next day we retreated. Exhausted by five weeks of fighting, I fell asleep in a shallow trench. Airplanes dropped bombs and killed all the men around me. I was in a drugged sleep, and did not even hear the explosions.

The enemy had captured the heights, and we were being driven down slowly to the seacoast, but we still fought every inch of the way among the foothills. We came to the village of Ceanuni, not far from Barazar. The village had been heavily bombed. The telephone poles lay crazily across the roofs of the houses. There was no one alive in the village, no one at all. It was dusk, and there was only the burned-out village, the emptiness, the desolation. Suddenly we saw something we never dreamed we would see. Slowly, along the bombed road, came two oxen dragging a motor ambulance. The doors of the ambulance were swinging open. Two dead men had been thrown over the roof of the ambulance, but how they got there we never knew. We looked inside. The ambulance was filled with the dead, and the blood dripped down on the road. The oxen went on in the gathering darkness, and the blood continued to drip down on the road.

We made our way down the hills below Barazar. There was a lot of skirmishing, and the airplanes kept coming over. We were in heavy heart, for we had sent a detachment of cavalry to Barazar—the only time we used cavalry in the war—and the airplanes found them. After the bombing, there was not one cavalryman left alive.

We were in the hills when we saw a priest coming up toward us. He was a good priest, and wanted to be helpful. He was carrying blankets and three knapsacks on his back, and four or five rifles under his arms, and somehow balancing a machine gun on his shoulder. He was quite young, about twenty-six years old, and he had seen things that made him want to fight. It was hot that day, and he was wearing a heavy cassock.

"Why have you come here, Father?" I asked him.

He smiled pleasantly and said he had come to fight. He lifted the machine gun from his shoulder and put it down on the ground. The barrel of the machine gun was bent, and it was quite useless.

"No, Father, you shouldn't be here," I said. "Go down into the valley. The wounded will need you down there."

He sighed and wandered down through the woods, leaving the machine gun on the ground.

About a week later I was sent to Monte Sollube, overlooking the fishing port of Bermeo on the coast not far from San Sebastián. The Italians had captured Bermeo, and it was our job to get them out of it. So we made them fight in the thick pines of the mountains. It was enjoyable fighting, for we liked to lead the Italians deep into the mountains and then cut them up piecemeal. The days were clear, and every night it rained, and that was good, too. The Italians fell into all our traps, and at last we were able to throw them off the mountains and back in Bermeo. For some reason the Basque government refused to let us go in for the kill.

We kept fighting them all round Bermeo until they were begging for mercy and jumping into the water. We refused to let them get away. For us Basques it was the one great moment of victory in the war. But the Nationalist navy came up and bombarded the mountains from the sea. For the first time I saw a whole mountain catch fire. The mountain was our base, and we were forced to make our way through the mountain paths, choking and coughing and crying. And when Franco was tired of shelling the mountain from the sea, he dropped incendiary bombs from the air, and fired at us with artillery from his shore batteries. Ships, airplanes, batteries—they were throwing everything they had against us. We had the sweet memory of the Italians begging mercy at our hands, but we lost too many men in the mountains to take any pleasure in it.

At the beginning of May I was back in Bilbao. Suddenly my detachment was ordered to move to the main square of the city: to occupy the square and see that no one came in or out. No one explained why we were being sent. We were ordered to carry no heavy luggage, and no blankets. We decided we would be regrouped in the square and then sent to a nearby sector. We were shock troops, accustomed to being sent up the line at a moment's notice.

There were no air raids that night. It was a beautiful, mild night. There was no movement in the streets. We reached the square, and received our orders—we were to surround the Engineering School.

We obeyed the puzzling order without asking any questions. We knew, of course, that the Engineering School since the beginning of the war had become the headquarters and main supply depot of the Anarchists in Bilbao. So far the Anarchists had fought for the government. They fought well.

The Engineering School was a huge yellow building occupying one side of the Plaza de la Casilla, dominating the square which is filled with trees and fountains. The square was silent and dark, very quiet. We took up our posts and waited. Our guns were trained on the school.

So we waited, and one by one, and sometimes in small groups, Anarchists made their way to the school, and we disarmed them. Nearly six hundred heavily armed men attempted to enter the square that night. We took their arms. We filled up two or three trucks with their hand grenades, pistols and rifles. They cursed us, but we took them.

We were beginning to get some inkling of what was afoot. We posted machine guns and mortars on the houses facing the school, gradually accumulating enough firepower to blow it sky high. But everything was done quietly. We knew the Anarchists were up to some mischief, but we did not know what kind of mischief.

Around seven o'clock in the morning there was a surprising development. About ten yellow trucks arrived, filled to bursting with armed men—they were Anarchists, and there must have been nearly six hundred of them in the buses. We halted the buses and ordered them to surrender their arms, and they refused. Altogether we were four companies in the square, about five hundred men. So we were very nearly equal in numbers. But there was no fighting. They cursed us as we had never been cursed before. They looked tired and battle-weary, and we thought they must have come from the front, but they did not tell us where they came from—this we learned later. If we had known where they came from, we would have turned our machine guns on them and killed every single one of them.

It was broad daylight now, and we were all arguing, and there was that strange silence in the square. We did not understand what was happening. We did not know why we had been ordered to disarm the Anarchists. Something was being hidden from us. There were endless conferences, and in the end it was decided to let them through with their weapons. They went into the Engineering School and disappeared.

There followed more and more conferences. One of our officers, Major Mario—he was tall, handsome, and absolutely reckless—decided to go into the school and investigate. He told us: "If you hear a shot, don't worry about me! You'll know what has happened! Burn the whole place down!" About this time a very old Anarchist came out of the school, carrying a carbine. He was white-haired, and tears were streaming down his face. He walked across the square, shouting: "What's happening? Has everyone gone mad?" Then he took the carbine and smashed it against the wall, and it fell at his feet in two pieces. Then he vanished, and we understood no more than we understood in the beginning.

At ten o'clock we were ordered to return to our barracks. Sometime later during the day we learned what had happened. The Anarchists, in their strange fashion, had intended to come out in open revolt, following the example of the Anarchists in Barcelona. But we were luckier than the people in Barcelona—there was no bloodletting in Bilbao. The government got wind of the plot in time, and that was why we were sent to disarm them. We prevented an Anarchist uprising which would have been just as senseless and wasteful as the uprising in Barcelona.

We did not know until later that the Anarchists had fallen back on Bilbao after abandoning their positions in the Peñas de Udala. They were deserters. We lost many men when we tried to hold back the enemy, who hurried through the gap.

In those months our lives were spent in frantic efforts to hold back the enemy. We thought we had built an iron ring round Bilbao, but we had neither the men nor the material to man the ring. Worse still, the engineer who built the defenses went over to the enemy, and this was specially galling, because we believed him to be a close friend of the President of the Basque Republic.

We were sent up to the hills overlooking the Valley of Llodio, and we fought there for a month and a half, while Bilbao fell, and our losses increased until we were only a handful of men defending an impossible position. We could see the enemy in the distance with their tanks and planes and heavy artillery—they mounted one of their heaviest guns beside the great statue of the Virgin of Orduña— but we held out much longer than we expected. We took San Pedro from the Moors at the point of the bayonet. We fought along the cliffs, three hundred feet high, surrounding the valley. And when their heavy guns found our positions, there were shell craters next to shell craters, and no place where a man could live.

We attacked and fell back, attacked again and fell back again, and we were sleepless and had no food and our ammunition was running out.

So we came at last to Santander, the last town remaining in our hands. It did not remain in our hands for long. For the first time I saw a population given over to despair. People were drunk with despair and drunk with wine: so we went out and smashed every single wine bottle we could lay our hands on. I saw a young soldier embracing his girl for the last time, and then the hand grenade he was holding in his hand exploded. I saw a ship leaving the jetty, crowded with refugees, with soldiers, with everyone who could board the ship, and the captain was signaling to us frantically, for he knew the ship was overloaded, but none of the passengers would get off; and the ship sailed away and sank and all were drowned.

There is a special atmosphere in a town which knows it is doomed. There is a strange look on the faces of trapped people. Santander seemed to lose its life before our eyes.

Then the Italians marched in as though they were on parade, marching in long lines, very stiff and formal in their beautiful clothes, with their guns and their tanks. They did not look as though they had fought a single battle, and they were well-fed. We surrendered the town to them, and I became a prisoner.

That was the end of the war in the Basque Provinces.

Explosion in Barcelona

*I*N *the spring of 1937 cracks were beginning to appear in the façade which the Republicans showed to the world. A kind of weariness born of intense excitement was already setting in. The Republican Government, continually faced with insoluble supply problems, forbidden to receive arms from abroad by the Non-Intervention Committee, and at the mercy of irreconcilable philosophies, seemed powerless to control the forces at work. There was no one man of outstanding ability who could weld these forces together. The Republic was menaced from within and without. Sooner or later the temperature would reach flash-point.*

The explosion took place on the night of May 3rd, when the Anarchists came out in open rebellion against the government. The uprising seems to have been planned swiftly, without taking thought of the consequences, and was sparked by the determination of Azaña and Companys to take over the Telefónica in Barcelona, which had been in Anarchist hands from the beginning of the war. Jaume Miravitlles describes how he came to learn about the uprising:

Those early days at the beginning of May 1937 were wonderfully clear and sunny, with crystal blue skies. Barcelona was enjoying the quiet glory of spring. The war seemed far away.

Yet gradually and almost imperceptibly the tension was gathering. The power of the Communists was increasing, that of the Anarchists was slowly fading. Those happy people, consisting very largely of refugees from the farmlands of Murcia in the south, dreaming of fraternity and the collective life, with no one earning more than 10 pesetas a day—these people with their equalitarian philosophy, their boldness, and their extraordinary courage, thought the millennium was at hand, or would come soon. And they were learning that the millennium was bitter to the taste, and their philosophy of unbridled individualism was dangerous. They were the rulers of Barcelona, but their days were numbered.

In Barcelona they controlled all transportation, all (or nearly all) the factories, all communications. They controlled the Telefónica which stands in a strategic position in the Plaza de Cataluña. There, especially, their influence could be felt, and this influence spread out through the whole of Catalonia like the ripples when a stone is flung in a pool.

On May 2, the President of Republican Spain, Manuel Azaña, then living in the parliament house in Exposition Park, talked by telephone to the President of Catalonia, Luis Companys, who was in his office in the Palace of the Generalitat. The conversation had been going on for some time, when it was sharply interrupted by an Anarchist in the Telefónica who said: "This conversation will have to stop. We have more interesting things to do than listen to your stupid conversations." The line was then broken. The two Presidents put down their receivers, both determined to put an end to Anarchist interference: for if they continued to submit to Anarchist control of communications, they would be abdicating all their powers.

That night troops from the Guardia de Asalto prepared to take the Telefónica by force. Simultaneously the Anarchists gave the orders for a general uprising.

Within a few hours the city was in the hands of the Anarchists, who tore out the street stones and erected barricades at all the crossroads. There were altogether about a hundred barricades, each five feet high and two feet thick, all of them placed with a superb knowledge of the proper strategical position. Only heavy artillery could destroy the barricades. Light mountain guns have been known to shell them without effect.

I had heard about the conversation between the two Presidents, and I knew something about the intention to take over the Telefónica. I did not know about the general uprising until the next morning when I switched on my radio and heard Companys saying that the city was in the hands of the Anarchists. All members of the government were ordered to proceed at once to the Palace of the Generalitat. I was Secretary of Information, and it was my duty to reach him by whatever means were possible.

At that time I was living in a house near the Plaza de España, almost in the suburbs, far from the Generalitat. The streets were deserted. No streetcars were running. The only people in the streets were the Anarchists guarding the barricades. The first barricade was 200 yards from my house. They stopped me, asked who I was, pointed their guns at me, and for two pins they would have killed me. I explained I was on my way to the Palace of the Generalitat at the summons of the President. I was unarmed. They let me through. So I went from one barricade to another until by some miracle I had passed through nearly all the twelve barricades which separate the Plaza de España from the Generalitat.

I was annoyed and angry. As I walked through those completely silent streets, I marveled at the audacity of the Anarchists, and their stupidity. It was clear that the philosophy of unbridled individualism would have to give place to a more realistic philosophy. One does not embark on civil wars behind the lines without impunity. The black and red flags of the Anarchists fluttered at the barricades. There was no other movement in the streets.

I reflected, too, about my chances of reaching the Generalitat. They were very slim. At one or other of the barricades I was likely to be shot. They discussed killing me. They were trigger-happy, ignorant, bitter, fanatical. It would have pleased them to see my body lying beside a barricade.

At last the Palace of the Generalitat came into view, and there was only one more barricade to pass. They told me this last barricade was defended by a machine-gunner belonging to the POUM, then in alliance with the Anarchists. They told me he had orders to let no one pass. He would shoot to kill.

"How do I get in touch with him?"

"You can call the pharmacy at the corner. He may answer."

So I called the pharmacy and said: "I am Jaume Miravitlles."

The machine-gunner said: "Are you Señor Miravitlles?"

It was astonishing to hear the unrevolutionary word "señor." Suddenly I guessed I was speaking to one of my old mathematics students at the Workers' University. No one else would have used the word.

"Are you one of my students?" I asked.

"Yes, señor."

"Will you let me pass?"

"Of course, señor."

In that way I reached the palace. I was the first to reach the side of President Companys that morning.

He asked me what I had seen in the city.

"I saw nothing but FAI and POUM."

Companys nodded.

"It will change," he said.

So it did, for in the course of the morning government forces and the Socialists, together with Communists, began the counterattack. Fighting broke out all over the city. It was particularly bitter in streets where an Anarchist and Socialist or Communist building stood close together. The hate between the factions had risen feverishly during the night. The cars belonging to the unions were marked in large letters with the appropriate initials: POUM, FAI, CNT, UGT. Cars belonging to enemy factions were picked out with machine-gun fire until Barcelona became full of bullet-riddled cars.

At the corner of the Vía Layetana and the Calle de la Princesa I saw the ambush of two Anarchist cars. The Anarchist cars came roaring along the Vía Layetana, filled with armed men. There must have been ten men in each car. They felt safe because the whole of the Vía Layetana was in their hands. But suddenly from the high balcony of a CGT building at the intersection machine-gun fire broke out. The cars swerved crazily, and men jumped out. They did not jump out in any recognizable way. It was as though, in each car, an enormous compressed spring had suddenly been released. They hurtled out, they seemed to fly in the air while assuming fantastic attitudes and gestures, waving their arms and their feet like dancers. It was incredible to see them spinning in the air, and then falling slowly on the road, where they assumed new attitudes, as fantastic as before. The machine gun did not pause. They continued firing until all the men were shot to pieces.

At that moment a small rain fell, and slowly, from each body, red stain began to trickle over the square. The red stains met and ran into one another, and soon the entire square became a lake of blood. The funeral chant for these dead and crumpled Anarchists was provided by the wild blaring of the klaxons of the cars they had so swiftly abandoned. The rain continued to fall, and the blaring of the klaxons went on and on, without end.

Of this strange and shapeless civil war behind the lines, George Orwell, on leave in Barcelona, was an involuntary witness. He had joined a POUM brigade, and was therefore caught up in the fighting on the side of the Anarchists.

About midday on 3 May a friend crossing the lounge of the hotel said casually: "There's been some kind of trouble at the Telephone Exchange, I hear." For some reason I paid no attention to it at the time.

That afternoon, between three and four, I was halfway down the Ramblas when I heard several rifle-shots behind me. I turned round and saw some youths, with rifles in their hands and the red and black handkerchiefs of the Anarchists round their throats, edging up a side-street that ran off the Ramblas northward. They were evidently exchanging shots with someone in a tall octagonal tower—a church, I think—that commanded the side-street. I thought instantly "It's started!" But I thought it without any great feeling of surprise—for days past everyone had been expecting "it" to start at any moment. I realized that I must get back to the hotel at once and see if my wife was all right. But the knot of Anarchists round the opening of the side-street were motioning the people back and shouting to them not to cross the line of fire. More shots rang out. The bullets from the tower were flying across the street and a crowd of panic-stricken people was rushing down the Ramblas, away from the firing; up and down the street you could hear snap—snap—snap as the shopkeepers slammed the steel shutters over the windows. I saw two Popular Army officers retreating cautiously from tree to tree with their hands on their revolvers. In front of me the crowd was surging into the Metro station in the middle of the Ramblas to take cover. I immediately decided not to follow them. It might mean being trapped underground for hours.

At this moment an American doctor who had been with us at the front ran up to me and grabbed me by the arm. He was greatly excited.

"Come on, we must go down to the Hotel Falcón." (The Hotel Falcón was a sort of boarding-house maintained by the P.O.U.M. and used chiefly by militiamen on leave.) "The P.O.U.M. chaps will be there. The trouble's starting. We must hang together."

"But what the devil is it all about?" I said.

The doctor was hauling me along by the arm. He was too excited to give a very clear statement. It appeared that he had been in the Plaza de Cataluña when several lorry-loads of armed Assault Guards had driven up to the Telephone Exchange, and made a sudden assault upon it. Then some anarchists had arrived and there had been a general affray. I gathered that the "trouble" earlier in the day had been a demand by the Government to hand over the Telephone Exchange, which, of course, was refused.

As we moved down the street a lorry raced past us from the opposite direction. It was full of Anarchists with rifles in their hands. In front a ragged youth was lying on a pile of mattresses behind a light machine-gun. When we got to the Hotel Falcón, which was at the bottom of the Ramblas, a crowd of people was seething in the entrance-hall there was a great confusion, nobody seemed to know what we were expected to do, and nobody was armed except the handful of Shock Troopers who usually acted as guards for the building. I went across to the Comité Local of the P.O.U.M., which was almost opposite Upstairs, in the room where militiamen normally went to draw their pay, another crowd was seething. A tall, pale, rather handsome man of about thirty, in civilian clothes, was trying to restore order and handing out belts and cartridge-boxes from a pile in the corner. There seemed to be no rifles as yet. The doctor had disappeared—I believe there had already been casualties and a call for doctors—but another Englishman had arrived. Presently, from an inner office, the tall man and some others began bringing out armfuls of rifles and handing them round. The other Englishman and myself, as foreigners, were slightly under suspicion and at first nobody would give us a rifle. Then a militiaman whom I had known at the front arrived and recognized me, after which we were given rifles and a few clips of cartridges somewhat grudgingly.

There was a sound of firing in the distance and the streets were completely empty of people. Everyone said it was impossible to go up the Ramblas. The Civil Guards had seized buildings in commanding positions and were letting fly at everyone who passed. I would have risked it and gone back to the hotel, but there was a vague idea floating round that the Comité Local was likely to be attacked at any moment and we had better stand by. All over the building, on the stairs and on the pavement outside, small knots of people were standing and talking excitedly. No one seemed to have a very clear idea of what was happening. All I could gather was that the Assault Guards had attacked the Telephone Exchange and seized various strategic spots that commanded other buildings belonging to the workers. There was a general impression that the Assault Guards were "after" the C.N.T. and the working class generally. It was noticeable that, at this stage, no one seemed to put the blame on the Government. The poorer classes in Barcelona looked upon the Assault Guards as something rather resembling the Black and Tans, and it seemed to be taken for granted that they had started this attack on their own initiative. Once I had heard how things stood I felt easier in my mind. The issue was clear enough. On one side the C.N.T., on the other side the police. I have no particular love for the idealized "worker" as he appears in the bourgeois Communist's mind, but when I see an actual flesh-and-blood worker in conflict with his natural enemy, the policeman, I do not have to ask myself which side I am on.

A long time passed and nothing seemed to be happening at our end of the town. It did not occur to me that I could ring up the hotel and find out whether my wife was all right; I took it for granted that the Telephone Exchange would have stopped working—though, as a matter of fact, it was only out of action for a couple of hours. There seemed to be about three hundred people in the two buildings. Predominantly they were people of the poorest class, from the back-streets down by the quays; there were a number of women among them, some of them carrying babies, and a crowd of little ragged boys. I fancy that many of them had no notion of what was happening and had simply fled into the P.O.U.M. buildings for protection. There was also a number of militiamen on leave, and a sprinking of foreigners. As far as I could estimate, there were only about sixty rifles between the lot of us. The office upstairs was ceaselessly besieged by a crowd of people who were demanding rifles and being told that there were none left. The younger militia boys, who seemed to regard the whole affair as a kind of picnic, were prowling round and trying to wheedle or steal rifles from anyone who had them. It was not long before one of them got my rifle away from me by a clever dodge and immediately made himself scarce. So I was unarmed again, except for my tiny automatic pistol, for which I had only one clip of cartridges.

It grew dark, I was getting hungry, and seemingly there was no food in the "Falcón." My friend and I slipped out to his hotel, which was not far away, to get some dinner. The streets were utterly dark and silent, not a soul stirring, steel shutters drawn over all the shop windows, but no barricades built yet. There was a great fuss before they would let us into the hotel, which was locked and barred. When we got back I learned that the Telephone Exchange was working and went to the telephone in the office upstairs to ring up my wife. Characteristically, there was no telephone directory in the building, and I did not know the number of the Hotel Continental; after a searching from room to room for about an hour I came upon a guide-book which gave me the number. I could not make contact with my wife, but I managed to get hold of John McNair, the I.L.P. representative in Barcelona. He told me that all was well, nobody had been shot, and asked me if we were all right at the Comité Local. I said that we should be all right if we had some cigarettes. I only meant this as a joke; nevertheless half an hour later McNair appeared with two packets of Lucky Strikes. He had braved the pitch-dark streets, roamed by Anarchist patrols who had twice stopped him at the pistol's point and examined his papers. I shall not forget this small act of heroism. We were very glad of the cigarettes.

They had placed armed guards at most of the windows, and in the street below a little group of Shock Troopers were stopping and questioning the few passers-by. An Anarchist patrol car drove up, bristling with weapons. Beside the driver a beautiful dark-haired girl of about eighteen was nursing a submachine-gun across her knees. I spent a long time wandering about the building, a great rambling place of which it was impossible to learn the geography. Everywhere was the usual litter, the broken furniture and torn paper that seem to be the inevitable products of revolution. All over the place people were sleeping; on a broken sofa in a passage two poor women from the quayside were peacefully snoring. The place had been a cabaret-theatre before the P.O.U.M. took it over. There were raised stages in several of the rooms; on one of them was a desolate grand piano. Finally I discovered what I was looking for—the armoury. I did not know how this affair was going to turn out, and I badly wanted a weapon. I had heard it said so often that all the rival parties, P.S.U.C., P.O.U.M., and C.N.T.-F.A.I. alike, were hoarding arms in Barcelona, that I could not believe that two of the principal P.O.U.M. buildings contained only the fifty or sixty rifles that I had seen. The room which acted as an armoury was unguarded and had a flimsy door; another Englishman and myself had no difficulty in prizing it open. When we got inside we found that what they had told us was true—there *were* no more weapons. All we found there were about two dozen small-bore rifles of an obsolete pattern and a few shot-guns, with no cartridges for any of them. I went up to the office and asked if they had any spare pistol ammunition; they had none. There were a few boxes of bombs, however, which one of the Anarchist patrol cars had brought us. I put a couple in one of my cartridge-boxes. They were a crude type of bomb, ignited by rubbing a sort of match at the top and very liable to go off of their own accord.

People were sprawling asleep all over the floor. In one room a baby was crying, crying ceaselessly. Though this was May the night was getting cold. On one of the cabaret-stages the curtains were still up, so I ripped a curtain down with my knife, rolled myself up in it and had a few hours' sleep. My sleep was disturbed, I remember, by the thought of those beastly bombs, which might blow me into the air if I rolled on them too vigorously. At three in the morning the tall handsome man who seemed to be in command woke me up, gave me a rifle and put me on guard at one of the windows. He told me that Salas, the Chief of Police responsible for the attack on the Telephone Exchange, had been placed under arrest. (Actually, as we learned later, he had never been deprived of his post. Nevertheless the news confirmed the general impression that the Assault Guards had acted without orders.) As soon as it was dawn the people downstairs began building two barricades, one outside the Comité Local and the other outside the Hotel Falcón. The Barcelona streets are paved with square cobbles, easily built up into a wall, and under the cobbles is a kind of shingle that is good for filling sand-bags. The building of those barricades was a strange and wonderful sight; I would have given something to be able to photograph it. With the kind of passionate energy that Spaniards display when they have definitely decided to begin upon any job of work, long lines of men, women, and quite small children were tearing up the cobble-stones, hauling them along in a hand-cart that had been found somewhere, and staggering to and fro under heavy sacks of sand. In the doorway of the Comité Local a German-Jewish girl, in a pair of militiaman's trousers whose knee-buttons just reached her ankles, was watching with a smile. In a couple of hours the barricades were head-high, with riflemen posted at the loopholes, and behind one barricade a fire was burning and men were frying eggs.

They had taken my rifle away again, and there seemed to be

nothing that one could usefully do. Another Englishman and myself decided to go back to the Hotel Continental. There was a lot of firing in the distance, but seemingly none in the Ramblas. On the way up we looked in at the food-market. A very few stalls had opened; they were besieged by a crowd of people from the working-class quarters south of the Ramblas. Just as we got there, there was a heavy crash of rifle-fire outside, some panes of glass in the roof were shivered, and the crowd went flying for the back exits. A few stalls remained open, however; we managed to get a cup of coffee each and buy a wedge of goat's-milk cheese which I tucked in beside my bombs. A few days later I was very glad of that cheese.

At the street-corner where I had seen the Anarchists begin firing the day before a barricade was now standing. The man behind it (I was on the other side of the street) shouted to me to be careful. The Assault Guards in the church tower were firing indiscriminately at everyone who passed. I paused and then crossed the opening at a run; sure enough, a bullet cracked past me, uncomfortably close. When I neared the P.O.U.M. Executive Building, still on the other side of the road, there were fresh shouts of warning from some Shock Troopers standing in the doorway—shouts which, at the moment, I did not understand. There were trees and a newspaper kiosk between myself and the building (streets of this type in Spain have a broad walk running down the middle), and I could not see what they were pointing at. I went up to the "Continental," made sure that all was well, washed my face and then went back to the P.O.U.M. Executive Building (it was about a hundred yards down the street) to ask for orders. By this time the roar of rifle and machine-gun fire from various directions was almost comparable to the din of a battle. I had just found Kopp and was asking him what we were supposed to do when there was a series of appalling crashes down below. The din was so loud that I made sure someone must be firing at us with a field-gun. Actually it was only hand-grenades, which make double their usual noise when they burst among stone buildings.

Kopp glanced out of the window, cocked his stick behind his back, said: "Let us investigate," and strolled down the stairs in his usual unconcerned manner, I following. Just inside the doorway a group of Shock Troopers were bowling bombs down the pavement as though playing skittles. The bombs were bursting twenty yards away with a frightful, ear-splitting crash which was mixed up with the banging of rifles. Half across the street, from behind the newspaper kiosk, a head —it was the head of an American militiaman whom I knew well—was sticking up, for all the world like a coconut at a fair. It was only afterwards that I grasped what was really happening. Next door to the P.O.U.M. building there was a café with an hotel above it, called the Café Moka. The day before, twenty or thirty armed Assault Guards had entered the café and then, when the fighting started, had suddenly seized the building and barricaded themselves in. Presumably they had been ordered to seize the café as a preliminary to attacking the P.O.U.M. offices later. Early in the morning they had attempted to come out, shots had been exchanged and one Shock Trooper was badly wounded and an Assault Guard killed. The Assault Guards had fled back into the café, but when the American came down the street they had opened fire on him, though he was not armed. The American had flung himself behind the kiosk for cover, and the Shock Troopers were flinging bombs at the Assault Guards to drive them indoors again.

Kopp took in the scene at a glance, pushed his way forward and hauled back a red-haired German Shock Trooper who was just drawing the pin out of a bomb with his teeth. He shouted to everyone to stand back from the doorway, and told us in several languages that we had got to avoid bloodshed. Then he stepped out on the pavement and, in sight of the Assault Guards, ostentatiously took off his pistol and laid it on the ground. Two Spanish militia officers did the same, and the three of them walked slowly up to the doorway where the Assault Guards were huddling. It was a thing I would not have done for twenty pounds. They were walking, unarmed, up to men who were frightened out of their wits and had loaded guns in their hands. An Assault Guard, in shirt-sleeves and livid with fright, came out of the door to parley with Kopp. He kept pointing in an agitated manner at two unexploded bombs that were lying on the pavement. Kopp came back and told us we had better touch the bombs off. Lying there, they were a danger to anyone who passed. A Shock Trooper fired his rifle at one of the bombs and burst it, then fired at the other and missed. I asked him to give me his rifle, knelt down and let fly at the second bomb. I also missed it, I am sorry to say. This was the only shot I fired during the disturbances. The pavement was covered with broken glass from the sign over the Café Moka, and two cars that were parked outside, one of them Kopp's official car, had been riddled with bullets and their windscreens smashed by bursting bombs.

Kopp took me upstairs again and explained the situation. We had got to defend the P.O.U.M. buildings if they were attacked, but the P.O.U.M. leaders had sent instructions that we were to stand on the defensive and not open fire if we could possibly avoid it. Immediately opposite there was a cinematograph, called the Poliorama, with a museum above it, and at the top, high above the general level of the roofs, a small observatory with twin domes. The domes commanded the street, and a few men posted up there with rifles could prevent any attack on the P.O.U.M. buildings. The caretakers at the cinema were C.N.T. members and would let us come and go. As for the Assault Guards in the Café Moka, there would be no trouble with them; they did not want to fight and would be only too glad to live and let live. Kopp repeated that our orders were not to fire unless we were fired on ourselves or our buildings attacked. I gathered, though he did not say so, that the P.O.U.M. leaders were furious at being dragged into this affair, but felt they had got to stand by the C.N.T.

They had already placed guards in the observatory. The next three days and nights I spent continuously on the roof of the Poliorama, except for brief intervals when I slipped across to the hotel for meals. I was in no danger, I suffered from nothing worse than hunger and boredom, yet it was one of the most unbearable periods of my whole life. I think few experiences could be more sickening, more disillusioning or, finally, more nerve-wracking than those evil days of street warfare.

I used to sit on the roof marvelling at the folly of it all. From the little windows in the observatory you could see for miles around— vista after vista of tall slender buildings, glass domes and fantastic curly roofs with brilliant green and copper tiles; over to eastward the glittering pale blue sea—the first glimpse of the sea I had had since coming to Spain. And the whole huge town of a million people was locked in a sort of violent inertia, a nightmare of noise without movement. The sunlit streets were quite empty. Nothing was happening except the streaming of bullets from barricades and sand-bagged windows. Not a vehicle was stirring in the streets; here and there along the Ramblas the trams stood motionless where their drivers had jumped out of them when the fighting started. And all the while the devilish noise, echoing from thousands of stone buildings, went on and on and on, like a tropical rainstorm. Crack-crack, rattle-rattle, roar—sometimes it died away to a few shots, sometimes it quickened to a deafening fusillade, but it never stopped while daylight lasted, and punctually next dawn it started again.

While George Orwell was standing on guard, unashamedly frightened and perplexed by the uprising, someone else was also showing signs of fear—Manuel Azaña, President of the Republic of Spain. That lonely old liberal, who no longer controlled events, regarded the uprising with a mixture of fastidious loathing and panic fear. Jaume Miravitlles describes a visit to the President at the height of the fighting:

By some miracle the telephone system was still working. Suddenly the telephone on the desk of President Companys began ringing. He picked up the receiver. He heard the nervous, agonized voice of President Azaña speaking from the parliament building in Exposition Park. The President of Spain was complaining bitterly against the Anarchists. He was terrified for his life, and inclined to put the blame on Companys, who was at that time employing all his resources to put down the rebellion. Companys believed the rebellion would collapse in a few hours, or at most in a few days. He was not afraid of it. Azaña was frightened out of his wits.

Azaña had seen groups of Anarchists making their way through the park. He believed they were about to attack the parliament building, where he was living. He already regarded himself as a prisoner of the Anarchists, dying at their hands.

Companys tried to humor him.

"No doubt there are a few Anarchists prowling around the park," Companys said. "They won't harm you, I promise you. I give you the assurance that you are under the protection of the Catalan authorities, and therefore in no danger."

"Can you guarantee my life?"

"Your life is in no danger."

"It is easy to say that, but how can you prove it? I am in an intolerable position. The President of Spain should not be placed in such a position. How can you prove to me that you are in control of the situation?"

We stood around the table, watching Companys. We could hear the rumbling voice of Azaña speaking from the park.

Companys was busy with the civil war, but he felt that at all costs he must reassure the President of Spain.

"Very well," he said at last, "I will send three of my associates to your office. They will come by car. In this way we shall show you that the streets are clear and we are still exerting our authority."

So it happened that Josep Tarradellas, the Premier, and I were sent on a mission through the barricaded streets to the President of Spain. We went in a car marked: GENERALITAT. We went slowly, stopping at each Anarchist barricade to show our credentials. We knew very well that the Anarchists might fire at us if it served their purpose. They were trigger-happy, and we could hear the sounds of firing in the distance. At one of their barricades we picked up an Anarchist friend of mine, who rode with us to the park, waving the black and red Anarchist flag to show we were under their protection. At last we came into the presence of Azaña, the man who had upheld through the dictatorship of Primo de Rivera and over many years the tradition of liberalism.

He was a heavy-set ugly man, flabby, jowly, his face black with moles. He did not carry himself like a President. He was shaking, and pale with fear.

"The situation," he said, "is absolutely intolerable. The Catalan Government is not exercising its authority properly. It is intolerable to let the Anarchists take over power."

There was a good deal more in the same strain.

We did our best to convince the old man that the Anarchist uprising was only a temporary phenomenon, and all the proper precautions were being taken. Elite troops had been summoned from Valencia, and in a few hours it would all be over. We explained, as best we could, that although the Anarchists had won a resounding victory, they were incapable of using it. They lacked any power of decision. They were like a band of dangerous children who had thrown their parents out of the house, but they were incapable of running the household. Companys had told the Anarchist leaders: "All right, kill me, kill every member of my government, but what do you do then?"

They did not know what they would do, and so inevitably the victory would fall from their hands.

In Azaña's expression there was no trace of the familiar elegance we associated with him. He looked bitter, angry, terribly frightened. Yet he was a little more tranquil when we left him.

We returned to the Generalitat. The Anarchist barricades were still up. Stores were closed. The streets were absolutely deserted. The firing was still going on.

For three days the Anarchists held Barcelona. On the evening of the third day, they sent out peace feelers. Augustín Souchy, one of the bravest of the Anarchist leaders, recorded the last frustrating hours of victory:

Thursday, May 6th.

At two in the morning the government had still failed to answer the proposals, awaited with so much impatience and anxiety. . . . Twenty minutes past two. No answer. . . . Half past two. No answer. . . . A quarter to three. . . . Three o'clock. Still no answer. They were discussing the resumption of work in the outlying districts where the fighting had stopped. The traffic could not start unless the barricades were pulled down. The delegates of the transport workers union were awaiting the answer of the government in order to give the order to start work again. . . . A quarter to four and still no answer. . . . At five minutes to four, in the morning, the Provincial Committee communicates that they are ready to hold up the troops from Valencia. . . . Four o'clock. No answer.

At last, at a quarter past five, the government answered. They agree to the armistice. All parties shall leave the barricades. Patrols and guards retire to their headquarters, unions and fortified positions. Both parties to release their prisoners. The Patrols to resume their functions.

Everybody relaxed. But . . . could one trust the sincerity of this answer? Would the workers in the telephone exchange continue to function as before? Would everything come out all right again?

Neither victors nor vanquished. That is the will of the Syndicalists and Anarchists. The antifascist front shall not be destroyed. War against fascism. Unity of all workers. That is the firm wish of the workers on the barricades. And the resolutions of the committees were based on this wish. The Regional Committee issued the following note over the radio:

"To all the workers of the CNT: Having reached an understanding with both the political and trade union representatives, we wish to notify you that you will receive instructions from your responsible committees regarding the establishment of complete peace and calm. For the present we urge you to keep the calm and presence of mind that the situation requires. Do not answer the provocations of those who seek to perpetuate the existing state of disorder."

While the results were still being discussed, new fears arose as the shooting broke out again to disturb the enveloping silence of the night. Two cars were driving down Vía Durruti. As they passed the police prefecture, they were shot at. They were able to pass the headquarters of the Regional Committee undisturbed, but a short distance away, the shooting broke out in full violence once more. Rifles, machine guns, hand grenades came into play. A bad sign. A strange contrast to the assurances of a peaceful solution of the conflict. Only half an hour till 6 o'clock. Will we be able to pacify the suspicions and the tempers of the comrades? At six o'clock, shots could still be heard.

We switched off the lights. A beautiful morning. Barcelona slept in silence.

Friday, May 7th.

A few hours later, Barcelona had undergone an almost complete change. True to their agreement, the workers had left the barricades. In many places the barricades had already been torn down. They had withdrawn from the buildings. But they were keeping their arms.

In the center of the city, however, the air was still tense. The barricades of the Assault Guards, of the Catalan Nationalists, and of the PSUC remained intact. And guarded. Taking advantage of the good will of the workers, groups of Assault Guards were walking about, disarming workers wherever they could get hold of them. New friction arose between the Assault Guards and the Libertarian Youth in the Plaza del Pino and the Puertafer. And once more it was thanks to the initiative of the Anarchist Youth, who went unarmed to the headquarters of the Assault Guards to negotiate, that finally, after hours of discussion, the Assault Guards decided to show a more peaceful attitude and the barricades could come down.

The center of the city was like a fortress. High buildings had been used as fortifications by the various groups. Out of walls of sandbags, mattresses and cushions, rifles and machine guns poked their barrels. The Assault Guards had opened the churches and used them as fortifications.

But the populace could breathe more freely. For three days they had been forced to remain in their houses. Now everybody was walking about in the streets. The masses of people pushed their way through the barricades. Children played at revolution, rolling up a rock in a piece of paper and throwing it at the counter-revolutionists from behind the barricades. Everybody was discussing the situation in the bars and cafés.

At twenty past eight the Assault Guards from Valencia reached Barcelona. They drove down the Vía Durruti in motor trucks, and were welcomed at the Police Prefecture. What will their attitude be toward the workers? And what attitude will the workers take? As they passed the headquarters of the Regional Committee, a shot was fired from one car, while from another came the cry, "Viva la FAI." Obviously their feelings and attitude toward the workers, toward the Syndicalists and Anarchists of Catalonia, were as mixed as their composition.

The workers had put down their arms, and they did not think of taking them up again.

The negotiations between the Anarchists and the Catalan Government were witnessed by Jaume Miravitlles, who once again walked through dangerous streets.

The end came swiftly. When it became clear to the Anarchists that there was nothing they could do with their victory, they clamored for a cease-fire. Companys said he would discuss the cease-fire only if they came to the Generalitat.

Now it was their turn to be frightened. Like Azaña, they wanted the assurance that the Catalan Government could protect their lives. I was sent to the Anarchist headquarters to accompany them to the Generalitat.

It was not a pleasant task, and I had no fondness for it. It is terribly dangerous to be walking about Barcelona during a time of Civil War. The Anarchist headquarters was perhaps 400 yards from the Generalitat, but I counted each one of those yards. Companys had telephoned to the people in all the buildings along my route, telling them I was on an official mission and must not be fired at.

I could see the machine guns on the balconies slowly turning as they followed me.

The streets were deserted. There was a terrible emptiness in the air.

When at last I came to the Anarchist headquarters, which was formerly the club of the powerful Catalan industrialists, I could see faces peering at me through the windows. They were the people who had brought about the rebellion. I heard myself shouting: *"Visca la República!"* They replied with the same words, but without enthusiasm.

They came to the door, and I accompanied them back to the Generalitat. Among them were Santillán and García Oliver.

The guns slowly turned from the balconies, following us.

At last they came into the presence of Companys, and the terms of the cease-fire were worked out. It was agreed that there should be no reprisals.

But in fact the Anarchists had committed suicide. By this uprising they had shown themselves incompetent. They had caused the bitterest fighting known up to that time in Barcelona—it was more severe than the fighting during the rebellion in October 1934 or during the uprising in July 1936. No one knows how many people were killed during those three days of fighting in May. We counted 1,500 dead, but there may have been many more.

Brunete

WITH the war in the Basque territory over, and the battlelines in the rest of Spain relatively stable, the Republicans determined to make a frontal attack on the enemy lines near Madrid. The battle of Brunete, fought through most of July 1937, in intense heat, was as savage as any of the battles fought during the Civil War, with positions changing hands many times over. In the end the Republicans gained a small advantage at the cost of shattering losses. Here Ralph Bates, on a tour of inspection of the front lines, describes a strange incident in the battle.

Momentarily blinded, I was seized by a violent fit of coughing, barbs were tearing out my lungs; then, as I flung myself against the river bank I saw a figure blundering down through the dust.

"Get down," I yelled but at that instant another bomb fell. A terrific blast, furnace hot, followed the white flash, then darkness. I thought I was blinded, the skin of my face was peeling off, burnt away; and then I touched it with clay-daubed fingers and opened my eyes. Higher up the bank two bombs crashed. Something huge, black and writhing swept through the air, and I was caught up and hurled backwards into the shallow water. Struggling frantically beneath the surface, I yet heard the bombs crashing, then my head came above water and I gasped, eyes shut, gulping deep, painful breaths. The thorn hedge at the top of the bank had been blown into the river like a thrashing serpent; my exposed flesh was torn, I was caught in its briars and could not gain the cover of the bank. Desperately I struggled towards the bank, slipping on the smooth rocks of the river bed. Again dense yellow dust swept down the bank away from the crashes and all went dark. I heard the terrified screaming of a mule, there was an earth-splitting crash behind me to the right and I was flung head-first on to the bank by the sheet of water blown out of the river. The screaming mule plunged up the bank and I could not get out of its way; as I fell, I clutched at its neck. There was another crash, and another. Crash—crash—crash, and the mule was lashing about somewhere in the shrieking night of dust and smoke. I lay on the wet clay, the water trickling back around me. I clasped my hands over the back of my neck, trying to think, "This is noise, no more than noise, pure sense data, nothing goes with it"; but this time it didn't work. Solipsism, dear comrades, is anterior to tri-nitro-toluene. Then I heard the double thwack of our anti's, like a backfire in a garage, and there were no more crashes. The dust began to settle and I got up out of my vomit and the mule's blood, my knees weak and tired; oh God, tired; tired.

It was Heinrich, with whom I had discussed Malraux's *Days of Contempt* the night before, who had been coming down the bank. I felt him over, the small of his back was a dusty red mush; a lump of metal had punched out his spine. Some god-damned fool words of verse came into my head, exasperating me, no, maddening me, as if I had been repeating them for weeks. "Your bowels are like jewelled lizards . . ." my brain churned over. "Your bowels are like jewelled lizards, your bowels . . ." It was the fragility of this body of watery cells and delicate filaments, and the hard sharpness of metal, which made me think of that verse, but it was the thought, not the words, that had been with me all these weeks, coming to life gradually, like a winter's beetle under the stone of my will. Heinrich would have nar-rowed his eyes and nodded, had I told him this. Ah, Heinrich, the days of contempt are over, *They* have learnt now, raging at our Brigades. "Blessed be he that taketh their children and dasheth them against the stones." That last night of your life you were singing "By the waters of Babylon," and you looked up and said: "No, our psalm of blackest hate should be, 'Blessed be he that taketh their children and teacheth them the truth.' " And you meant hate, or that is how I understood you then. Heinrich said, "I also heard music in prison; and I heard the voice of a salmon before a monstrous fall, leaping in vain. The music was of their triumphant hate, thundering down upon me, like Zambese, Nyanza, Niagara."

I found the staff in a dry gully above the river, stunned as I was. Klaus was fumbling with a torn-up bush, I picked up a bush also; its leaves were dusty. We gaped at one another, and our voices when we spoke were farcical, I wanted to laugh at the silly squeaking of our voices, but laughter would have been a rat's call. The ringing in our ears was like the lingering of a nightmare when one awakens.

"I sent Heinrich for you," Klaus mumbled, he was behind a wall of glass.

"He's dead." He nodded, and threw the bush away, it toppled over upon the maps.

"There's a machine-gun team hanging behind, up on the ridge," he said. "They're Belgians," and my mouth was choked with cotton wool. The dust was bitter on my lips.

"Show me," I said, and looked down at the map, covered with dust and shrivelled leaves.

"You speak French," Klaus mumbled, struggling to make contact with me. I got out of the gully and looked back at him. He grinned and said, "Your eyebrows are gone." They were scorched off, but some of my moustache was left.

I went up the slope. The chaser which had looped over us to whistle up the wind of death, was away over on our right, towards Brunete, describing the signal we had decided was a call to their artillery. Some Spanish troops were straggling back from the ridge and I blundered over to them waving my arms, but when I reached them I was too weary to speak. God; I was tired, tired. My brain was a kaleidoscope of red glass, shifting round, presenting a different pattern at every moment, but always of sharp triangles and pentagons of red glass. Glass that lacerated the inflamed cells of my brain. Fatigue, after that sleepless fortnight of red battle on yellow blazing hills was not weakness but pain, red glass in the brain and glass dust in the eyes, splinters of glass in the muscles and flakes of glass sawing at the stretched nerves; glass in the joints, mixed with the marrow of my bones.

"Hold the ridge," I gasped. "Get back, it's this ridge we must hold." They stood dazed, like cornered deer, and the booming on the front faded away and there was silence round us.

"Comrades," I said, and tried to find strength for a speech, but the glass in my brain suddenly turned to morphine and I sat down on a boulder. "Comrades," I drooled, and one of their non-commissioned officers wheeled about and began to exhort them. They were alongside of me when next I noticed them, and the sergeant was asking for

advice about positions and the front was booming. Shrapnel began
to rocket over the ridge; stamens of smoke hung down from the inverted lilies of the shrapnel bursts. I wondered what the Spanish
comrades would do when they walked under the shrapnel; they belonged to an unseasoned brigade. Then there was a faint popping
above us and I looked up, the shrapnel bursts were like a cloud of
gnats following a sweating man, but too high up; most of the stuff
fell outside of the area we covered. Then the shells burst lower and
men began to scream and fall down, but our helmets of scorching
steel were good against it. The Spanish comrades walked onto the
ridge and tried to dig in. It was a ridge of calcined rock, quivering in
that fierce July heat; they took it lying on the idiot stone, their rifles
popping against the enemy's whirlwind of machines.

I found the Belgian engineer Vandenburg on the ridge; he was in
command of the American battalion then. I said, "There's a small
white house somewhere about here, where the Franco-Belge were."
The bullets slid by like schools of invisible fish slipping through glittering water. I pushed Vandenburg towards a litter of rocks.

"Tous les balles vont haut," he said, his voice soft and apologetic
as when one June evening, swinging our legs over the plaza wall in
Ambares, we had argued about a gold cigarette case he had bought
in Madrid. . . .

"There's your white house, on that ridge," Vandenburg said, pointing across the crackling valley. The high explosive fire that followed
the shrapnel was running wild through the holm oaks in the valley,
smashing the trees, tossing them up through the puffs of smoke. All
the guns which they had opposite us were tearing up the wood.

"Any way round the valley head?" I asked.

"No . . . the enemy holds it," Vandenburg said, offering me a
cigarette; the smoke scorched my sore lungs.

The trees shook in the height of a fever, their glistening leaves
rained upon the slippery rocks. Twice I heard the thud of venomous
metal against a tree trunk; branches plunged down through the ragged
tops of the trees; the smashed rocks reeked like burnt powder. All
this was nothing. Fatigue, mortal fatigue, when tears will not flow and
quickening fear has disappeared; fatigue that is a glass blade, with
exact knowledge nicking at the million nerves, prodding at the nerves
of the eyes, at the nerves below the teeth; ah, this is the truth of the

war. When the brain sleeps in the moving body and fear goes, and the heart barely throbs in the knifed chest.

At the top of the slope there was a wounded comrade writhing beneath the bushes, lips chewed to bleeding shreds. I drew my pistol and held it to his ear and blessed him with sweet death; sweet death that is comfortable as polished china upon white linen; beautiful as golden evenings and the hoot of outgoing ships upon a gleaming estuary; sweet death, like the song of a thrush among wet-leaved apple trees beside my home; ah, God, master of blessings, like birds round my home. I stood up from the bushes of peace.

Then fatigue pinched out the flickering butt of thought; yet I knew rifle bullets were zipping by. The white house was before me and I was going towards it, but I was a shell, a husk that the dreary, drifting winds of indifference would blow away from the hard rocks of belief. I hated my will, the murderer of my belief, that had driven me till my body was beyond the refreshment of sleep. My pride, insane and laughing in its madness, shoved forward my creaking body.

I pushed upon the side door of the house as the machine-gun opened fire again. Upon the floor lay one of the comrades, wounded, and another was bent over him.

"Withdraw," I bleated.

"Withdraw?" the boy beside the gun, he was only a boy, looked at me nervously, his hands nursing the belt through the lock of the gun.

"You are to withdraw, the line is across the valley now."

"He says we are to withdraw, Jean," the feeder shouted and the gunner jerked his head round; his lips were tight pressed, there was no blood in his freckled face. It was a mask of weariness also. The shelling suddenly stopped and the gunner switched his head round.

"Can't withdraw now, they're advancing all along the sector, look!"

They were going to storm across the flat-topped ridge. That was why they had been shelling so furiously, but their maps must have been incorrect. I could not accept death, that before had seemed sweet, yet my will had not force enough to compel those comrades to withdraw.

The belt was out and the feeder inserted another and flung the empty one behind him. "Fill it," his lips said, but I heard no sound. I began, but I had had no practice and could not fill quickly.

"Here, I'll attend to him," I croaked, pulling the comrade away from the wounded man. I bent over his shoulder; the comrade's tunic was open, the vest ripped. I saw the breast of a young girl, soft, pink-nippled, and I caught my breath and knelt beside her. Fear came into her face; her comrade suddenly grasped the belt and began to fill it.

"Comrade," I whispered, "you should not be here," but I did not feel what I said; something was moving in my drugged brain, warmth creeping into my heart. God, the contact of smooth skin upon hot, trembling fingers, tears were coming to the surface of my husk of flesh. In that moment I saw all their story, the four of them setting out from a slum in Antwerp, the tender, strong, shaven-headed girls in their lovers' clothing, crossing a fog-hidden canal by night into France. Dodging through France, hiding by day from the French police, at the command of despicable men. Crossing the phantom hills of midnight into Spain, and the months of fighting, of hurried loving, of fear, of weeping during the "nightwatches" and now this approach-ing thunderstorm of death. . . . Tears were watering my inner self, washing away the lacerating crystals of fatigue.

We had never permitted women to enlist in the International Brigade; the Government had ordered their withdrawal from the militias before we began to organize our brigades. Often I had seen this comrade, and debated whether to investigate concerning his age, believing him to be younger than the limiting age of 21 years.

"You should not be here, comrade," I repeated, all my heart swell-ing in my breast. Her lips moved and I bent over her.

"Number Two is my sister," she whispered, "send her away, too, if you must."

"I must," I murmured. "Dear comrade, come lift yourself." I helped her to sit up, her shoulder was not yet giving her severe pain.

"Withdraw, stop firing," I ordered and the feeder ran over to me and put her arm round my neck, pleading mutely, like an animal that does not know what it pleads, yet craves nearness.

The gunner was crying, I saw; yet he would not abandon his gun. "Take them both away, comrade," he said hoarsely.

"She's your lover?" I asked.

"No, Berthe is mine, Marie belongs to Paul," he answered. Number Two gazed at me sadly, her hands feeding the belt skillfully.

It was then that resolution came into me, and it was my heart that resolved. My spirit cried on God for His mercy, for the warmth of love that flooded into me, and I turned upon conscience and my will and cast them out of me like alien things. Number Three, the filler, was lifting Comrade Marie to her feet, her little breast still naked. The intensity and tender purity of my love for her moved me more than my belief; and I wept openly. My love for them cast out discipline and I was glad, ah, God; joy swept through me. I turned to the gunner and said, "Come, they shall go to the rearguard and work. You shall all go." I was robbing the Brigade of a magnificent team, yes, yes, I was depriving our retreating men, and the advancing men of the future, of a splendid gunner, but I rejoiced, and my life was given back to me.

"Quick, comrades," I shouted, and there was the laughter of the old days in my voice; my heart ached with happiness. Jean and Paul carried the gun and Comrade Berthe and I helped Marie, the wounded girl. Thank God the gunners I had brought back to the ridge opened fire as the enemy swept past the white house; that was Vandenburg's work, I knew, for I had not placed them correctly for such fire. We stopped below our guns while I tried to draw our men's attention; I could not do so. "We must chance it, comrades; Marie and I will go in front, they'll see she's wounded," I said, and motioned Berthe away.

She came close to me and said, "You mean what you said, comrade commissar, you will order them?" and I nodded. I gathered Marie into my arms and climbed the last slope towards our guns. As I topped the ridge the Americans came into action with their machine-guns and then I heard Vandenburg's whistle. He gave me another cigarette.

I brought the team to the Staff gully and wrote the passes for the three comrades; Klaus was too weary to ask what I was doing.

"Go to my office in Madrid," I ordered them, "and tell Albertini to lodge you. When this is over I shall come." The enemy plane was signalling overhead as I put them on the track that led back to Villanueva.

When I returned to the Staff, Klaus beckoned me. "Go up to the Americans and find out how their left flank contacts are," he ordered. "The telephone is broken, I can't get Major Cunningham."

"Where's the American Headquarters?" I asked and he closed his eyes and shuddered before replying; fatigue was poisoning his brain. "Nelson reports he's in a gully near Cunningham's post. . . . It's important that the left flank holds for two more hours."

I climbed out of that *barranco* and ran across the slope as the first shells searched for the Staff. There was new strength in me, because of that weakness; because of that indiscipline, I accepted our discipline anew. And pride, which is our curse and often our prison, was gone. I was weary, ah, God, I was weary as I staggered across that brazen hill, but in my heart was the love, and the awareness of man's need of man, by compulsion of which we were fighting.

The Prisoner

THOUSANDS upon thousands of men died in Spanish prisons during the Civil War. The classic account was written by Arthur Koestler, who was arrested in Málaga in the house of Sir Peter Chambers-Mitchell on February 9, 1937:

The prison at Seville had been built in the first few years after the Spanish revolution, in 1931 or 1932. The young and ambitious Republic wished to emulate, and, if possible, to excel, the civilized West in everything. Among its finest achievements must be counted reforms in the sphere of penology, up till that time on a medieval level in Spain. The "model prisons" which were built in Madrid, Barcelona and Seville are, in fact, the best and most up-to-date in Europe.

We crossed the lovely garden in front of the main gate, rang—here too there was a night bell—and the gate was opened.

Three long corridors radiated out from the entrance hall; one leading straight on, the others to the right and to the left. The corridors were flanked by long, monotonous rows of cell doors, two tiers of them on either side. The cells on the upper floor opened on to narrow steel galleries which were reached by steel staircases. Each cell door bore a number and a name-plate, and was fitted with a spy-hole. Everything that met the eye was of steel and concrete; everything looked fantastically standardized, symmetrical, machine-like. Gazing at this framework of steel one might have imagined oneself in the engine-room of a warship.

In the middle of the hall, facing the entrance, was a kind of glass case: the office. For the third time I went through the procedure of having my particulars noted, my person searched and my finger prints taken. The demeanour of the officials made one feel one was not in a prison, but in an income-tax office, in the midst of a group of polite and slightly bored clerks.

The gorillas took their departure. A young, friendly and taciturn warder took charge of me and led me down the central corridor. The first cell to the right which we passed—Cell No. 44—bore the name Caballero.

Largo Caballero was at that time Prime Minister of the Government in Valencia. I knew that his son, whom the insurrection had taken by surprise in Seville, was being held as a hostage by the rebels. Some days before I had left Paris the newspapers had reported that he had been executed. So this news was false; for here on Cell No. 44 was the visiting card of Caballero Junior. This seemed to me very gratifying, and I had a positive urge to knock on his door and call out: "Doctor Livingstone, I presume?"

We passed cells Nos. 43 and 42; they bore Spanish names. At Cell No. 41 we stopped, and the warder unlocked the door. This, then, was my new home.

It was, if the adjective is in place here, a room of pleasant, square proportions. The first thing that struck me was the big window opposite the door. It was let into a kind of alcove in the wall and began at the level of the head, so that by supporting one's elbows on the slant of the wall one could look out quite comfortably. The window gave on to the patio, a very large and dusty prison courtyard. It was protected by a solid iron grille, and outside the grille was fixed fine wire netting, rather like a steel mosquito net.

Against the wall to the right was the iron bedstead, which could be folded back against the wall to allow more room for pacing up and down; opposite it was a steel table with a chair welded to it, also collapsible. At the foot of the bed was a large wash-basin with running water; opposite it the W.C.

The warder tested the straw mattress, to which was attached a linen tab with a date stamped on it, obviously to show when the straw had last been changed and the mattress cleaned. He brought in a good woollen blanket and said he would change both mattress and blanket for clean ones next morning. Then he wished me good night and carefully locked the door from outside.

After Málaga it seemed to me that I was in a luxury hotel.

I went to the window and looked out; it was a starry night, and the courtyard was still and peaceful. Opposite my window, along the wall at the further end of the court, a guard patrolled up and down with fixed bayonet, smoking a cigarette. With a small effort of imagination one might have fancied that he was promenading out there not in order to guard us but to protect us.

It was half-past two. I lay down on the straw mattress, revelled in the wonderful luxury of possessing a blanket, and fell contentedly asleep.

I was awakened by a bugle-blast; it was a quarter to seven in the morning. I assumed that it was the signal to get up, but feigned deafness and went on sleeping. The next time I woke up it was nine o'clock, and the sound of shouts and clattering feet came in through the window. I looked out; the courtyard was full of prisoners, who, with true Spanish fervour, were engaged in a football match, some as players, some as spectators.

There may have been three or four hundred men in the courtyard. They were not in uniform, and they were moving about freely in the great quadrangle, which was about a hundred yards by sixty. It was only some time later that I picked out a uniformed warder among them, who, a revolver in his belt and a rubber truncheon in his hand, patrolled up and down, exchanging a word here and there with the prisoners, or even walking about in conversation with one of them. The prisoners all wore civilian clothes and yet created a fairly uniform impression, for the overwhelming majority of them appeared to be young Andalusian peasants and wore the same kind of clothes; bluish-green faded linen shirts and jackets. A uniform effect was created, moreover, by their unshaven state, their bare heads and bronzed faces. The young lads who were playing football chased across the courtyard after the ball, which was made of rags bound together with string. Another group was engaged in a game of leapfrog along the opposite wall. When, under the force of the impact, one of the "frogs" fell flat on his stomach together with the jumper, there were roars of laughter. The warder stood by and joined in the fun. The more sedate elders were shying little pebbles at a target; others were sitting in the narrow strip of shade, reading.

And all this festive activity was going on just outside my window, which was on a level with the ground. After the bloody nightmare of Málaga it all seemed like a dream. For five days I had crouched in my isolation cell, which stank of blood and excrement, had not seen a single human countenance except that of the warder, had not heard a single human sound except the oily voice of the invisible herald of death. The hullabaloo in the courtyard, the change of scene, the plenitude of faces and human destinies that offered itself to the view, positively dazzled and intoxicated me. I leaned on my elbows in the alcove and called out to the courtyard. At first the fact that no one heard me or seemed to want to hear me did not worry me. Nor for the moment did it strike me that no one passed directly by my window; indeed, that an empty space several feet wide was left alongside the wall separating me from the courtyard.

There was a rattling at the lock of my door. I turned away from the window to see who was coming; for the first time since my arrest I heard the cell door opening without my heart's being constricted with fear. It was the warder who had taken charge of me in the night; he looked round the cell and began to curse me for not having got up at the first bugle-blast and washed the floor.

He roared until the walls shook, but it was nothing to worry about. He swore at me as a corporal swears at a recruit, and involuntarily I answered like a raw recruit who has just arrived in barracks and doesn't yet know the routine. He quickly calmed down and explained to me that I must first sweep the flagstones with a broom and then scour them with a pail and floor-cloth.

I took the broom and began to sweep, assuming an air of distinguished incompetence, until the warder had had enough of it and said he would call the orderly to show me how to set about things. Opening the door he called out into the corridor:

"*Angel, Angelito!*"

The "angelkin" thus evoked came shuffling up and set about sweeping the floor with ape-like agility. He had the face of an old woman; his skin was like crinkled parchment and his figure that of a twelve-year-old child. He never once looked either me or the warder in the face, and as he crept about the cell on all fours, his eyes darted about swiftly, like the eyes of a shrew. In less than two minutes the cell had been swept, swilled with water and apparently thoroughly scoured. It was positively a star turn. When warder and angelkin had departed and the floor began to dry I could see that the flags were as dirty as before.

Shortly afterwards breakfast arrived: a tin bowl full of appetizing coffee, ladled out of a huge tub, and a white roll.

It was Angelito who brought the breakfast round. He seemed to be maid-of-all-work here. I asked him to report that I should like to be shaved, so as not to look like a bandit at my trial; for I was expecting hourly to be at length brought to trial. But Angelito vouchsafed no reply and slammed the door in my face.

I once more took up my observation post at the window and watched the activities in the courtyard until midday. Bit by bit I began to pick out single individuals from the anonymous crowd. An old man was the first to rivet my attention; he must have been over seventy; he walked with a slight stoop and wore a warm woolly ulster. He immediately won my sympathy. Then there were a few boys of no more than thirteen or fourteen. I thought they must be hostages from Red families. Three or four strikingly elegantly dressed men with immaculate creases in their trousers and brightly polished shoes paced up and down apart from the others, with portentous expressions. I christened them "the dandies" and wondered what could have brought them here.

I wondered, too, whether all these men were political prisoners or criminals. Their faces seemed to suggest the former; but I noticed that about nine or ten of them were wearing a strip in the Bourbon colours on their shirts, and that these were by no means shunned by the rest. This did not fit in with my ideas as to the atmosphere amongst political prisoners.

Everyone in the courtyard was smoking, and tobacco and cigarette paper were being handed round freely. After having been treated to cigarettes on the journey, I found my renewed abstinence particularly hard. I bored a tiny hole with my index finger in the wire mosquito net in front of my window—large enough for a cigarette to be pushed through. It was quite easy; I had only to force the wires apart a little. I knew that the inside of my cell must appear dark from the courtyard and so I pressed my face against the iron bars and began to make signs to those outside that I wanted something to smoke.

At first I had a feeling that it was only by chance that no one looked in my direction. I began to call out, but there was such a din in the quadrangle that I found it difficult to make myself heard; for after all I did not want to shout. All the same, those nearest to me must have heard. But no one responded.

To be ignored in this way gave me a very uncomfortable feeling. Now I noticed, too, that some of the prisoners could perfectly well hear and see my signals as they passed, but quickly averted their heads. And once more it occurred to me that no one came within ten paces of that part of the wall where my cell was.

At last I saw one of the peasant lads in a linen jacket drawing the attention of some of the others to my window. But he did so very discreetly. Three or four of his companions looked stealthily in my direction. I gesticulated more vehemently and signed to them to pass a cigarette through to me. They seemed embarrassed and at a loss to know what to do, and looked round anxiously at the warder, although he was at the further end of the courtyard. Then one of them quickly put a finger to his lips and shrugged his shoulders, and the group hurried off.

It takes some time to make out details in the chaotic bustle and stir of a courtyard containing three or four hundred people. Thus it was not until now that I noticed that a faded and scarcely visible white line, rather like the marking on a neglected tennis court, was drawn parallel to my wall. The line began at the end of my row of cells, in front of No. 44, the cell containing Caballero, ran past my window, and ended some cells further to the left, as far as I could tell in front of Cell No. 36. Further down, from No. 35 downwards, the prisoners approached the wall quite freely and spoke to the inmates of the cells through the windows. But from Nos. 36 to 44 there was a no-man's land ten yards wide between the wall and the white line. The cells opposite this line, which included mine, were obviously taboo.

And now suddenly I realized that the men in the courtyard were afraid. Afraid of being watched. They obviously knew that every one of their movements was being spied upon. They could see what I could not see; that from the upper storey windows watchful glances were cast at the courtyard below. There must be something peculiar and uncanny behind all this demonstrative gaiety.

And now I couldn't understand what was happening. What ghostly carnival was this? Were all these men, playing leapfrog and football and strolling about in the bright sunshine of the patio, were they only waiting for the second cock-crow—or waiting for an oily voice to call out their names?

Why had I been put into a taboo cell? Why was I not allowed to join the others in the court and why were the prisoners in the court so afraid of looking in my direction? Was it indeed fear—or was it the embarrassment with which the healthy avert their gaze from the gravely ill, who bear the stamp of death on their brows?

And now at last I admitted to myself what had gradually been dawning on me from the start. I had been put in one of the condemned cells.

Friday, April 9th.

A new promenader has appeared in the patio during the siesta. A little Andalusian peasant with a wild black stubble of beard and soft, blue, slightly prominent eyes. He kept with Byron and the consumptive; Carlos stalked around the courtyard by himself.

My heart no better; today the sixth day . . .

Have thirty pesetas left. Shall buy no more extra provisions, only cigarettes and soap.

Ever since I have been ill time has passed appallingly slowly. Two or three times as slowly as before. It not only limps, it drags a leaden weight behind it. This is because I am unable to read, to write, to concentrate—in brief, to forget time. This theorizing about time is gradually becoming an obsession. When I was still young in this prison I tried to lie in wait for the hands of my watch, to experience pure time. Now I know that an inexorable law prevails: increasing awareness of time slows down its pace, complete awareness of time would bring it to a standstill. Only in death does the present become reality; time freezes; he who succeeds in experiencing "pure time" experiences nothingness.

Saturday, April 10th.

I have always thought it very funny when old ladies say that they cannot read war books, because they upset them too much. But now certain passages in *War and Peace* cause me such palpitations that I have to stop reading. When I read the passage describing the shooting of prisoners after the taking of Moscow by Napoleon I had to be sick. But all I got up was greenish bile.

Sunday, April 11th.

Since for the moment I am unable to go on reading the bloodthirsty Tolstoy, I have started making up crossword puzzles. It is much more amusing, but also much more difficult than solving them.

For one combination I got "Eumene." This certainly means something, but what?

. . . I was still puzzling over "Eumene" when the Governor sent for me. He said he would try "to get my case expedited." He said that I looked seedy, and asked if I were ill. I replied that I had chronic heart trouble, but that it would certainly improve. He said he would try to get permission for me to be allowed into the fresh air now and again. I said that I should like nothing better.

The Governor also looked seedy and I asked him how his operation had gone. He said he was still very weak and that the best thing he could do would be to get himself prescribed a rest cure in a cell. Everyone laughed. When I got back to my cell I felt quite cheerful.

Then came Mass, accompanied by choral singing. The singing—the first music except for "Ya la-ee-la," which is not music at all, but rhythmical moaning—stirred me thoroughly.

Monday, April 12th.

A day of great, world-shaking events . . .

First of all, I was shaved. During this operation a new warder was on duty—a youth in Falangist uniform, with pince-nez, whom I had seen yesterday strutting about like a turkey-cock in the patio and bullying one or two wretched peasants. When the shaving was over, he stayed in my cell and went on with our conversation. Later Don Ramón and the librarian joined us, and it became a regular tea-party.

The youth in pince-nez indulged at intervals in charming witticisms, brandishing his revolver right under my nose and saying that sooner or later I would be shot, anyway. Don Ramón, who was sitting behind him on the bed, signed to me not to take him seriously, and even went so far as to tap his forehead. "If you were in my place and I were the warder," I said, or something like it, "you would find such jokes exceedingly distasteful." "That's true," he said, astonished, and from then on mended his manners somewhat. He abused the "Reds," and said they tortured their prisoners, put out their eyes, etc. I said that was absolutely untrue; I had imagined the same of the opposite side; one always thought the worst of the enemy. He said that also was true, and then added, with a grin: "Here in prison you're all treated like gentlemen, until you're shot; but if one of you falls into the hands of the Moors at the front it's no laughing matter, I can tell you."

I asked him, whether as a Catholic, he approved of the torture of human beings. "Well, no," he said with an embarrassed smile. And so it went on for a while; in-between-times we talked about England, about Darwin, and whether men would ever fly to the moon.

This visit lasted nearly two hours. I wondered what it could all mean.

Then the mysterious librarian told me his story. He was not a professional boxer at all, but the proprietor of an advertising agency in Paris. Shortly before the outbreak of the Civil War he had gone bankrupt and had fled to Spain. His creditors had got on his tracks, and the French Government had requested the Spanish Government to arrest and extradite him. He was arrested in Seville a week before the Insurrection. The librarian—we will call him "Henri"—appealed against his extradition. Then the Civil War had begun, conditions in prison "had undergone certain changes," as he discreetly put it, and now it was Henri's dearest wish to be handed over to the authorities of his own country. All the more so since his creditors, touched by his dramatic story, had declared themselves ready to compound. The French Consul in Seville had done his best to get the lost sheep sent home again, but now the rebel authorities were unwilling to let him go. To them a Frenchman is a "Red," and the place for a "Red" is the prison patio. The ludicrous thing is that Henri alleges that he is a member of the "Croix de Feu," Colonel de la Roque's Fascist organization.

Henri told me his story with an air of injured innocence, and we kept having to laugh, Don Ramón, the youth with pince-nez, Henri and I. The two warders must have known the story inside out, for they nodded benevolently at every sentence as though listening to a well-worn anecdote. When he had finished, the Falangist declared that Henri too would be shot sooner or later, and then the tea-party broke up. As I saw my guests to the door, Don Ramón beckoned with his finger and allowed me to get a glimpse of the outside of my cell door.

I had been given a new plate; my name was on it—but *"Ojo"* and *"Incommunicado"* had vanished.

Round about seven the Falangist returned, and informed me officially that from tomorrow morning onwards I was to be allowed to walk in the patio during the siesta hours, from one to three. I asked if I might now at last write to the Consul. He said "Yes," but letters must be written in ink and I could not buy pen and ink until tomorrow, as the canteen was closed.

Eureka!

Monday night.

A moment ago—10 P.M.—the *jefe de servicio* was here. A *jefe* that I have never seen before, an elderly man with grizzled hair. He said that the office had received instructions from the military authorities that from tomorrow on I was to be allowed in the patio with the other prisoners, that is to say, the whole day long.

Better still!

Tuesday, April 13th.

I was up by six and I waited in a fever of impatience for the moment when I should at last emerge from my hole. The prisoners appeared in the courtyard at 8 o'clock as usual—but my cell door was not opened. I drummed on the door—in vain. At last, at breakfast, the warder explained that a different *jefe* was on duty today . . . and that he said he had received no instructions with regard to me. I asked for pen and ink—this too was refused, "since the *jefe* had no instructions." I asked to speak to the *jefe*. He sent a message to say he was too busy.

I was about to fly into a towering rage.

Tuesday evening.

At 12 o'clock Angelito suddenly came in with a message from the *jefe* to say that the military authorities had phoned through confirming that I was definitely to be allowed out on the patio between one and three . . . he had received no instructions, however, to let me have pen and ink.

A fresh period of feverish waiting until one. At last the whistle sounds, the prisoners in the patio line up four abreast and are led indoors. The patio is empty. In ten minutes' time, at the most, Byron, the consumptive, Carlos and the newcomer must appear; and then at last my cell door will be opened. . . .

A quarter-past one comes, half-past one, a quarter to two, nothing stirs. The others do not appear in the patio either.

I cannot contain myself any longer and I start beating out a tattoo on the door—hammer with my tin bowl on the steel and kick it till my feet are sore. It makes a hell of a din. After two minutes of this the door opens and Angelito, the *jefe* and "Captain Bligh" appear. They storm at me in chorus; Angelito loudest of all. (He has not had a tip for the last few days and knows that I have only twenty pesetas left.) I explain why I have been drumming on the door. "Captain Bligh" thunders that he will let me out when it suits him, and if it doesn't suit him he won't let me out at all; and if I behave like this again he will stamp on me, trample on me, crush me like a worm.

All this takes place in the open doorway. Byron, the consumptive and the newcomer, who have obviously just been let out of their cells, stand listening in the corridor. Then we are all four allowed out into the courtyard.

I feel the hot sun on my face, inhale a mouthful of air—and then everything suddenly turns grey, green, black before my eyes, and I find myself sitting on the ground. The other three set me on my legs again. Byron and the newcomer grasp me under the armpits; and after a few steps I am all right again.

We stand about together in a group, opposite Cell 36. At first I can do nothing but breathe in the air. Real air again for the first time—instead of the dense gaseous mixture, compounded of the odour of the stuffy bed, the smell of stale food and the stench of the lavatory on which I have existed for the past two months. Then we start talking.

My first question is, of course, what sentences they have been given.

"*La muerte*—death," says Byron, and grins.

"*La muerte*," says the consumptive. He is a well-known Republican politician, and Byron was formerly his secretary; they have both been waiting three months to be shot.

"*La muerte*," says the third man. He is a little Andalusian peasant, a Militiaman, taken prisoner on the Almería front.

Carlos was not there; presumably he is ill.

Carlos is an Italian, a lieutenant in the Italian contingent fighting under Franco's leadership. His arrest seems to be somehow connected with his German friend.

The Militiaman is called Nicolás. He was taken prisoner ten days ago and sentenced three days ago. He was charged, as are all prisoners of war, with *"rebelión militar"*—armed rebellion. Nicolás told us, as we paced up and down the patio, of his trial in the Seville court-martial.

It had lasted three minutes. The President had read out the prisoner's name, birthplace and the name of the place where he was captured. The Prosecutor had demanded the death penalty, and had added: "I only regret that I cannot send this *rojecillo*—this miserable little Red—in a cage to Geneva before he is shot, in order to show the League of Nations what pitiable objects are these so-called fighters for justice and democracy."

Then they had marched him off.

Nicolás had somehow managed to get hold of a stalk of lettuce; he nibbled away at it as he told us his story, and offered us each a leaf. I refused—thinking of my heart; the two others accepted with alacrity. "When do you think they'll shoot me?" asked Nicolás. "*Paciencia,* my boy," sad the Republicans with all the contempt of old inmates for the greenhorn. "One must not expect too much. We've been waiting three months now."

But then we all three began to comfort him. He was more afraid, even, than we were, for the ink was scarcely dry on his death sentence. We told him stories about how death sentences were only passed as a joke, to frighten people, and actually no one was ever shot; we three, who had been in prison an aggregate of eight months, and were not dead yet, were living proofs of this. He was only too glad to believe it, and in the end we believed it ourselves. We became quite gay, and Byron suggsted that a notice should be hung in the patio between one and three:

"No admittance except to those showing death sentences."

I offered to lend Nicolás a book, but he said that he could not read. He stroked the cover of the Tolstoy lovingly with his horny peasant's paws, and his eyes took on a stupid, sad look. He said he had hoped, once the war was won, to have an opportunity of learning to read.

Tomorrow is the anniversary of the proclamation of the Spanish Republic. The consumptive and his secretary are racking their brains wondering what sort of flags the foreign consulates in Seville and Burgos will fly. From the tone of their discussion I gather that this argument has been going on for weeks; they share a cell. Little Nicolás enquired despondently if they had nothing better to worry about, whereupon Byron drew himself up like a Spanish hidalgo and flashed at him: "No, señor."

The air smelt glorious; it smelt of spring and the sea.

We were not taken back to our cells until half-past three.

At seven o'clock Angelito arrived with pen and ink. I had given him a five-peseta voucher to change for me, but he forgot to return me the three peseta change.

Wrote my letter to the British Consul in Seville, but hear that it cannot be posted till tomorrow morning. Tomorrow when the letter has gone off, I rather think my heart will improve.

Tomorrow will be the tenth day of my illness.

Wednesday, April 14th. (Anniversary of the proclamation of the Spanish Republic.)

Gave letter to warder at breakfast-time, but he brought it back from the prison censor's office, saying that it must be written in Spanish. The merchant from Gibraltar who interpreted for me before was called in to help me to write it in correct Spanish. Afterwards he told me that he had come to Seville some weeks ago with a Spaniard on business in connection with the delivery of war material—whereupon they had both been arrested. There are three of them in No. 33; the third is the representative of a big American automobile firm, and he is also there for currency smuggling. They obtain food, wine and even coffee from the hotel, and in addition Angelito buys from forty to fifty pesetas' worth of goods for them every day in the canteen. They are the aristocrats of the prison; I hate them. The fellow promised to have some coffee and a chicken sent to my cell—am convinced he will not keep his promise. (P.S. I was right.)

He went on to say that he and his friends "hoped shortly to move into No. 39," just as though he were talking of rooms in an hotel. He said, further, that Angelito was a bloody bastard who would murder his own brother for a tip.

At midday my letter at last went off—I saw Don Antonio post it in the box in the corridor, after it had been censored. He says that the Consul is certain to come tomorrow.

A nauseating set-to with Angelito over the three pesetas. He said I could do what I liked with my beastly money, but again did not return it.

Then, shortly after one, pretty punctually this time, I was let out into the patio again. The two Republicans were there, and Carlos.

But Nicolás was missing.

I was about to ask the warder what had become of him, but the two others urgently advised me not to. Carlos kept at a distance from us; he had cut a swastika out of paper and stuck it in his buttonhole, and he stumped up and down alone by the outer wall.

Finally I did ask the warder after all. He shrugged his shoulders and said nothing. . . .

Requiescat in pace, Nicolás. Let us hope it was all over swiftly and that they did not make you suffer too much. They chose a solemn day for your execution. I wonder what flags the consulates flew?

Little you were, a little Andalusian peasant, with soft, slightly prominent eyes, one of the poor and humble; this book is dedicated to you. What good does it do you? You could not read it even if you were still alive. That is why they shot you: because you had the impudence to wish to learn to read. You and a few million like you, who seized your old firearms to defend the new order which might perhaps some day have taught you to read.

They call it armed rebellion, Nicolás. They call it the hand of Moscow, Nicolás. They call it the instinct of the rabble, Nicolás. That a man should want to learn to read.

My God, they should have sent you to Geneva in a cage, with the inscription:

"Ecce Homo, Anno Domini 1937."

Teruel

A LL *through the summer and fall the fighting went on along eight separate fronts. Bilbao fell in June, but the war in the Basque provinces went on, and the northern campaign did not end until October with the capture of Gijón. On all fronts the Republicans were pressing hard, gaining space in the east, and Franco's determined efforts to drive a wedge between Madrid and Catalonia were so far unavailing.*

The war burned with a slow flame. Day after day reports from the various fronts read: Sin novedad (*nothing new*). *While Franco planned great simultaneous offensives toward Guadalajara and southward to Madrid, and a thrust at the Mediterranean coast, the Republicans planned to drive against Saragossa and to break his eastern salient. Their eyes were on Teruel, and in December they captured it.*

The battle of Teruel was the turning point of the war. The fighting in those treacherous chalk hills took place in the dead of winter, the worst winter Spain had endured for twenty years. The snow fell, blizzards raged, and the fighting went on. Men died of the cold. They would be walking and talking, and suddenly they would drop dead with a frozen look in their eyes. There were snowdrifts six feet deep. The Republicans attacked on December 15th, and by New Year's Day most of the town was in their hands, but this was only the beginning. For more than seven weeks, until there was hardly a building left standing, the battle went on. At last, on February 17th, General Yagüe was able to cut off the town from the north, and four days later he had wrested it from the Republicans. The long battle was over.

Here Henry Buckley, an English correspondent who took extraordinary risks in order to cover the battle, describes the early days in

December, when the Republicans were fighting their way into the city:

Teruel is a bleak town if ever there was one; it is a sort of Spanish Buxton. It stands on a small hill in a basin surrounded by blunt hills nearly all of which are treeless. In normal times Teruel always scores by having the lowest temperatures of any other important town in the country each winter. It is about sixty miles from Valencia with its pleasant climate and its orange groves. It is also famous for a legend of two lovers. The poor boy, so the story runs, loved a rich man's daughter. He was given a certain length of time in which to make a fortune. He achieved this, but arrived just a little late and only in time to see his loved one married to another. He killed himself and the girl died of grief before she was possessed by her husband.

The unsentimental Spaniards have evolved a popular couplet which says:

> "Los amantes de Teruel
> Tonta ella y tonto el!"

That is to stay:

> "The Lovers of Teruel,
> She was stupid and he as well!"

There is a grandeur about this town perched on the top of a low hill, alone in this desolate terrain. It is a lovely sight seen on a winter's evening with the sun setting and the hard, surrounding landscape bathed in a soft, rosy glow. I knew something about Teruel for I had Spanish friends there. It is the capital of a very poor province, although there is richer ground in the direction of Saragossa. It was tremendously reactionary as far as I could find out. My friends certainly were. As soon as I got into Teruel I tried to find them but the first man I asked said to me very curtly: "My God, you have strange friends, young man." I found out that my friends were all in the Seminary where the Nationalist troops were resisting.

The Government lines had been near the town since the first days of the revolt. They occupied the heights of the Puerto de Escandón, about six miles from the town. The lines were even nearer round about Valdecebro to the North-East. The town was shelled occasionally and had been bombed, although not very much I think.

The operation was begun by a very neat and well executed cutting off of the town by Major Lister who repeated similar moves done at Brunete and Belchite but this was on a major scale. The attack made, I think I am correct in saying, at three o'clock on the afternoon of Friday, December 17, started a battle which raged almost unceasingly until Teruel was retaken by General Franco on February 22. The first step, made in broad daylight, consisted of sending troops across country from Valdecebro to beyond Caudete but without taking either this town or Concud and then sending part of the troops due south along the crest of the great rolling hill known as the Muela de Teruel (the tooth of Teruel) until they met another detachment coming up from the Republican front line near Villel. At seven o'clock in the evening Teruel was surrounded completely in a large circle which contained probably some 15,000 troops who had not yet come into action and probably about 20,000 civilian inhabitants.

How it had been possible for the Republicans to bring up at least forty or fifty thousand fresh troops, with all the corresponding equipment, to this front without the Insurgents finding this out remains one of the mysteries of the war. Their own and their allied spy systems either did not work or their warnings were disregarded. The weather when the attack was launched was terrible. It snowed almost the whole of the first day and all the roads were ice-bound. The Republican troops had to perform miracles to move their materials forward.

The officer responsible for the Teruel attack was the commander of the Eastern Army, Colonel Juan Hernández Sarabia, formerly in command of the Presidential Guard and once War Minister for a brief period. He was promoted to General after the capture of Teruel. A mild-mannered little man, he was always most pleasant to deal with but I never got the impression that he was a very efficient soldier. The strategy of the move had been planned by General Vicente Rojo, former teacher of strategy at the Toledo Infantry Academy and the man who had been General Miaja's chief of staff in Madrid throughout the defence of Madrid and later in the Battles of Jarama and Guadalajara. His handling of the situation at Guadalajara had been exceptionally good. Personally, he was very modest and retiring.

Sad little Teruel with its some 14,000 inhabitants and five or six thousand soldiers which had suffered already the anguish of shelling and bombing for one and a half years, had also suffered from the "white terror." The Left estimated about 2,000 of their people shot, but this probably was an exaggeration. Certainly some hundreds had been shot according to all the evidence available. One shooting had apparently taken place in the Plaza de Torico in the presence of hundreds of people. Women also had been executed. A Republican Councillor told me that of seven Republican Councillors only he and another one had escaped death; these two had managed to cross the lines to Republican Spain.

I went into Teruel twenty-four hours after the first troops and kept my eyes open for corpses on the outskirts of the town. I only saw one, a thin little man dressed in black, maybe about fifty. Some people standing near said that he was "a Fascist" who had been shot.

On the whole every effort was made to avoid reprisals. The population streamed out of the town by back roads while inside fighting went on around the Civil Governor's office, the Bank of Spain, the Convent of Santa Clara and the Seminary where in all maybe some 4,000 people were shut up.

For over two weeks I stayed up there watching the drama of this little mountain town which had suddenly become a world name. Each night I motored down to Valencia to telephone to London. I was in Teruel the day they brought out the governor of the local gaol and along with him the spy he used to have among the prisoners—who were nearly all political and therefore Left-Wingers—and the spy was crying and the governor, dirty and unshorn and indeed a tough-looking piece of work, bawled him out and called him a coward for crying. I found a shop where they had seven hundred hams and two soldiers were on guard. The owner was a nice little fellow; we smuggled his youngest son aged fifteen into Valencia in our car as if he were a journalist. I suspect that he had been a member of the Falangist Youth but he seemed a nice kid and we were glad enough to do a turn to the father who gave us a good deal of useful information.

Then there was Christmas Eve and the staff of a brigade asked us to supper in a tumble-down barn with a big wood fire. What nice young fellows they were, few of them over thirty; nearly all university students or clerks who had now been trained as officers and were full of enthusiasm. The troops provided a rondalla, or choir of guitar players and singers in the Aragonese fashion, who played and sang magnificently. There was a young Swiss with them. He had been brought up in Spain where his parents had a business, but he had of course no need to do service. He thought it a good idea to strike a blow for Democracy. Despite good wine and singing I was sad, for these boys were so earnest and out beyond the Pyrenees who cared about them? Paris would be in the whirl of the réveillon, champagne, balloons, concertinas, kisses. London would be asleep preparatory to great trencher feats the next day.

As I lay rolled in blankets in a car before I fell asleep I wondered where I should be next Christmas Eve and whether the world would still be sloughed deep in its egoism, those who have, greedily feeding, indifferent to the hunger and misery around them in the world. Two thousand years, nearly, since Christ was born and even to-day who follows His teachings?

At first there was little danger at Teruel—if one kept away from the strongholds where the Insurgents were holding out—but soon Franco massed for counter-attack. Fiat chasers raked the roads with machine-guns. Huge Caproni and Junkers bombers appeared in the sky with dawn and were still there when dusk fell; as one flight unloaded, another one would be coming up with fresh bombs. The Franco counter-offensive began about December 28 in a furious attempt to drive down at Teruel from the North and West and reach the town.

Report had it, I have no idea with what extent of accuracy, that Germans and Italians were against the idea of counter-attacking but would have preferred to have gone on with steady preparations for the vast spring offensive planned, instead of milling around a town which strategically was not of great value to a weak opponent such as the Republicans were.

But it must be remembered that General Franco had his own problems. He must by this time have had considerable debts not only to Germany and Italy but in London, New York, Paris where he received credits to buy petrol and other vital necessities. As he must continue to be able to rely on credits against the belief that he would eventually win, it was very necessary for him never to admit defeat and during the war on more than one occasion he sacrificed purely military considerations to political ones.

New Year's Eve was grim beyond measure, the Insurgents hurled their best troops forward in a tremendous effort to smash their way through. The Government forces stood their ground like heroes. Despite a gale which in the afternoon developed into a roaring blizzard, the Nationalist airplanes bombed and machine-gunned without cessation until all visibility went soon after three o'clock. I stayed up on the Puerto de Escandón, above the town around which shells were falling thickly, for the Insurgents had their artillery so far forward now that they could shell behind the town, and make the trip in and out highly unpleasant. Soldiers flocked past. Assault Guards with submachine-guns turned them off the road and ordered them to prepare camps. But actually there was no collapse although it looked like it. These men were mostly from fortification units which had been working on the other side of Teruel and had had to retreat.

Down in the valley, although we only heard of it later, a shell had hit a car containing our "opposite numbers" on the other side and Mr. Edward Neil of Associated Press, Mr. E. R. Sheepshanks of Reuter's and Mr. Bradish Johnson, Paris correspondent of *Spur,* were killed. Mr. Harold Philby of the *Times* was injured. The Nationalists were so sure that they had the town and indeed the snowstorm gave them a magnificent opportunity to take the Government troops by surprise, but the Republican defence was so good that the attackers desisted when only little over two miles away. That must have been a great disappointment with their 4,000 supporters resisting so near and yet they could give them no help.

The icy gale blew for two days and snow was four feet deep in drifts before the blizzard eased. It was several days later before a passage was cut and normal communications with Valencia restored. Six hundred vehicles had been blocked in one long jam half-way up from the coast. Sefton Delmer and myself went down to Teruel to see how things looked and I, at any rate, had my heart in my mouth. The Nationalists were kind and did not shell or bomb us on our way in although the trail of dead mules on the ice-bound road leading into the town told its own tale. But inside that town there were plenty of things happening. Bombers hovered the whole time and bombed the outskirts steadily. Chaser planes swooped down every once in a while and machine-gunned the streets. Sporadic shells from the Nationalist batteries landed. Around the Seminary and the adjoining Santa Clara Convent there was the devil's own inferno. Green-clad, unshaven carabineros who had been fighting fifteen days without rest, hurled bombs down into the cellars of the buildings, both of which were complete wrecks. Those below fired back with rifles. From a church tower we looked out over the countryside and had the front pointed out to us, very little over two miles away. The Nationalists had taken part of the Muela de Teruel, but their impetus had failed at the critical moment and they did not make even the outskirts of the town. Government planes dashed across and bombed the Insurgent lines and scurried away chased by angry pursuit planes. Puffs of black smoke from the German anti-aircraft batteries filled the air.

It was nearly all up with the defenders. Sr. Prieto had insisted that so far as possible the people within should not be harmed and this had greatly slowed up the attack for it excluded drastic measures with really big mines and meant slowly driving the people back and back from one building to another until they could not move. This had happened now, for the Seminary was a heap of ruins and there were about 1,700 in the cellars of the Santa Clara Convent with a wrecked building on top of them and, so I understand, no water. There were about 3,000 also in the Bank of Spain and an adjoining building. On January 3, the Civil Governor's office had fallen and those within had escaped to the Bank of Spain. On January 7, Lieutenant-Colonel Rey d'Harcourt, the senior Nationalist officer, surrendered. All those within were evacuated. Teruel was now completely empty except for the Government soldiers and they resisted there stoutly until February 22.

Rey d'Harcourt was viciously attacked as a coward and traitor by his own side, but it is difficult to see what else he could have done with 2,000 civilians, old people, women and children, under his care and neither food nor water for them. I saw their position just before they emerged and as I pointed out higher up, they were literally buried under ruins with Government soldiers on top of the ruins. They would all have been dead long before February 22. Poor Rey d'Harcourt met a sad end for he was, along with Bishop Anselmo Polanco of Teruel and some sixty other prisoners, shot, apparently by Anarchists, near the French frontier while being brought towards France during the final days of resistance in Catalonia.

For six weeks a fierce battle raged before the Nationalists finally managed to drive the Republicans well back from the mountains to the north of Teruel and so free their communications. The International Brigades who had not previously been used, Sr. Prieto wanted this to be an "all-Spanish effort," were thrown in including the Washington-Lincolns, the Mackenzie-Papineaus (Canadians) and the Major Attlee Battalion (British). Many British lost their lives up in these hills in fighting which was never properly reported because of the difficulties of reaching the scene and of moving from one sector to another.

One thing worth pointing out, I think, in considering the Battle of Teruel is that the very strict instructions issued by Sr. Prieto to the effect that as far as possible the defenders and the refugees inside the buildings which held out for nearly three weeks should be taken alive and that ruthless measures should not be adopted, made the defence of the town tremendously difficult from a military point of view. This arose from the peculiar situation of Teruel which is perched on a hill. Communication with Valencia is from the southern part of the town over a bridge which passes over a deep and wide gully. The other main road which runs from Saragossa to Cuenca does not actually enter Teruel but runs along the Valley of the Guadalaviar (a contraction of the Arabic for White River; the same river is called the Turia lower down and plays a great part in watering Valencia's fertile *huerta*) which runs along the western edge of the town.

Consequently this road was under complete domination from the people in the Seminary and Santa Clara, even when they were downstairs, for the ground shelves down precipitately at that point, and these buildings are on the western edge of the town. They could fire with rifle, machine-gun or trench-mortar on to this road and on to the branch road running down from the Valencia road.

So the troops in Teruel had no road communication whatever either to the North or South or in front of them. If, for instance, Colonel Leopoldo Menéndez commanding the troops in the town, wished to send a piece of artillery to a position on the Muela de Teruel, say at two miles from his headquarters, this gun had to travel back to Puebla de Valverde, then across a villainous mountainous road through precipitous country to Villel, then up the Cuenca-Saragossa road back to the Muela. About seventy miles in all! The same held good for the North. Valdecebro could only be reached by a very bad road from Puebla de Valverde and the northern sectors of the Teruel front such as Alfambra were supplied from a road running inland from Tortosa. It was an incredible situation.

General Hernández Sarabia, who had his headquarters in a train which was pulled considerably into a tunnel near Mora Station, must have had enormous difficulties in moving supplies and in keeping communication with his men and in organising the defence of the town, which it must be understood had to be organised from the two wings for the people in the town could only move backwards towards Valencia, they could not go forward or sideways. All this could have been avoided, of course, if the Government forces had gone ruthlessly forward and concentrated numerous batteries on the buildings or placed large mines underneath, for the town had a labyrinth of underground passages. Fire or tear gas might also have been employed if really drastic measures had been decided on.

Here Valentín Gonzáles, known as "El Campesino," describes how his men fought their way out of the besieged town when the battle was nearly over:

The Fascist offensive against Teruel, directed by Franco in person, lasted from January 21 to February 9, 1938. The advanced positions were lost, and I quickly found my force of 16,000 men surrounded. Outside the town, Lister and Modesto commanded six brigades and two battalions. They could have helped me. They did nothing of the kind. Even worse, when Captain Valdepeñas wanted to come to my rescue, they prevented him from doing so.

But I have little taste for martyrdom. I fought back. Shut up in Teruel, besieged and encircled by the Fascists, my men fought on splendidly. Of the nine hundred men of my One Hundred First Brigade, who bore the brunt of the attack, only eighty-two survived. I decorated all of them when the battle was over.

At the last stage, fighting was going on inside Teruel itself, around the bull ring. All the nearby buildings were in ruins. In these ruins, the Fascists were intrenched on one side, we on the other. I was directing the defense from a cellar.

Then word was brought to me that the Fascists were shouting across to our men, "El Campesino is dead—surrender! We've killed El Campesino—surrender!" I ran out of the cellar, jumped on to the rubble which was our parapet, and shouted, "Where are those bastards who say El Campesino is dead? Here I am! Do you think I look dead?"

The Fascists were so surprised that they did not even remember to fire at me. Then my aides got hold of me from behind and pulled me back just in time. The bullets started whistling overhead just as they hustled me back into my cellar.

There was no hope of holding Teruel any longer. Now the task was to try to save my men and as much as possible of our equipment. We fought our way out, through the encircling forces, at the cost of a thousand men.

Among our casualties was one of my aides. He fell at my side, killed instantly. I wanted to save his body and took it on my back. But I soon realized my folly and laid the body down in the snow. My cloak was soaked with his blood. I threw it away. This act gave rise to the second report of my death. My cloak was of a special pattern, made for me in Madrid to look like those the Russians wore. My men recognized me by it in the field. Also it had the stars of a commander in chief.

This cloak was picked up and brought to Franco. He called in newspaper correspondents and showed them the bloodstained cloth and the identifying stars. The report went out: "El Campesino is dead." Even the Republican Government believed it. An official telegram informed my wife that I had been killed in action.

As soon as I had led the survivors of my command to safety, I rang up Prieto. "El Campesino speaking," I said. "I've broken out of Teruel with most of my men and a good deal of our material."

"You're joking," said Prieto. "El Campesino is dead. Who is that speaking?"

"Go to bloody hell," I started, but Prieto interrupted me: "Now I recognize you," he said. "I know you by your vocabulary."

An officer of the Republican Army describes the frozen landscape and the attack on the molar-shaped hill called La Muela, which dominated Teruel.

A week before my unit was sent to the front of Teruel, I was summoned to army headquarters. That day there had been a downpour, the rain had quickly frozen into ice, and in the bright wintry glare of the Castilian sky the trees assumed the shapes of strange crystals forming a complicated pattern of transparencies and refractions. The road from Cuenca to Mora de Rubielos was like a blinding mirror, dazzling us as we drove at a snail's pace.

Then in the middle of the day it began to snow while we were crossing the Sierra de Camarena along an improvised road which had been built hurriedly to connect on the south flank of the front the roads linking Teruel to the cities of Cuenca and Valencia. This road led across a wild and desolate landscape of sharp mountains, scrub and villages old as poverty. In that snow, on that impossible road, with its fabulous gradients and precipices, one had the sensation of being outside time, leaving reality altogether and entering the kingdom of allegory. The people seemed to have lost themselves in the seclusion of their mountains, for their gestures, and the way they held themselves, and spoke to us with a shy dignity, somehow suggested a complete remoteness. While the snow fell, it was good to smell the food they cooked on their open fires, and it was good to talk with them, and good to see there were still places not yet invaded by the war.

When my unit was sent to the front, the snow had been falling for days. The glassy road winding through the mountains was crowded with trucks inching their way toward Teruel. We forgot the beauty of the place when three of the trucks slipped over the precipices and fell into the ravines below. Then we knew it was bitterly cold, and there was no more dangerous road anywhere on earth. The convoys crawled. There were no guardrails—only the winding road and the mountains and Teruel a few miles away.

I saw a lot of that road, for I went up and down it on a motorcycle, and I knew the sufferings of the men and felt compassion for them.

Very late in the day I was able to concentrate my unit in a bombed village at the foot of a ravine, but the ravine formed a chimney for the wind, and it was probably colder there than in the mountains. The gutted walls provided no shelter. The men slept by the side of the cliff, huddled together. In this way each man had three or four blankets over him. It was the best way.

Meanwhile I found a small house on the other side of the ravine, and went there to get some sleep. I might have done better in the open. There were sixty men huddled round a fire, and the wind howled through the open roof, and the smoke clogged our eyelids. But we slept a little, and before dawn we were on the march.

Our object was to take La Muela de Teruel, the flat-topped hill on the south bank of the Guadalaviar River, overlooking Teruel. We needed the hill, for it was an excellent observation post and dominated the valley. It was very nearly impregnable, scored with small ravines, and the sides were almost vertical.

We attacked during a blizzard, the temperature below zero. Our men had somehow to climb and grapple their way up the steep slopes of the hill, arm over arm. There was a biting wind and blinding snow, but somehow they succeeded in establishing a foothold, and by midday they were occupying half of the hill. It was the better half, looking down on Teruel. It was December 31st, 1937.

The horror was in the cold, the wind, the snow, the absence of footholds. More than half our casualties came from frostbite: many had to have their toes amputated. Still, half the hill was in our possession. I could have pressed my men to take the whole hill "whatever the sacrifice," and perhaps we might have taken it, but it was impossible to demand any more sacrifices from them. We had to content ourselves with our slice of the hill, with the enemy no more than a few yards away.

It was a strange position up on La Muela, with a wavering serpentine line dividing us from the enemy, our men digging shallow trenches and taking what cover they could.

On one of my inspection tours of the front I found the hill blanketed with fog. I was unable to see more than three or four yards ahead, and often much less. Later the sun burned the fog away, and the whole hill stood out perfectly. I continued my tour of inspection along the erratic forward line, the enemy perhaps three hundred feet away. All this time my orderly was acting in a way beyond my understanding. He kept moving round me. Sometimes he was on my left, sometimes on my right, sometimes behind me or in front of me. I suddenly realized my orderly was trying to protect my life with his own, and I was alarmed. It was strange and wonderful that he should have thought he could protect me on that exposed hill, against bullets which would slice through two men as easily as one. And I marveled.

Teruel is the coldest town in Spain, but the hill was colder. La Muela was absolutely barren: no trees, no grasses, grew on it. All around Teruel there is this eroded land with deep gulleys, harsh and uninviting. But we clung to our hill.

Once, many centuries ago, the fields around Teruel were probably covered with thick pine forests. Now there were men in their ice-cold pebbly trenches, keeping low to the earth, shivering, waiting for the next artillery barrage, the next burst of rifle fire, the next mortars and machine guns, and the inevitable attacks.

One day I accompanied General Hernández Sarabia on one of his visits to another sector of the front. We stood on a hill and watched the preparations for the enemy's coming attack. The whole snowy countryside seemed to be boiling under the heavy concentration of fire, from aviation and artillery. Because the ground was covered with ice and the earth was frozen, there was no black smoke in the explosions. All along the front thick white clouds erupted and dissolved and flared up again and melted and reappeared elsewhere, and there was no end to the weight of armor hurling down over the plains of Teruel.

General Sarabia was a quiet man. For a while he watched in silence the pounding of our lines, and then he could contain himself no longer. He leaned forward and muttered between his teeth: *"Co-bardes! Así se puede ganar la guerra!* Cowards! Is that the way to win a war? Why don't you fight man to man, as we do?"

There was no end to those pure white explosions filled with smoke and ice and expanding gases and the remains of human beings, and no end to the general muttering: *"Cobardes! Que den el pecho, como nosotros!"*

André Malraux

Already a world-famous archaeologist, revolutionary, and novelist,
André Malraux became one of the chief organizers of Republican
resistance in the air. He bought planes for the Republic and flew them
in battle, and his novel Man's Hope, *based on his journals and written*
with extraordinary immediacy while the war was still being fought,
is a work of classic scope and enduring brilliance. The following notes
were published in Collier's *in the spring of 1937.*

It is the Epiphany, the feast of the Three Kings, the great festival of
the children of Spain. In the morning when I came to the War Ministry
all the streets were filled with armored cars. They have been passing
by all day long, while one hundred kilometers away the International
Brigade and the columns of militiamen captured, lost and recaptured
the Teruel cemetery. It is the first children's feast since the birth of the
new Spain, and the trade unions have wanted to give them a celebra-
tion such as they have never had before. For a week the workers have
been busy all night making cardboard figures taken from the animated
cartoons which the children have been clamoring for, and, in addition
to the traditional cake fortresses, the old bulls, the king and the play-
ing-card characters, twelve-foot figures of Mickey Mouse and Felix the
Cat have on this occasion invaded Valencia.

My car is taking me back from the War Ministry to the front. It is
three o'clock in the morning. In the starlight that breaks through the
clouds one senses the tall buildings around the great square, grounded
in the night like the prows of old Spanish galleons. The blue wartime
lights, like the blue lights of deep-sea fishes, cast a faint glow over the
square and the shadows of Mickey Mouse figures are swallowed up
by the asphalt that is wet from the last brief shower. When the auto-

mobile reaches the broad boulevards that encircle Valencia we are stopped by the heavy traffic. We turn on our headlights for a moment: all the characters that people the dreams of children, from the early dreams of Christianity to those of American children, from the Magi to Mickey Mouse, are there in a jumble; and between their legs some of the thousands of children who have come for the feast of the Epiphany have sought refuge from the rain that may start again any moment and have fallen asleep.

Here and there for miles we come upon these great phantoms of childish dreams abandoned in the night, as if the genii of all races were to come here to fetch them for the dreams of all the children who sleep. On each base, around their legs, the dimmed automobile lights reveal in passing a cluster of children, calmly asleep—stretched out like the wounded of Teruel a little farther on, on the same ground.

The dull explosions from the cannon of Teruel, that seem imperceptibly to shake the earth, seem at the same time to shake these frail phantoms above the serene slumber of all the motionless children, their arms relaxed in gestures of the dead.

A battalion of militiamen is leaving for the front. They are heading toward the Prado, and the loud strains of the Internationale draw nearer. When they are almost immediately below my window, at the moment when the singing should be loudest, it subsides, only to pick up again a little farther on, on a lower note, muffled. I go to the window; a blind man, holding his white cane out in front of him, is walking down the middle of the street. None of those adolescents on their way to the battle front has dared to push him aside, and he advances against the current of the marching militiamen who go around him on both sides, and stop their singing. After they have passed him and gone on a little way their song again breaks out, in a more sober strain. The blind man continues forward, throwing back his shoulders as almost all blind men do, distressed by this crowd which he cannot see, and which is silenced by his presence—and, surrounded by an empty circle as by the respectful terror with which the blind men of old were regarded, not understanding and wanting to escape, he walks faster and faster; and the militiamen swerve aside before he touches them, as though to let Destiny pass by.

I saw him again. The Moors were in Carabanchel—at the gates of Madrid. Those of us who had fought in the infantry and were used to hearing the tom-tom of the Moors at night opened the windows to listen; but the wind was coming from Madrid, and we could hear nothing in the rainy night, not even the rattle of machine guns. After nine o'clock the patrol of the thoroughfares was extremely strict, and the streets were almost wholly deserted.

From the top of one of the big hotels, no doubt for the benefit of the police, a searchlight periodically swept the street. Suddenly before me, in the vast flood of light, appeared two enormous hands, hands fifty feet long, that vanished into the night. The police and the militia-men no doubt knew the blind beggar and had let him pass. He was without a cane and was protecting himself with his groping hands; he was barely visible in the beam from the searchlight, but his out-stretched hands, trembling like those of a god of the night, seemed to be seeking the living and the dead with a frightful maternal gesture.

On the outskirts of a village between Madrid and Talavera the dynamiters were awaiting the enemy tanks.

Messengers would come and give them the warning signal. For the time being there was nothing to do but wait. They were in a deserted bar, telling each other stories:

"I took part in the retreat with Gorde and Sabranek. They are both miners in the country where they come from; they were assigned to the company at our rear back of the village. At that time there weren't any dynamiters. They had both been machine gunners in the army, and so they were put on the machine guns. The first day of the attack their company of machine gunners was detailed to hold a small wood. Hell was popping right and left, when they suddenly noticed that their two flanking companies had been pushed back and that they were surrounded by Moors. There was nothing to do but to take to their heels and try to get through; make a three-hundred-yard dash, stop, fire a roll, make another three-hundred-yard dash. So off they went, jumping like rabbits, taking their Hotchkiss with them. After the first three hundred yards they stopped and began to fire. It was Gorde who was at the gun. He shot his roll. The Moors were falling in their tracks, just like in the movies, but they were bound to catch up to them.

" 'Beat it!' shouted Sabranek. The other continued to tinker with his roll.

" 'Beat it, for God's sake!' He continued to tinker with his roll, sitting 'way back in the saddle, and then opened fire. The Moors once more began to go down. Exasperated, Sabranek let go with his booted foot and kicked him in the pants again and again. The other got up, hesitated a moment. And again Sabranek kicked him in the tail. Then with both arms Gorde grabbed his machine gun and took to his heels, running full speed right into the enemy, with Sabranek behind him still yelling at the top of his lungs. And they both disappeared over the ridge held by the Moors, like Laurel and Hardy. I can't get over seeing them again here. I thought they'd been killed."

Others, outside, are sitting or lying down with their horse blankets wrapped round them, giving the effect of a Mexican army, minus the sombreros. The flames at intervals light up the faces, as in engravings of the Napoleonic wars.

"Pedro was in the Asturias in '34 with Gonzáles Peña. We were fighting with one bullet to every five men. When the cartridges were empty the women gathered them up, put them in their salad baskets, and the baskets went off in a truck to be reloaded with bullets. The enemy planes chased the armored trains that scurried into the tunnels, waited till the planes went back to refuel, and then made a dash for another tunnel. And so on. The peasants were fighting all around Miejes. It was the last day. Nothing more could be done. But they needed three hours to prevent the outer flanks of the Moorish guard which was advancing like a crescent toward Miejes from closing together, and to evacuate all who could be evacuated.

"There was still quite a bit of dynamite that came from the mines. But nothing to make bombs with. No copper, no steel. The Moors were advancing. In a little peasant hut the committee was deliberating. The Moors were advancing. A strange rumbling was beginning to make the walls tremble. It was not an earthquake: the walls were trembling, but not the ground. And it was not cannons: it was a dull, but multitudinous sound, like thousands of muffled drums. Pedro went outside, and the moment he opened the door the noise of machine guns, like the ripping of cloth, could be distinctly heard in the room beneath the rumble that was growing louder and was as mysterious as ever. Suddenly a cow appeared in the main street, hesitated, passed in front of the central committee shack and fled down the other end of the street. A bull ran after her, with the jerky, nervous gallop of the *corrida*. And when Pedro saw a rabbit scurrying toward him, he understood.

"To encircle the town, the Moors were advancing as for a roundup. Game and cattle, thrown back on Miejes by machine-gun fire, were beginning to pour in among the peasant huts on the outskirts, toward the center, and it was the sound of thousands of hoofs that was making the ground shake. The cattle were coming down the mountain with the rumble of great herds returning from pasture. And now, seemingly rising from the ground, the sound of bells could be heard.

"The animals all carried bells—the heavy, deep-sounding bronze bells of mountain cattle, like those of the Moslem herds. In a moment tables, chairs, boards, objects of all kinds were thrown out through the windows of the hut or brought from near-by houses. The rumble was growing louder: the cattle were coming. The materials gathered for the barricades were feverishly piled up. From all sides the peasants were converging for the building of a new barricade—the barricade against the cattle herd.

"The herds were stopped. One by one the peasants unfastened or tore off the heavy bells, which sixty dynamiters transformed into bombs. And they began to take their places in all the hollows in the rocks along the path of the Moors.

"For more than three hours they held them off by hurling cowbells from the hollows. The fighting population scattered into the interior of Spain or crossed the frontier into France. Fifty-eight dynamiters were killed."

"I was in Talavera," said another. "We were being bombarded by their planes as we had never been before. Around Saragossa there are holes like those in the valley of the moon; here there were twenty-five-pound bombs all over the place—unexploded. During the bombardment only one out of ten went off. It was an amazing sight. The Fascists were bombarding almost entirely with light bombs. No doubt they had no heavy ones left. The bombs came out of their holes like handfuls of grain, fell right on us, and here and there one of them would burst, as if by accident. It was as if the Fascists were bombarding us with enormous darts. On the embankment of the road where our trucks passed they must have bombarded us fifteen times, in small squadrons of five to nine; on both sides the bombs were piled up as if they were there ready to be carted away. They had fallen on top of each other and had not exploded.

"It was rather odd. When a few don't explode it's more or less natural; but with so many it was uncanny. Some of our men had been aviation mechanics; they had often helped with loading the bombs on their planes. They began to unscrew the percussion fuses to examine the bombs. The first one turned round, excited as a windmill, holding out a little slip of typewritten paper to show to the second one who, no less excited, was holding a similar slip. It was the message of the Portuguese workers: 'This bomb will not explode.' "

The messengers had just arrived. It was the signal for action. The dynamiters scurried off with their bombs. I thought of an Annamite I had known several years back who had been killed in his first elephant hunt: the animal was charging, and it had seemed to my friend that a man was so slight a thing before this great mass that he had dropped his gun and run; the elephant had killed him with one blow of his trunk. So slight a thing before the mass that was coming down on him. . . . The men continued to advance to the firing line, one behind the other, their bombs on their backs or under their arms. We heard what sounded like distant motors. And with our eyes fixed on the broken crest of the hill in front of us we waited for the first armored car to appear.

"There's a peasant who wants to talk to you. He's come over from the Fascist lines."

I follow him to where the peasant is standing, surrounded by aviators who are questioning him. His answers come reluctantly. As I approach I see his face in full profile—the long, dark, lean profile of the Spanish peasant: of the men who fought Napoleon; to complete the illusion one has merely to imagine the visored cap he is wearing replaced by a knotted kerchief.

"You say you want to speak to me?"

"No. I've come to speak to the commander of the air squadron."

"That's him," the aviators tell him.

The peasant is suspicious. My outfit—the planes will be leaving in half an hour—bears no insignia of rank.

"Can you give the word for the planes to take off?"

The pilots stand round him, some friendly, others suspicious; he comes from the enemy lines. I draw him aside. He has been sent to me by the People's Front of León. The Fascist planes are in the vicinity of his village. He has just gotten through the lines and has gone to notify our people in León; they have immediately sent him to me.

I have one of the men get a phone connection through to the People's Front headquarters in León to check the story, and come back to the peasant.

"Where are the planes?"

"In the woods. The Fascists have made clearings under the trees where they can keep them out of sight."

"What's the field like?"

"Where they take off?"

"Yes."

He makes a drawing. Long and narrow.

"The soldiers have been working since yesterday to make the field wider."

"How does it run?"

He thinks for a moment.

"East and west."

"And the wood?"

"To the east."

This means that the enemy planes have to take off from east to west. The wind, which is very strong, comes from the east, and it is undoubtedly the same in Olmedo. The enemy planes would have a hard time taking off from the field which the peasant has described.

"How many planes are there?"

"There were twelve large ones and six small ones last night. We managed to find that out through some of our boys."

We have only four planes at our disposal. If the peasant is telling the truth it is worth attempting to surprise the enemy camp. If he is lying the enemy planes will be able to take to the air before we discover them, and we will not return. A telephone operator comes, bringing the answer from León. The man does, in fact, come from Olmedo, but the León people don't know those in Olmedo. It is up to us to decide what to do.

"It's near Olmedo," he repeats.

I show him a map; as I supposed, he is unable to read it.

"Take me to Olmedo," he says: "I'll show you. I can guide you right to the spot."

"Anyone in your family been killed by the Fascists?"

"No. Take me in your plane."

In such a situation spies are likely to betray themselves—in aerial warfare enemies cannot choose their victims. Olmedo is an hour and a half away. Our planes hold enough fuel to last five hours.

"Have you ever been up in a plane?"

"No."

"Aren't you nervous?"

He didn't quite understand.

"Aren't you afraid?"

"No."

"You think you will recognize the way?"

"From Olmedo, yes. I know the country better than a dog."

We have no pursuit planes, but the sky is overcast and we may be protected by the clouds.

The three other planes that follow us in triangle formation disappear from minute to minute in the clouds that grow increasingly dense as we approach the Sierra. The inverted plowshares of the highest crests rise above the great expanse of piled-up snow; up there the enemy scouts are awaiting us with the rockets that will warn their pursuit planes. But no doubt the sea of clouds is compact on the other side and separates the scouts from their observers. We fly amid the clouds, emerging from time to time so as not to crash into the mountains—as sperm whales come to the surface to breathe. Above us and the enemy scouts, far above the subterranean agitation of war, is a wonderfully clear sky of autumn morning. An almost biting cold finds its way into the plane; these combats that were to have lasted only a few weeks settle on the invisible earth like wounded men in their beds, and in the wind that strikes our faces winter once more passes its hands over the old face of war.

The clouds draw nearer. The peasant looks at me. I know that he is thinking: "How am I going to guide you if I can't see anything?" But he asks nothing. I yell into his ear:

"We'll cross above Olmedo."

He looks at the Sierra, looks below him and waits. In each plane the crew commander, his eyes on the crest rising above the clouds, watches for the rockets.

We are now above the Sierra. On the other side the sea of clouds forms a compact mass.

We navigate by the compass, but the compass does not record the drift caused by an oblique wind. If we are carried twenty to thirty kilometers out of our course the enemy planes may have a chance to take off. I will try to reconnoiter the country without completely getting out of the clouds, rise again to pick up the other planes, rectify our course, and head for Olmedo. Then it will be up to the peasant to show the way.

We have passed the Sierra; we are over enemy territory. Now any accident to the motor is fatal. The Moors have a special predilection for wounded aviators. Beneath the radiant sky, buried under the clouds, lie torture and death. Behind us the other planes, still in triangular formation, follow us with the comradeliness of two arms of the same body.

We are approaching Olmedo. The clouds, the sky, still the same serenity. . . . We enter the clouds. As soon as the mist envelops us it seems as if the battle were beginning. The plane descends slowly, so as to stay within the clouds as much as possible; at the fighting posts the machine gunners and the bombers are now on the lookout. And the pilots and I watch the compasses and the altimeter with more intensity than we ever watch a human face.

The altimeter drops: 800—700—500—400—375—350. We have not yet pierced through the blanket of fog. If we continue to drop and we are not exactly over Olmedo (which is probable) we are going to crash—there are hills throughout this region.

We begin to take on altitude again. Before dropping I have observed that the sea of clouds was punctured here and there. We shall wait, circling over the point where we are, till a rift appears below us.

Our plane loses all contact with the earth. Until now we have been advancing, our eyes and our minds always turned to what lay before us, fascinated by what we were approaching; for the first time now we must wait. The planes circle above the bank of clouds that extends beyond the distant crests; but the clouds advance with a movement that gives the illusion of being the movement of the earth itself, and it seems as if men, earth, destiny, flow away with that immensity that is gliding beneath us, while high up, beyond the world, the planes circle with the fatality of stars.

Yet at the same time the old savage instinct of the bird of prey has taken hold of us. With the centuries-old wheeling flight of hawks we circle as we wait for a break in the clouds, the eyes of all the crew looking downward as though we were on the lookout for the entire earth and expected it presently to appear in a sudden rift. And it seems as if the whole landscape of clouds and mountain peaks is turning with the slowness of a planet round our motionless machine.

A cloud darker than the rest, and greenish in hue, approaches. It is the break. Like a worn and dirty map, the earth begins to appear.

Olmedo is not immediately below us, but a few kilometers to our right, russet because of its tiles, like an old smear of blood on the shredded surface of the clouds. My plane beats its wings—the combat signal—and we swoop downward.

All heads are stretched forward, parallel like those of ancient bas-reliefs. We are above the church; below us, the houses rush past at full speed like a herd in flight.

The peasant looks, his whole body tense, his mouth half open, and tears zigzag down his cheeks, one by one; he does not recognize anything.

Some distance away large puffs of shell smoke appear, like fragments of the clouds from which we have just emerged. The enemy antiaircraft guns are beginning to fire. The battery is no doubt close to the enemy camp, but there is no trace of smoke on the ground. We have two minutes at the most. The peasant said that the field was north of Olmedo. I put the signal on the command dial square north; no one in the other three planes is aware that we don't know where we are going.

For a brief moment I bank the plane 90°. Our path is parallel to the main street of Olmedo. I point it out to the peasant:

"There's the church. The street. The Ávila road."

He recognizes all that in passing, but can't get his bearings for the direction we have to take. What will he be able to recognize when we no longer have even the buildings? Below the immobile upper half of his face from which the tears are flowing his chin quivers convulsively.

The Fascist pursuit planes are surely getting their motors started. The first one that takes off will show us the field; but if its attack allows the others time to leave the ground, none of us will return. It is now a question of seconds.

There is only one resort: give the peasant an angle of vision that he is used to. Perpendicularly he does not recognize the country; on the ground—horizontally—he would recognize it at once. We must get a view as close as possible to that which one gets from the ground.

I shift the course a few points off north and drop to thirty meters.

The machine guns rattle, but that doesn't matter. The antiaircraft guns have ceased firing—we are too low, below their range. Soldiers and farm animals scurry off frantically below us like snow shooting sideways from a snowplow. If one could die of looking and seeking, the peasant would die. He catches hold of my arm, points with a taut, crooked finger which he does not manage to straighten at a large publicity billboard, black and pale yellow under the low sky. And he pulls me to the right, with his whole might, as though I were the plane. I put the command signal east. The peasant shouts. None of the men turns his head. The peasant yells, but does not speak, and with his finger which is still crooked points to a wood.

"Is that it?"

He answers yes with his whole head and shoulders, without relaxing his outstretched arm. And there, next to the wood, is the oblong field which he had drawn for us before our take-off. A pursuit plane and a bombing plane are out in the open. The propeller of the pursuit plane is in motion.

We are approaching in the very direction in which it must take off. In order not to be brought down by our own bombs, we take on altitude, and in a few seconds we will again become targets for the antiaircraft shells. As we pass over the field we drop a few light bombs— enough to cut the path of the pursuit plane and prevent it from taking on speed. We circle and turn back dropping a string of light bombs. It's impossible to aim, but our blind firing cuts the path of the Fascist plane. We drop bombs as we pass over the wood, where a cluster of figures is trying to push the bombing plane. We bank as we did a while ago above the clouds and come back. As the field comes into sight again, the pursuit plane is lying on its side: a heavy bomb from one of our planes must have struck close by.

At full speed the four wheeling planes in oblique formation pass again one after the other over the wood and rise toward the shells which are beginning to form a barrage—as though we were deliberately going to meet them. Our bombs fall on the wood, where we can make out nothing. Undoubtedly the pursuit planes from the nearest enemy airdrome, advised by telephone, are already in the air. Our machine gunners watch the sky, the pilot and the bombers keep their eyes on the ground; the round continues.

We are suddenly jolted as by an air pocket. Has a shell just burst close by? There is no puff of smoke near us. But down below, from the wood, a thick, black smoke begins to pour, which I immediately recognize: gasoline. Directly or indirectly, we have struck the enemy depot. Still we see nothing of what we are bombarding. The enormous smoke begins to rise as if subterranean beds were burning beneath the quiet wood that looks exactly like all the others in the late morning. A few men come running out of the wood—and, in a few seconds, hundreds of them, in the same headlong animal flight as the flocks of cattle a while ago. And the smoke, which the wind beats down as if the sky would fling every trace of war back toward the wretched world of men, begins to spread. Beside me, shivering with joy and cold, the peasant stamps his feet in the fuselage.

Madrid is being bombarded. I am following a man who lugs a manuscript as big as himself. People rarely write on paper of that size, and such a large manuscript naturally interests a writer. I stop the man:

"What is that manuscript of yours?"

The sound of airplane bombs reaches our ears.

"It isn't a manuscript," he answers gently. "I'm changing the wallpaper in my apartment."

The Crossing of the Ebro

*W*ITH *Teruel lost to the insurgents, and Valencia threatened, it became increasingly necessary for the Republic to prevent the eastern march of Franco's forces.*

The loyalist soldiers were therefore ordered to hold existing lines at all costs, while all through the spring and early summer preparations were made for a massive thrust across the Ebro. The planning of the campaign was in the hands of General Vicente Rojo, while the overall command of the troops was entrusted to Colonel Juan Modesto.

With startling suddenness, at a quarter past midnight on the night of July 24, 1938, along a ninety mile front joining Mequiñenza in the north to Amposta in the south, the army of the Ebro went on the offensive. Only at Amposta was there a slight resistance. In six days an area of 270 square miles was conquered from the enemy. Dizzy with long-awaited success, the Republicans dreamed of a time when Franco's army would be rolled into the sea. For four months the bridgehead was held against seven powerful counteroffensives, and then the exhausted Republicans were thrown back to the Pyrenees, and the war was lost.

The crossing of the Ebro was the last triumph of the Republicans. Here is the diary of Edwin Rolfe, a young American poet, attached to the Lincoln Battalion:

25th July

Up at 6:30, start march along dried river bed of Río de Torre. Breakfast, but not able to eat. Order march. Bamboo growth along shore. See our shelling of Asco across river. Shells begin coming close to our river bed, where we're resting, at 8:05. Then crossing. Lamb first over in boat "All Right." Wolff last out of boat.

March on road toward crossroads to Gandesa. Turned off road, led nowhere. Have left road at crossroads where first squads of bombers and strafing planes appeared in sky and went over mountain and up another where we sent out scouting party to contact 3rd division.

Still waiting for signal from them. Losing valuable time.

26th July

6 A.M. ordered to rise again and reach peak of hill where, in an old farm hut, the Plana Mayor was located. Five more prisoners, ten in all captured. At 11 entered town of Fatarella. Got food, cigarettes, cigarros, cake, clams and octopus in tins, snails, tuna fish, sardines, beef in tomato sauce. Contacted brigade of 3rd Division about 2:30. All got shoes at Fatarella. Moved off at 3 P.M. down road to Gandesa, on which two companies of enemy had been spotted. Attacked, and 1st Company took 240 prisoners.

In evening, marched on till night on way to Gandesa, stopped to rest along country path, sent out patrol. Many shots, for two minutes panic. (Milt Robertson, Paolo, three others wounded.)

27th July

Deployed after three kilometer march against positions on hills held by enemy. Drove them from wooded height, then over another hill where our command post was established. Then, our men drove them off another ridge. Lamb, Hoshooley, Tabb, Mendelsohn wounded.

28th July

All day in same position. Command post moved one hill ahead on flank away from enemy under large figtree against a stone terrace wall. (Figs unripe)

Attacked. Men wounded lay in sun all day. Murra, Tom Page, others badly wounded.

Three attacks: 6-7 A.M., 10:30 A.M., and afternoon.

29th July

24th Brigade moved up today. Wolff, who is splendid officer, talked over plans with him. Other attacks—none successful. Quiet day.

30th July

At 5:30 A.M. two battalions of 24th Brigade attacked through our positions, drove fascists off hill ahead four times, but did not follow up, so enemy returned each time. Lay in gully till 10:30 when Brigade orders came for us to march away. Then order countermanded—we are to attack. But in meantime enemy attacked before we could return to our position, which we did rapidly. Now at 11:15 A.M. attack of enemy still on.

Enemy artillery shelled our ridge, two mules killed, no men. Shells fell right near our command post.

At 8 P.M. five three-motored bombers dropped load in valley behind our hill. Heavy.

All night flurry of fighting, bombs, artillery, etc. Our own artillery fell short, *behind* our lines.

31st July

Moved at dawn to another hill, behind Spanish positions. Had breakfast, then to sleep, wakened at 5:30 when shell landed 20 meters away from our stone house. Stayed around all evening. Shelling and bullets whistling by all time for days.

1st August

Moved across hill at 3:30 A.M., took up positions under artillery fire on side of hill behind Spanish battalion. At dawn our command post moved ahead to our former observation post, which directly faced the enemy. Our own artillery opened up, and at 11 A.M., after a short barrage, the Spanish moved up, went through our lines, and into attack. Lincolns went to their positions over "Valley of Death." Enemy artillery bombarded us all day. Our planes came over three times, bombing Gandesa. They told me the town was three kilometers away. It appeared to be much closer.

Evening, enemy shelled again in "Valley of Death" (Moors and Tercios). Place stank with dead. Enemy shells came over our ridge into valley behind, killing evacuated wounded, men with canteens at waterhole. Shells screamed directly overhead, as we lay against rock wall of a terrace, dropping twenty, thirty, fifty meters away. Hugged wall. As dark came, enemy began to use tracer bullets in rifles and machine-guns, the shells tracing a horseshoe against the sides of the bottle-neck-shaped gully systematically. Bodies stank. Bullets popped overhead, red tracers seemed to move slowly through air. Men screaming: *"Socorro, socorro!"* or groaning: *"Madre mía!"* long drawn out. Kept up all night long, intermittently, with hand-grenades, machine-guns, artillery just over in valley. Men dead by hundreds, mostly the enemy. Milman, commander of 24th, killed, bullet clean through head. Frank Stout badly wounded, trench mortar fragments in gut and groin.

Longest day I've ever spent.

2nd August

Battalion pulled out of line in A.M. (about 6). As usual, hasty distribution of food, all being handed out rapidly. Always the feeling we may move again, and then all our rations would be wasted. Mick almost in frenzy trying to hand out stuff rapidly AND systematically and *justly*. Lolled around.

Now, with almost three hundred losses, wounded, dead, and the threat of death hanging over the rest, our affection for those who remain has intensified. Each one is precious, almost in the way that one's wife is precious, and one fears for their safety as one does for the safety of a child. Men go out of their way to reassure, cheer up others, soothe, console them, lighten their fears.

They talk about cigarettes, lack of mail, food they're going to eat "if we ever get out of this," and their eyes smile, but they're deadly serious.

3rd August

Quiet day. Hot meals arrived, first time in ten days, since crossing the Ebro. At 8 P.M. twenty-nine enemy planes bombed the hill to the northeast where we rested two days ago. House now has shell-hole through the roof and side, where Wolff, Watt, others, myself, slept all day.

At 10:30 ordered to take up new positions on flank of Mac-Paps, on ridge along Corbera-Gandesa road. Moved after midnight, marching three kilometers. Slept under fire.

4th August

Quiet except for trench mortars, artillery, planes always overhead. Otherwise except for poker game with enemy money all quiet.

5th August

Quiet. Poker game all afternoon.

6th August

In morning telephone call to report back to Estado Mayor. Immediately Wolff suggested continuation of card game, since I'd won yesterday and he wanted to regain some of the dough. We played, and I kept winning, and meanwhile the enemy trench mortars opened up on us. I thought it would be ironic if staying on for the poker game would mean the end of us all.

After lunch walked to the Estado Mayor with Watt. On way he pointed out to me the spots where the Lincolns had split and decimated, just outside Corbera, in the April retreat.

7th August

Last night walked through Corbera. Place ruined, wrecked, after almost two weeks of intense artillery and air bombardment. City stinks with the bodies of the dead, unburied, in the ruins of houses, and horses and mules in the streets.

15th August

Arrived at Sierra de Pandols, one of higher hills, before dawn. Took over immediately positions vacated by 11th Brigade. Almost solid rock, couldn't dig in, no parapets, fortifications, etc. Dead still on ground.

Stayed on till 24th August.

The enemy were on higher hills to the southwest, looking down on us. They dug in with trenches, fortifications, barbed wire. We attacked next day, but couldn't get beyond the barbed wire. They had a great number of machine-guns and could throw hand-grenades down on us. Spent our nights fortifying—sand-bags, barbed wire. Sand-bags limited, little dirt to put in them. Third day opened up barrage with trench mortars, 81 millimeters, automatic artillery—six hours. Direct hits on machine-gun nests, blowing guns and men to pieces. A man's shirt and clothes were blown off, but he was unhurt except for slight shock and scratches on his arm. Always after bombardment we were still there, ready to stop any follow-up of artillery.

Next day similar bombardment two and a half hours.

Little water and bad food, which came up only at night.
No complaints, extreme fatigue, fighting and bombing all day.

*At this point Rolfe's diary comes to an end except for some scattered
and disjointed notes. One of them reads: "Knocked out. Spirit good.
No crabbing. Laugh and joke about it." But he was beyond laughing.
The tragedy of Spain haunted him for the few remaining years of his
life.*

*About the time Rolfe was moving up to a position on the Sierra de
Pandols, an English reporter, Robert Payne, found General Modesto
in his command post near Mora de Ebro:*

We reached Mora de Ebro in the afternoon, the bombed and
gutted village all black and green, with twisted iron bedsteads sitting
in the rubble. The sweet-sour smell of explosives hung everywhere.
Down river, the old concrete bridge was a heap of mangled wreckage,
but the pontoon bridge was untouched. It creaked crazily under the
wheels of the car, but it was wonderfully sturdy. No airplanes in
sight, and the sky like blue crystal.

All the way from Barcelona there has been that sharp blue crystalline light in the air, quick and fresh, and no sign of the war except for
the occasional farm-boys who spring out of nowhere to examine our
papers and then wave us on.

The farm-boys guarding the bridge at Mora de Ebro, with their
anti-aircraft guns hidden in the ruins, looked keen and alert. They are
immensely proud of their bridge, which is the life-line for most of
the Republican forces across the Ebro. They gave us wine from their
pigskins and showed us how to drink, lifting the skin high above the
head so that the wine reaches down to the back of the throat. They
have an unerring aim. Our own aim was unimpressive, as we splashed
the red wine all over our faces.

The question was where to find Juan Modesto, the commander of
the Army of the Ebro, known to have his headquarters somewhere
in the neighborhood. From one of the ruined buildings there could
be heard a low voice speaking in that peculiar timbre which is used

only on telephones. So we waited, and gathered the small dusty blue grapes from the vines, which were very sweet. For mile upon mile we had seen these vines withering in the sun.

About ten minutes after reaching Mora de Ebro a young lieutenant told us the road was clear.

"Clear to where?"

"To Modesto," he said, and smiled. By the way he smiled it was quite clear that he had an extraordinary affection for Modesto.

"But where is he?"

"Just follow the road. You'll know when you get there."

We were there twenty minutes later. "There" was a red bluff with zigzag trenches covered with the usual camouflage netting, and beyond the red bluff lay a farmhouse. Some peasants were working in the fields, or perhaps they were soldiers. Except for the zigzag trenches, there was no sign of a war—only the red earth and a quiet farmhouse and the rows of vines going into the distance. And the man standing on the red bluff silhouetted against the sky did not in the least resemble a general. He wore a white shirt open at the neck, khaki trousers, sandals. There were no badges of rank. He was tall and well-built with black hair streaming back from his forehead, his face deeply tanned. It was a powerful face, beautifully modeled, with a square jaw and high cheekbones; he looked less like a farmer than a young landed proprietor. He smiled easily and well, and walked with a spring-like motion—he was a superb physical specimen. Until three years ago he was a journeyman carpenter. Now he commands the Fifth Army.

He shouted like a boy as he led us down into the trench, his official headquarters, with maps and telephones littered on the plank tables. We were, I believe, the first correspondents who had seen him since the victorious crossing of the Ebro on July 24th, and the Spanish correspondents kept asking him questions about the crossing, and he answered quickly, his eyes shining. He was very pleased with his men, pleased with the progress of the war, pleased to have these young and eager correspondents around him. Wine was brought out. He traced the battle-lines on the maps, using the wine bottles to mark the point of furthest advance.

"We threw everything we had at them," he said, "and took them by surprise. Half our men crossed the Ebro swimming, and the other half went over in Catalan fishing-boats. We used every weapon we could think of, including *chevaux de frises*—a mediaeval instrument of torture specially calculated to frighten the Moors."

I hadn't the faintest idea what a *cheval de frise* is, and learned later that it was an iron ball with spikes, much feared by horsemen.

He was full of questions about Barcelona: how people were doing, what they were eating, and whether they were holding up against the bombing. He cursed planes and bombs. Then he talked about General Rojo, the chief of staff, the man most responsible for the crossing of the Ebro. "What a man! He knows everything! He is the bravest of the brave!"

"Did he cross the Ebro?" someone asked.

"No, he stayed in Barcelona. At a time like this, you understand, to stay in Barcelona is the real heroism." He went on: "It is much easier at the front. The food's better. The atmosphere is better. You're not so frightened. I pity a man who has to stay at his desk in Barcelona. There is no man in the world I have more respect for."

I had met General Rojo two days before at the Ministerio de la Guerra in an enormous baroque room with tapestries on the walls and a carved table which seemed at first to be littered with a vast jungle of maps, but on closer view the maps were neatly spread out. In the face of an entrenched enemy Rojo had planned the campaign which threw the Republican forces across the Ebro on a ninety mile front. He was a small, neat, precise man with a grey mustache and deepset eyes which looked infinitely weary.

There must have been a lull in the fighting, for no telephones rang, and no one came down into the trench with reports. Modesto decided to stretch his legs, for he had shown us the maps and it was time to relax. So we walked out over the red bluff, looking down on the sunken road.

What was astonishing was the quietness and loneliness of the scene. The farmhouse seemed to be deserted. The guards, squatting on their heels among the vines, were out of sight. Occasionally a car drove past, and sometimes on the distant hills there was the bright silver glint of a heliograph, as one company of troops near the front signalled to another. The heat came beating up from the earth, the mountains trembled in the heat-haze, and far off, skimming over the vines, making for the Sierra de Pandols, were the little snub-nosed yellow fighter-planes called *chatos,* belonging to the Republican Army, which resembled grasshoppers. When I said something about the quietness of the place, Modesto laughed and said: "We have to have time for sleep. We fight at night." Then for the first time I saw that his eyes were bloodshot.

Actually the silence was deceptive. Behind the green shutters of the farmhouse, behind the coils of barbed wire and the camouflage netting, behind the vineyards eternally stretching sunward, there was ceaseless activity. Sappers were burrowing into the earth, soldiers were cleaning guns, telegraph wires were humming, military dispositions were being made. The spies were sleeping, but at night they would make their way through enemy lines, and their sleep was a form of violent activity, just as the recharging of batteries is a violent activity; and along the red roads of Catalonia the peasants were carrying their pots and beds to Barcelona, shuffling through the heavy dust, very slowly but with the power of pistons.

We were walking across the bluff, looking at the *chatos* vanishing in the perfectly blue sky, when a boy came up, saluted smartly, and presented a report. Modesto read it, smiled, and gave the report back. The boy looked about fourteen, with a humorous mouth and a dark, sunburned face. There was an extraordinary paternal look in Modesto's eyes as he spoke of how the boy had made a long journey through enemy lines and returned with an important report on enemy installations. The boy's face turned the color of red litmus paper, while Modesto talked about him and the correspondents took notes.

The shadows were falling, and we were all conscious, I think, that the day was already passing into history. This lull was only temporary; and the boy's happiness was only temporary. There was something insufferably oppressive in the harsh sunlight, in the absence of any traffic along the road, in the decaying vineyards, in the flashing river winding below, and in the burned green and black village of Mora de Ebro. The air was somehow exhilarating and oppressive at the same time; and the sun's heat struck through our flesh and bones.

And then the attack came, or rather there were two very nearly simultaneous explosions. First three glistening Savoia-Marchettis came out of nowhere and dive-bombed the pontoon bridge we had crossed only a little while before, and the bombs falling on the river made a sound like millions of pieces of silk being torn to shreds. The air quivered, streaked with silver. There was no time to dive into a slit trench. We flung ourselves under some vines, those small stunted vines planted in neat rows close to the command post, cowering in the thin shadow of a two-foot high tree. Modesto had vanished, quick as lightning, into his command post. We crouched there, making ourselves as small as possible, curling up, trying desperately to be the size of a leaf. I remember, just before, talking to a young Spanish poet about Arthur Rimbaud, who seems to me the greatest of all modern French poets, and in an extraordinary way, between the staggering explosions, the whining of the bombs as they fell, and the crack of the anti-aircraft guns, we somehow succeeded in continuing the discussion, shouting ourselves hoarse.

Altogether twelve passes were made at the Mora de Ebro bridge by the three Savoia-Marchettis, and all of them failed. When the bombing was over, we saw the three beautiful silvery-blue planes vanishing over the hills, and the darkening sky was smeared with hundreds of grey smudges of smoke which the high winds overhead turned into strange shapes of wings and horses' heads and letters of the alphabet.

Afterwards—and this was a sound I never heard during the bombings of Barcelona—there was a beautiful rushing sound not unlike the sound of the wind springing up in a forest. It came, I think, from millions of little crumbs of dislodged earth as they settled quickly back again after being dislodged during the explosions.

When we had brushed all the dust and earth off our clothes, and seen the last of the three airplanes vanishing away, and heard the last of that soft whispering rushing sound which followed the bombardment, we had a little time to pause and to feel ourselves, to see that we were whole. The soldiers were shouting with glee. They had learned that the pontoon bridge remained undamaged and no one had been hurt in Mora de Ebro. Modesto was walking across the red bluff, silhouetted against the violet sky.

The wind must have been very strong high above us, for soon there was no trace of wings and horses' heads in the sky.

Then the second attack came.

Far away across the valley stood the sharp-toothed Sierra de Pandols, a bare bleak ominous mountain on which, as far as I could see, nothing had ever grown except perhaps a few small stunted trees. By day the mountain seemed to be made of burnished copper; in the evening light it glowed with a rich purple color. The top of this mountain suddenly burst into flame. It was something so entirely unexpected that we all wheeled round and stared with our mouths open; and the light of the flames stretched across miles of space and lit our faces, as we stood on the red bluff facing the dark valley already sinking deep into the night.

I could not imagine what could burn on the mountain, what the flames could feed on. At least twenty seconds passed before we heard the heavy rumbling of the artillery barrage, and by this time the bright flashing of the flames was already darkening into smoke, great billowing clouds of smoke. Gleams of fire continued to erupt along the top of the mountain, but they died quickly. Yet the mountain seemed to be alive, shaking and crumbling before our eyes, and the pounding went on. It was growing darker, there was no moon, but the first stars were coming out. The thin flames scrawled across the mountain-top were like the fringes of an immense black curtain which rose slowly until it filled half the sky. All round us the pigeons wheeled and moaned, confused in the shivering air.

Once again Modesto vanished. At the moment he heard the distant detonations, the rumbling, the strange heaving of the earth, he hurled himself into his dug-out. He made a single leap down into that underground chamber with its maps and tables and cane-bottomed chairs. There was a candle stuck in a wine bottle, and in the light of the candle he was studying the maps, while two or three other officers of the command-post stood around him. The telephone rang. I was standing on the third stair. I heard Modesto's clearcut voice: *"Bueno, camarada, bueno.* Hold on a little longer." Modesto looked very calm, his face clean against the candlelight. His left hand held the telephone, and his right moved across the map, pausing to pencil in a gun-position, a redoubt, a straggly defence line. He was giving orders, but all the orders were the same. "Hold on through the night. Supplies will soon be coming up. Hold on."

There must have been six or seven telephones all ringing at once, and he would pass from one to another easily, lightly, like a man accustomed to listening to desperate cries for help each night, knowing that he could offer no alleviation of suffering to the men who were crouching in dug-outs on the hill, while the flames roared out of the sky and the red-hot shells exploded all round them. His face in the candlelight was a mask, dead-white, strangely motionless.

I went out on the red bluff again and watched the mountain boiling with smoke, and now there were only a few startling gleams of fire, but the ragged ends of the smoke-cloud were black arms stretching across the sky. The stars were brighter now, and the rumbling of each exploding shell seemed to grow more distinct as the night wore on.

And then suddenly, inexplicably, there was silence. After eighteen or nineteen minutes the barrage ceased as shockingly as it began. There were no more flames. The smoke-cloud lifted itself off the mountain, the violet sky poured through, and the hidden stars came out again. Far away to the east a small fighter plane shot across a patch of somber light and made its way towards the mountains.

About five minutes later Modesto sent a message, inviting all of us down into the command-post.

With the map in front of him he pointed out the positions of the German guns and the line across the mountains held by the Republican troops. There had been some losses during the barrage, but the lines were holding. "They have tried hitting us there for a week," he said, "but our lines have been maintained." A young Spanish correspondent said: "How many heavy guns have they got?"

"Eighty-four," Modesto answered.

"How many have we got?"

"Three."

They were guns from warships which had proclaimed their loyalty to the Republicans.

"Is that bad?"

"Yes, it's bad. They're bringing up more and more guns, and more bombers. More and more."

His voice trailed away. The telephone bell rang again. This time it was Barcelona with some question about supplies, and when this was over, someone asked what would be the official communiqué for the day. He grinned and said: "Along the Ebro front, all quiet." High up on the Sierra de Pandols, Moors and Foreign Legionaries were being fought back by the weary and battered Republicans.

It was dark now, and there was some talk of where we should eat and where we should put up for the night. There were more telephone calls, this time to Lister's headquarters, and we heard later that we were invited to dine with Lister at his farmhouse further along the road. With a soldier on the running board to direct us, with headlights no more than faint blue slits, we drove at a snail's pace along the winding road. As we climbed higher we could see far away a ghostly blue flicker extending about a mile along the road from Mora de Ebro—the heavy supply-laden trucks were coming over the bridge.

We crawled along the road for about three miles and then turned down a narrow path leading to a large farmhouse sheltered by a spur of the mountains. The farmhouse gleamed in the starlight. Cedar trees stood in front, and there were guards everywhere. In this mysterious silent place I had the feeling, unlike the red bluff where Modesto had his headquarters, that every approach was guarded and booby-trapped. The place smelled of gasoline and grapes. It was a large, well-built farmhouse, but Lister was not inside. He was in the court-yard, and to our eyes this was the most fantastic courtyard we had ever seen. It was fantastic because against all the rules of probability it was brightly lit with kerosene lamps, and was open to the sky.

We were blinded when we entered the courtyard after an hour of peering cautiously into the thick murkiness of a sunken road. Lister was sitting at the head of an immense table, which was being pre-pared for dinner. He was in his shirt sleeves, a heavy man with his back towards us. He must have heard our car coming down the drive-way, and he knew we were there, and he was quite properly paying no attention to us, immersed in some problem of his own. Then, very slowly, with one hand on his knee, the other on his revolver holster, he turned towards us—a beautiful, studied action.

You could feel the electricity in the air, the electricity which Lister generated. He was a powerful man, brutal, pock-marked, deeply sun-burned, with thick black hair, a broad forehead, a small nose, a heavy mouth. He had a boxer's shoulders and a boxer's grace of movement, but he was growing fat. Modesto was pure Castilian and resembled an aristocrat; Lister, an Asturian miner and *dinamitero,* resembled a peasant. They were like people from different worlds.

There was something grotesque about this courtyard open to the sky, filled with so many lamps, with the white cloth on the table and the gleaming cutlery. There were rifles stacked in the corners, and there were guards armed to the teeth with revolvers in their belts and hand-grenades hanging like buttons all over their uniforms. In the light of the kerosene lamps the shadows jumped all over the court-yard, and somewhere a dog howled.

Lister was enjoying the impression he made. He was the perfect host. He introduced his staff: they were all very young, none of them more than thirty, and most of them were Asturians. He had a habit of leaning back in the chair and sticking his fingers in his belt. They were powerful fingers the size of sausages. I kept thinking of the stories I had heard about him. They said he was one of those who had attacked the Montaña barracks in Madrid during the early days of the war, and it was Lister who had picked up the Fascist officers on the third floor and simply thrown them down to the ground, thus killing them without wasting any ammunition. Three or four times he had stopped a retreat by killing his own men out of hand as a warning to others. He was completely and perfectly ruthless, but as he moved about the courtyard he was like those very strong men who behave with exaggerated gentleness for fear of crushing others.

I was awed by Lister, and so were the Spanish correspondents. There was none of the easy *camaraderie* we enjoyed with Modesto. We sat on benches round the table, while Lister sat in a plump, gilded chair which must have been taken from the manor of a great landowner: it was the kind of chair the Cardinal de Richelieu might have sat on. It was Lister's throne, but it did not look out of place in that courtyard.

The meal was enormous. There was duck soup followed by fish and lamb and an incredible *bombe* of ice-cream. There were four different kinds of wine, "all," Lister said, "captured from the enemy." I suspect that the *chef* was also captured from the enemy, for at our request he appeared at the end of the meal, and he looked a timid, frightened person, as much in awe of Lister as we were ourselves. But with this awe went immeasurable gratitude, for we had gone hungry in Barcelona.

"If I had known you were coming, there might have been time to give you a really good meal," Lister said, grinning.

It was a pleasant grin, and he talked well. There were people who said he was illiterate, and had been given a high position in the army only because he had a great following among the troops, but he was well-read and superbly intelligent on the one subject which interested him above all others—revolution. He talked of revolutions like a professor, analyzing them, always seeking the main lines of power. In his view Europe was passing through a revolutionary phase, and the Spanish Civil War corresponded to the revolutionary wars of France at the end of the eighteenth century. The same forces were at work; power was restored to the people, whose first task was to destroy their oppressors. The Terror, then as now, was the weapon of the people against their adversaries.

"But the Terror is terribly wasteful," I said. "They killed far too many people. I don't see the justification of the Terror which kills off people like the scientist Lavoisier."

"You don't?"

"No. Nothing will convince me that the problem can be solved by guillotining the best men in the country."

I should have known better. I was sitting next to Lister, and for some reason he took the words as a personal affront. He roared with rage, pounded the table with his enormous fists, while the blood rushed to his cheeks and his small eyes seemed to explode.

"Then you are a fascist!" he shouted. "Anyone who thinks like that must be a fascist! My God, do I have to shoot you—to put some sense in your head?"

His hand went to the revolver at his belt. He took it out and slapped it on the table. There was a terrible silence, broken by Boleslavskaya, the correspondent of *Pravda,* an extraordinary woman with her dyed red hair and enormous bust, who said quietly: "Put it away, put it away—" Lister was in no mood to obey, until she asked him about the attack on the Sierra de Pandols earlier in the evening, and then his rage against me gave way to a greater rage against the enemy massed behind the sierras. He shook his fists at the enemy. "Why do they come here?" he shouted. "Moors, Italians, Germans, what are they doing here? We don't want their dung here! Let them go! Let them go!"

A surprising thing was happening. The heavy face softened and all the roughness of his voice disappeared as he spoke about the Spanish earth he was fighting for. He even scooped up some earth from the courtyard and let it pour through his fingers onto the table, and all the time he was speaking about the young recruits he had molded into shape until they were able to form great armies.

"Who are they to come and take this earth away from us?" he said. "Who says we shouldn't kill these people? We have suffered enough from them—families, villages, whole towns wiped out." Then he added: "I don't hate them any more—it is an emotion too deep for hate!"

After dinner he spread the maps over the table and traced the enemy lines with his heavy fingers, and once more he showed us how the Fifth Army had made its way across the river deep into enemy territory.

Moths flung themselves against the whistling kerosene lamps, and all the time the heat seemed to be growing greater, the air windless and still, while Lister described those miraculous days when the Army of the Ebro went over to the offensive, telling us about these things so well that we could see the troops going over in the fishing boats and fanning out into the defiles through the mountains. It was about one o'clock when we left. We were taken to a neighboring farmhouse where mattresses had been thrown down on the floor. In the morning a messenger came from Lister, inviting us for breakfast. We asked when we could go up to the front.

"No one is going up to the front," he said, and then we knew that the situation was far more dangerous than we had thought.

Two days later we were back in Barcelona, attending a farewell party at the Hotel Majestic in honor of Theodore Dreiser, who had long ago come to the conclusion that all the troubles of Europe were due to Masons and Catholics acting in unison, and he insisted on haranguing us on his favorite subject. Hitler and Stalin were Catholics. Franco was a Mason. Did we know—did any of us know—the power of the Masonic conspiracy known as the Grand Orient?

Dreiser can rarely have enjoyed a more distinguished and respectful audience. André Malraux was there, his face convulsed in dreadful tics, his handshake limp, his hair damp and matted over his forehead. Ernst Toller was smiling his sad refugee smile, only his enormous warm brown eyes suggesting a ferocious compassion. There was Boleslavskaya of *Pravda* and Herbert Matthews of *The New York Times* and Louis Fischer, dark and saturnine, and sometime during the conversation James Lardner drifted in, looking pale and ghostly from his wounds. Dreiser could not be budged. He was going back to America and he was going to tell them about the great accomplishments of the Spanish Republic, but it was all the fault of the Masons and the Catholics. There was going to be a terrible war. There was nothing in the world which would stop this war, and he was glad to be going back to a country where people had more sense than to obey the orders of the Grand Orient and the Pope.

Dreiser's voice quavered with passion, and he evidently believed all this nonsense. He was a little drunk, for the Majestic had plentiful supplies of wine and almost no food. We lived on pale soup, bread cobs, squid and corn husks which pretended to be coffee.

"I tell you there's going to be a war more terrible than any war that has been visited on man," he said, his dewlaps shaking, the familiar old face assuming a strange aspect of pride. "There's no hope for Europe. The whole continent is riddled with the disease of war. I may not live to see it, but by God I know it's coming!"

I think Malraux was the one most perplexed by this diatribe. It was not that he did not believe Dreiser: it was simply that he saw deeper, and more perturbing, causes for the war which was coming. Toller, too, was uneasy, looking, as he often looked, like a hurt child. Matthews listened with appalled politeness, and only Boleslavskaya was gently amused by the sight of the doddering old man weaving his spell of doom, while the chandeliers tinkled overhead and the lights went out and the white-gloved waiters set candles on wine bottles round the table.

Toller was leaving for Madrid—a secret journey by air at night over occupied territory—and after dinner I went up to his room to help him pack. I thought it would be an uneventful evening, listening to Toller and drawing him out. We were halfway up the candlelit stairs when we saw a Negro leaning against the wall on a landing. He was evidently an American Negro from the International Brigade. He was leaning there out of weariness, and we heard the slow steady rise and fall of his breathing. He had huge black hands and a fine gleaming black face, and there was a submachine-gun under his arm. As we passed he must have heard our footsteps, for he was instantly awake, and he began waving the machine-gun at Toller. It had recently been oiled, and glinted in the light of the leaping candle-flames.

"You don't have to wave that thing at me," Toller said, as one might speak to a child. "I'm Ernst Toller."

"Hah, Ernst Toller, pleased to meet you, sah!"

The Negro, who wore a khaki shirt with his sleeves rolled up, put out one enormous and thickly veined black arm. Toller shook the hand firmly. The Negro's eyeballs were pure white. A look of suspicion crossed his face; his smile hardened; and perhaps he had forgotten where he was and thought he was back again on the Ebro. The black hand went slowly back to the oiled gun.

"You're just a fuckin' liar!" the Negro said, dead beat, leaning against the wall, the black fingers fumbling for the trigger as he waved the gun at us. He said in a tone of triumph: "Ernst Toller, sah? Ise read about dat feller! Writes poetry! How do I know youse the same guy?" He dug the machine-gun in the pit of Toller's stomach. I think Toller expected to be killed. There was an extraordinary look of compassion on his face. It was as though he was already forgiving the man about to murder him. The wind came down the stairwell, and sometimes the candle on the landing nearly gutted. It was the strangest place to die, there, on the third or fourth floor of the Hotel Majestic, with the candles spitting all round us and the tallest Negro I ever saw jabbing him with his machine-gun, and what made it all the more horrible was that the Negro was incredibly drunk with weariness, could hardly stand and had evidently returned from the Ebro only a few hours before, or perhaps he had only arrived a few minutes before. He was so powerfully built that he was like an enormous black statue with huge muscles rippling over his skin.

He gave one ferocious jab at Toller's stomach and said: "How do I know youse Ernst Toller, sah? How do I know? Let's hear your fuckin' poems!"

So Toller began to recite from the book of poems he wrote in prison, *The Book of Swallows*. He recited in German, speaking very softly, as though to himself, his eyes closed, swaying a little. The Negro listened with his huge bony head held a little to one side, then he let the machine-gun clatter to the floor, and said: "Ernst Toller, sah, pass on!"

Toller however continued to recite his poems. The Negro gazed at him as though fascinated. From downstairs there came Malraux's high voice as he ordered a car to take him to the Ritz Hotel, and somewhere on one of the distant landings a maidservant was walking stealthily on slippered feet, keys ringing from her belt. And then at last, with Toller still reciting his poems, the Negro slumped to the floor.

I thought that was the end of the excitement for one evening, but there was more—much more—to come. We went up to Toller's apartment, threw open the door, and saw an enormous man, stark naked, jumping up and down in one of those small hand-baths which were commoner in Victorian times than our own. He was pouring water over himself, and his whole body was glistening and shining in the light of candles he had stuck along the dresser.

In Barcelona in those days everything was unexpected, nothing at all happened according to rule and the sight of the huge hairy body glistening with soap was not particularly strange, though it startled us. Toller's room was already in an indescribable mess, for he had been packing at intervals during the day, so that the bed and the floor were covered with clothes and the innumerable mementoes he had picked up in the war. The visitor was General Hans Kahle, the famous General "Hans," late of the German Army, now one of the commanders on the Tortosa front on leave in Barcelona. He was almost as legendary as Lister, and in a rather brutal Prussian way almost as handsome as Modesto.

And then when he was dressed he told stories for hour upon hour, while we listened like children at his feet.

Once he said: "I'm not Lister. I can't shoot fear-crazed men out of hand. One does what one can. Not long ago, on the Tortosa front, my men were breaking. I didn't know what to do. In the end I told my orderly to bring me a large basin of water and a kitchen chair and set it up in the middle of the highway, and then very leisurely I sat on the kitchen chair and took off my boots and socks and let my feet soak in the water. The soldiers saw me, and the message went round that I thought the battle was going so well that I could afford to take off my stinking stockings and bathe my feet. And they were ashamed, and went back into the line. . . ."

Later that night Barcelona was bombed again.

The Last Days

DURING the fall of 1938 the Nationalists succeeded in accumulating overwhelming supplies of guns, tanks and airplanes on the Ebro front. The Non-Intervention Committee, which was introduced to prevent arms from reaching either side of the conflict, had long ago abdicated its functions, and the great powers had already written off the Spanish Republic.

The Republic fought on. The people of Barcelona were starving, and they were being bombed relentlessly by the Italian planes based on Majorca. Yet somehow the Army of the Ebro received food and ammunition from the hinterland. On December 23rd Franco opened the offensive which would take him to the Pyrenees.

With the equipment he had amassed he could hardly fail. Slowly, doggedly, fighting every inch of the way, the Republicans were thrown back, but even then it took Franco more than a month to reach Barcelona. Here is the account of the last hours of Barcelona, written by Dr. Marcel Junod of the International Red Cross:

January, 1939. The front rapidly came nearer and nearer to Barcelona. The prisons were chock full of prisoners the Republican troops had brought back with them as they retreated.

In the city air-raid warnings followed each other in constant succession. All the military and civilian services were paralyzed. In the villages along the coast, ten, twenty, fifty cars were waiting for supplies of petrol. When the sirens began to howl, mechanics, control officers, drivers, and passengers all fled to the countryside. The chaos was indescribable.

Returning to Barcelona one night, Marti and I were caught on the Caldetas road by an air-raid warning. All the headlights of our convoy were suddenly extinguished. Above the noise of airplane-engines we heard the sound of explosions not far away. Sudden flashes of light in the sky indicated the bursting of antiaircraft shells. For all we knew the planes were gliding overhead with their engines shut off, waiting for our lights to go on again. Or they might return. We waited for about a quarter of an hour in silence, our nerves tensed. Then we went on again, hunched up in our seats.

The streets of the town were filthy. The scavengers no longer removed the waste, and a disgusting smell arose everywhere. A shortage of water began to make itself felt. Most people stayed in their houses. Here and there mobs had begun to pillage the food stores. From my window I could see men and women scurrying along with sacks filled with plundered foodstuffs. Isolated shots sounded from time to time. *Paco* was the Catalan word used to describe them in imitation of the short sharp sound.

Requests for food came to us from the prisons. All we could send was a little flour and condensed milk. Our food stocks were almost exhausted.

The relatives of the imprisoned men were becoming more and more anxious about their fate. Some of them came to me to beg me to do everything possible to prevent a massacre or new transfers.

On January 19th I visited the British Embassy to try to find out from the British Minister if he knew anything about the intentions of the Republican Government toward the five thousand prisoners held in the town.

At the French Embassy I was referred to the assistant military attaché, a lieutenant. He was a little man and he received me with an air of importance.

"What are you so disturbed about?" he asked.

"But, Monsieur Lieutenant, the Nationalist forces are less than twenty miles away now. They can be here tomorrow, and the government . . ."

"That's not my opinion," he declared decidedly. "Barcelona will not fall."

I was dumfounded.

"On what do you base that opinion, Monsieur Lieutenant?"

"How shall I explain that? It's just an impression, like heat and cold."

I did not pursue the subject.

However, the French ambassador himself, M. Jules Henry, shared my misgivings and he got into touch with Juan Negrín. A reply came on January 23rd to the effect that there was to be a general transfer of prisoners. But the chaos was so great that the order was only partly carried out.

In the morning of January 26th, the governor of the women's prison of Las Cortes rang us up. She was at her wits' end. The relatives of the prisoners had been outside the prison in large numbers for three days, trying to stop any transfers. Five soldiers who had been ordered to remove a number of prisoners had had to abandon their task in face of the threatening attitude of the mob. She was unable to get into touch by telephone with the Central Prison Administration. There was no reply.

Marti and I did not hesitate. It was clear that we must go there.

We drove in our car toward the suburbs to the nearest point of the front line. On the Diagonal, the great highway of Barcelona, we passed several lorries full of soldiers. On entering the Los Hermános Badíos Square, we were stopped by a Republican control point. A line of cars drawn up along the pavement was guarded by militiamen armed with tommy guns. All the cars had been requisitioned to provide transport for the Republican rearguard.

"Bajen" (Get out), ordered a militiaman with a revolver in his hand.

I made a sign to the driver to stay at the wheel and I got out to negotiate.

"You can see that this is a Red Cross car," I said. "You have no right to requisition it."

The man hesitated.

"Where are you going to?" he demanded.

Again he hesitated and then he consulted his chief.

"Siga!" said the latter.

I jumped back into the car and we set off quickly.

At the prison of Las Cortes we drove directly into the courtyard. All around were the faces of women pressed against the bars of the cell windows.

"Long live the Red Cross!" they shouted excitedly. "Long live the Red Cross! Save us!"

I went to the office of the governor. She was a fair-haired young woman heavily made up. All the keys of the cells were together in a pile on her desk. Her wardresses were also present, looking awkward and dirty. The anxiety on their rather dull faces was hardly less than that which was finding expression in the shouts of the prisoners. They were no doubt asking themselves with good reason whether the roles were now about to be reversed. The release of the prisoners meant imprisonment for them, and they now begged me to afford them the protection of the Red Cross.

"I have always carried out my duties objectively," said the governor with her painted lips, "and I have done nothing but my duty." And then she added: "If you think I ought to open the cell doors and release the prisoners, I am ready to do so."

At that moment artillery opened up behind the prison. It was a Republican battery sending over its last shells. It was soon spotted by the Nationalist artillery, which returned the fire fiercely.

There was no time to be lost. I had seen a lorry standing in the prison yard, and when the prisoners were released I put the old and the sick women into it. But then they wanted to take their miserable things with them. One of them clung desperately to an old chair. They could not bring themselves to leave the wretched debris of their possessions behind in their cells where they had lived for months, sometimes for years. In the end I had to raise my voice imperatively.

The other prisoners, who were able to walk, went off on their own, surrounded by their delighted relatives.

Then we left. The prison stood empty behind us. I felt sorry for the governor and I took her along with me.

In the meantime another drama was being played out.

Dominating the harbor and the sea stands the ancient castle of Montjuich, which was used as a prison. There were about six hundred military and political prisoners held there, and all that was left of the guard was an officer and seven men.

Nationalist warships which had anchored broadside about three miles from the shore had opened fire on the fort in the belief that it was occupied by Republican troops.

From the Calle Lauría the members of our delegation had witnessed the bombardment, and one of our Belgian nurses, Madame Perdomo, had decided to drive out to Montjuich with our chauffeur to find out what had happened.

When she arrived, the bombardment was still going on. The excited officer in command immediately took her to the sick bay. A shell had entered through the window of one of the cells and exploded inside, blowing off one prisoner's head and wounding a number of others. Panic reigned both among guards and prisoners.

The shells came over pitilessly, one after the other, at regular intervals. In agreement with the officer of the guard, Madame Perdomo caused a white flag to be hoisted over the castle and the bombardment ceased at once.

The officer handed over the keys of the cells to our nurse and then, fearing to be seized by the prisoners, he fled with his seven men. But the hoisting of the white flag had also been observed in Barcelona, where it was supposed that the guard had mutinied. A detachment of sixty men was sent off at once to suppress the mutiny. On the way the detachment fell in with the officer of the guard and his men, and he was taken back to the castle with a revolver in the small of his back.

Arriving at the castle, the men broke down the gate with the butts of their rifles and then cautiously entered, fearing a trap. But all that awaited them in the courtyard was a Red Cross nurse.

Everything seemed quiet inside the fort. The prisoners were still in their cells, but anguished faces appeared at the bars.

"What are you doing here?" demanded the officer in charge of the detachment. "And what's the meaning of the white flag?"

"Señor Captain," replied Madame Perdomo, "I came up here during the bombardment to prevent the massacre of defenseless men in their cells. There were no more Republican troops on the hill, and I had the white flag hoisted to stop the bombardment."

The captain was dumbfounded, but the calm assurance of the woman impressed him.

"We thought there had been a mutiny," he declared. "I have been sent up here to shoot everybody. However, there's been enough bloodshed. But my orders are to hoist the Republican flag again. Barcelona has not yet surrendered."

The white flag was hauled down, the Republican flag hoisted in its place, and then the soldiers departed. The fighting was coming closer.

Half an hour later the bombardment opened up again even more heavily than before. There was now no hope of making the Nationalists believe in a surrender, so our nurse hurriedly tore off two strips of red cloth and sewed them on to the white flag. A prisoner then climbed up to the ramparts and hoisted it above the Republican flag. At once the bombardment ceased.

Six hundred men raised their eyes full of hope to where the red cross on the white ground fluttered from the mast.

On January 26th, at half past one, the first tank rolled down the street and came to a halt before our quarters. The crew consisted of German soldiers. Perched on top of the tank was a smiling woman giving the fascist salute to the crowd. I recognized her as one of the released prisoners from Las Cortes. It was a German Jewess who had been arrested and imprisoned as a Trotskyist.

During the afternoon red and gold monarchist flags began to appear on the balconies of Barcelona, and a great Nationalist standard was hoisted on the Tibidado hill. An endless column of Requetés in red berets, Falangists, and Moors with their patient mules moved slowly down toward the town.

By evening Barcelona was completely occupied.

On the day after the fall of Barcelona, Count Ciano, the Italian foreign minister, wrote in his diary that "the victory in Spain bears only one name, and that is the name of Mussolini." This statement was a half-truth, for the victory also bore the name of Hitler.

But though Barcelona was taken, there was still hope—a very small hope. The Republicans clung to the possibility of last-minute aid from England, France, or America, and they remembered previous wars in which Spain had succeeded in overthrowing its oppressors even after most of the state had been occupied. The mood of the Republicans, impersonated in the Prime Minister, Dr. Juan Negrín, was resistance to the bitter end, to the last drop of blood. Negrín had Churchill's bulldog quality.

As Franco's army swept toward the Pyrenees, hope grew dimmer. Madrid and Valencia might be saved, but Catalonia was close to defeat. There remained one final ceremony to be performed, and at Negrín's orders this took place in the castle of Figueras close to the border—a final meeting on Spanish soil of the Cortes elected with so much enthusiasm three years before.

Herbert Matthews describes the ceremony:

The Castle had been a fortress, prison, barracks, but never in its long history had it been the seat of government. It was built on a hill dominating the town—a huge rambling structure, with outer and inner walls, a drawbridge and deep cellars. Safe and powerful it certainly was, but completely devoid of any facilities for being the seat of government. Pieces of paper had been pasted up on various doors: *"Ministerio de Estado," "Presidencia de Consejo,"* and the like, and inside were bare rooms with plain tables and chairs. In contrast with the luxurious buildings in Barcelona, nothing could have been more depressing.

Indeed, every physical aspect of the whole situation was depressing. Figueras was a madhouse of bewildered officials and soldiers, struggling desperately, not only with their own work, but with those thousands of swarming refugees who filled every house and doorway and covered almost every inch of the streets where men, women and children slept through the bitterly cold nights with almost no food, and certainly no place to go.

The inevitable drift was toward the frontier, and there the refugees found the French Gardes Mobiles. My guess that day was that there were no fewer than 250,000 unfortunates strung out all along the road and in every village from Mataró to the frontier. That proved approximately right, but I never thought that virtually all of them would end up in French concentration camps. . . .

But, in spite of everything, there was that high, indomitable resolve which somehow gave a feeling of hope, despite the evidence of one's eyes. Negrín was so positive about it, and I knew the man too well to think that he was bluffing.

"The war will continue, the Army is establishing new lines; the rearguard is being reorganized," he told me. "This is where we stay as long as we can, and we hope it will be indeed long—that is, until we can get back to Barcelona and Madrid."

Foolish words, you might say, but the spirit that prompted them was the same as that which had saved Spain before. You cannot speak with contempt of people who do not know when they are beaten. At worst, they had the foolhardiness of Don Quixote.

However, there was no loss of authority, except in so far as the difficulties of communication hindered the transmission of orders. There were no mutinies or rioting or usurpations of power. The chaos did not come from that. The customs and police authorities were doing their duties as usual. The Army was taking orders from the Government. There was still plenty of money available. A recovery seemed possible, but only on one condition—and this everyone realized—that new materiel be allowed in. For a few days the Spaniards nourished the hope, despite all disappointments, that France would relent. . . .

When I went back to Figueras (from twenty-four hours in Perpignan) the hopes rose again. There had been a lull at the front and a line—a very weak one, but still a line—had been established, with the troops actually counterattacking in some places. Communications, although still bad, had improved. To Figueras had been given a new life, and one with genuine order. Traffic was being routed with reasonable speed, the refugees were being cleared out slowly but steadily, and those who remained were being fed free at the popular restaurants, where they received one dish per meal, of rice or beans and meat. . . .

A reorganization of the Army staff had taken place. Sarabia had been removed and General Jurado named to succeed him. The stories we heard in Perpignan of wholesale desertions or the flight of the Army were false. There had been some desertions, but relatively few in the circumstances, and I saw more soldiers returning toward their units than straggling toward the frontier.

Above all, there was the fact that the Cortes were to meet the following day, February 1. For those who had fought so hard and so vainly, that was somehow a symbol of hope and promise. It meant that the Second Spanish Republic still existed—against Franco and the whole world. The constitution was to be obeyed; the framework of democratic government, however weakened, was to be supported once more. A gesture was to be made, as truly Spanish as any ever made in the tragic and glorious history of the country of Don Quixote.

To go through Junquera alone was a matter of a full hour in a car, crawling by inches through swarming humanity, and often having to stop because of jammed traffic. Fires were springing up all alongside the road, in the fields and back in the hills. The scene was an unending gypsy camp, as those thousands of pathetic individuals, who had nothing to do with war except to suffer in it, settled down for another cold night.

We were back in Figueras early the next morning, for the meeting of the Cortes. No time had been set, because the Government did not want to send an invitation to the Rebels to bomb them. It was a day of tension, because everyone expected Figueras to be badly bombed. As we drove in, the trucks bearing the artistic treasures of Spain which the Government had so carefully packed and preserved through the war were lined up along the road, ready to be driven to safety. The weather was springlike, and the Government's protecting planes, working in relays from the airfield near Vilajuiga, were able to keep up a fairly constant patrol. . . .

Not even at Cadiz had the Cortes been held in so strange and picturesque a setting—down in the dungeon-like vaults of the old castle on the hill. At one time the place had been used for stables, and the stalls were still there, on one side of the low-ceilinged hall. The night was chilly, and some of the ministers and deputies kept their overcoats on throughout the session. The twelve ministers were squeezed together on a plain bench too short for them. Other benches and chairs had been placed facing them, and at right angles on their right, while on the left a dais and a rude tribune had been fixed up for Martínez Barrio, the President of the Cortes. . . .

Azaña, to his eternal disgrace, had refused to take the risk of being present. Some others, like La Pasionaria, were in Madrid and could not get there; others, like Portela Valladares, who had rallied to the Government when it seemed likely to win, had thought better of their loyalty; still others, like Caballero and Araquistain, were nursing their bitterness in other places. In all, there were present less than seventy of the full Cortes of four hundred and seventy-three deputies.

It was in this setting, with the Republican flag displayed for the last time at a Cortes of the Second Republic, with its tribune covered with red brocade, with cheap carpets on the stone floor and plain wooden seats, that Martínez Barrio tapped his gavel at 10:25 on the night of February 1, 1939, and the session began.

"You are meeting in difficult circumstances," he said. "You are the legitimate and authentic representation of the people. Keep your passions in check. This session will probably be historic in the life of Spain. You are writing a page of honor for the future of the Spanish fatherland."

Negrín was the first speaker, and the only one who mattered. Those of us who knew his state of physical exhaustion and discouragement wondered whether he would be able to keep on talking. Several times he had to stop to pull himself together, and sometimes he seemed almost too dazed to express his thoughts coherently, especially after his notes gave out when he was halfway through, and he had to speak extemporaneously. I do not believe any text of his speech has ever been published, and I have only my disjointed notes to go by.

He spoke of the "severe atmosphere" of war through which they were passing, but said that now "spirits were tranquilized and fears calmed." There could have been "a definite disaster," but it had been avoided. For a while "a wave of panic had almost asphyxiated the rearguard, paralyzed the Army, destroyed the Republic." There had been "a lack of communication between the Government and its people, and an exploitation of that panic by the enemy, but in fact there had been no rising against the Government. In fact, the contrary was true."

He then went on to explain why there had been a panic. There were "too many people in Loyalist Spain. Millions had fled before the Fascists, and that is the best proof of the feeling of our people. The massacre of Santa Coloma de Queralt demoralized the rearguard. It was no surprise, and the Government was prepared. After the fall of Tarragona it had asked the French Government to accept 100,000 to 120,000 old people, women and children, but had been refused.

"Public order has been maintained by public will, and not by force. The Government's energy is national. In three days it had solved the refugee problem, thanks to the French Government."

Again he spoke of the panic, which had affected many soldiers as well as civilians. They were taking "strong measures," but "the morale of the Army was good." There had been "a panic organized by provocateurs, by lies, which undermined morale. Those were our worst enemies, and we could not combat them for lack of means. There are few examples of an army that fought so long against such odds. Many were without arms, waiting for their comrades to die so that they could pick up their rifles. The lack was not their fault, nor the Government's." (This was the only time in his speech that he showed emotion, and for a moment it seemed as though he would break down.)

"Our terrible and tremendous problem," he continued, "has always been the lack of arms. We, a legitimate Government, had to buy arms clandestinely, as contraband, even in Germany and Italy! We managed to make some, and scrape along!"

Fixing his eyes steadily on us of the foreign press, he told of the Government's loyalty and how it had kept all its promises, hoping thereby that the democracies would change their attitude and give the Government a chance. With deep bitterness the Premier spoke next of "the farce of 'Non-Intervention' and the Italian withdrawal [of 100,000 men] followed by new shipments of men and materiel. . . .

"We are fighting for the independence of our country," he went on, "and also for democracy. This is a struggle of two civilizations, of Christianity against Hellenism. We are defending other countries—which are not only not helping us, but are causing us our greatest difficulties.

"To save the peace of Europe they let Austria go, and cut up Czechoslovakia. If the time came when Spain would provide one more sacrifice, would they be in a stronger position to meet the aggressors, to defend themselves? Here is where the answer will come to the question of whether a few totalitarian powers will control the world, or whether it will continue divided. Hitler and Mussolini are wrong in placing their support behind Franco, because the people are not with him, and because the fruits of victory will never be gained."

The Premier then offered three points which would be accepted by the Loyalists as conditions of a just peace: First, a guarantee of the independence of the country; second, a guarantee that the Spanish people would decide on its regime and its destiny; third, that when the war was over, all persecutions and reprisals would end.

"We will fight to save Catalonia," he concluded, "and if we lose it we will continue to fight in the central zone. Countries do not live only by victories, but by the examples which their people have known how to give in tragic times."

It was on that noble theme that the long speech ended. No one could call it an oratorical masterpiece; it was disjointed, and badly delivered, by a man so exhausted that he could hardly stand, yet it should take its place with the great documents of Spanish history.

Representatives of each of the major parties then followed, with brief addresses. Martínez Barrio asked for an explicit vote of confidence in the Government, which was passed unanimously, by acclamation.

So ended the last Cortes of the Second Spanish Republic.

The first Spanish Republic, which came into being in 1873, ended tragically less than two years later. The second Spanish Republic was a little luckier: it lasted for nearly eight years.

Meanwhile Madrid and Valencia were still holding out, and the Republic was still in nominal control of about a quarter of Spain. Negrín still hoped to keep on fighting. But in Madrid, where weariness and exhaustion had set in, and the growing power of the Communists was feared, a new Defense Council was set up by General Segismundo Casado, the head of the Republican Central Army. The council included representatives of all the political groups except the Communists, and its main task was to arrange a cease-fire and an honorable peace.

Negrín was in Valencia when he heard that the Defense Council had assumed supreme powers. Álvarez del Vayo, the foreign minister of the Republic, here recounts how the government took the news of the rebellion in Madrid:

The Prime Minister telephoned to Casado. "What is going on in Madrid, General?" he asked. "What is going on is that I have rebelled," was the reply. "That you have rebelled! Against whom? Against me?" "Yes, against you." "Very well, you can consider yourself relieved of your command," answered Dr. Negrín quietly. After all, he was still Prime Minister of Spain and Commander-in-Chief of the armies. Very soon he was to discover that the steps he could take to assert his authority were few.

This brief dialogue was followed by a series of telephone calls. The ministers who had been with Casado that afternoon and who had defended him at the Cabinet meeting against the suspicions of the Prime Minister refused to believe the news. "I'm coming over this very moment. Don't do anything until we have had a talk. All this can soon be settled"—this friendly request from the Minister of the Interior, Señor Paulino Gómez, merely provoked from General Casado the warning that not only would his journey be in vain, but that he would run the risk of being arrested on entering the capital.

While the rest of us returned to the meeting, the Prime Minister instructed the Under-Secretary of War to telephone the various chiefs of army corps in order to discover their attitude. A report from Cisneros, who on the news of the Cartagena rising that morning had been sent by Dr. Negrín to bring back Generals Miaja and Matallana by plane, was not very encouraging. Tired of waiting in the aerodrome for the two Generals, General Cisneros had driven over to Valencia, and had found General Miaja in his study with General Menéndez, leader of the Levant Army, and General Matallana, Chief of General Staff. All three were in a mood of great excitement, accusing the Government of a criminal "war-to-the-death" spirit, and proclaiming loudly that they were going to put an end to hostilities within twenty-four hours.

"But how?" asked General Hidalgo de Cisneros. "By surrendering?" "Yes, by surrendering. There's no other way out," replied General Matallana. A few hours later, however, this General—a man of fine character and a stern and disciplined soldier, who had fallen a victim to the manœuvres and capitulatory tactics of his companions—placed himself at the disposal of the Prime Minister in order to assist in carrying out the necessary measures for the suppression of the Cartagena rising.

The result of General Cordón's soundings was not at all satisfactory. It was obvious that the movement, which had been in course of preparation for some weeks, was a widespread one. Some of the army leaders, when called up by telephone, answered that they would remain with the Government, but only on condition that no proceedings were taken against Casado and that there were no clashes between the various military forces. General Menéndez, doubtless in the belief that we intended to hold General Matallana as a hostage, contented himself with demanding the latter's immediate "liberation" under the threat of fetching him himself and "shooting the lot of you." A sudden break in the telephone communication, no doubt engineered from Madrid, warned us that our situation was becoming increasingly precarious. Every possible means was tried to get in touch with the outside world, but it was not until two o'clock in the morning that a call from Casado to General Hidalgo de Cisneros put an end to our isolation.

On our instructions General Cisneros used all his diplomacy to re-establish communications, a matter of prime necessity. "But how was it you did this without letting me know?" he asked Casado, pretending to be offended. "I'll explain it all later; everything has happened so quickly. The reason I'm ringing now is to say that the Governor of Alicante informs me that the air force is all ready to bombard him." "They are carrying out my orders," replied Cisneros coldly. "But this is absurd," answered the other; "at all costs we must prevent any shots being fired." "Agreed," said Cisneros, "but in that case it is essential for me to get in touch with the aerodromes." In this manner contact was at least partly re-established.

There was, of course, no way of getting into touch with the two chiefs of army corps who had remained completely loyal—Colonel Bueno, who on account of his standing and authority was best suited for the Madrid command, and Colonel Barceló, afterwards executed by Casado. They were even more carefully watched and isolated than ourselves.

After five fruitless hours spent in attempting to make the contacts necessary to oppose Casado's coup, the Government set about making such preparations as the situation demanded. To remain there meant that we ran the risk of being cut off and arrested at any moment. Our forces consisted of a hundred guerrilla fighters brought over a few days previously to the Presidency—a building exposed on all sides and entirely unprotected. While orders were being given for the transfer of two airplanes to a new aerodrome whose whereabouts were not very well known to the authorities, I made use of the opportunity to give a full account of events to the only two foreign correspondents who had come to the Presidency—William Forrest of the London *News Chronicle,* and Marthe Huysmans, correspondent of the Brussels *Peuple* and daughter of the former Speaker of the Belgian Parliament. Both were trusty friends of Republican Spain, and up to the very last moment they worked loyally and well in their task of reporting the struggle of the Spanish people, a struggle of which almost any end might have been foreseen save the tragic one they were now forced to witness.

When I returned to the Prime Minister's study, General Matallana —whose situation was a very difficult one and whose embarrassment Dr. Negrín saw no real reason to prolong—was taking leave of his chief. Conscious of the approaching disaster, and bitterly regretting the break in the loyalist ranks, he said good-bye to us both with tears in his eyes and set off on the journey to Valencia. His departure forced us to hasten our own. While we had nothing to fear from him personally, any denunciation or indiscretion on the part of the chauffeur or one of his assistants might lead to our speedy arrest.

While we were waiting in the aerodrome at nine o'clock in the morning for the airplanes which were to arrive at any moment, Dr.

Negrín called me to his car, and under pretext of exploring the district we drove out in search of the one army headquarters where there was a chance of finding some of the loyal leaders.

This was the Dakar base, but a base in name only. It was a house on the highroad, exposed to the view of the whole countryside, and filled to overflowing with people, who had turned its terrace into the most public and democratic of meeting-places.

Here were assembled Generals Hidalgo de Cisneros, Cordón, and Modesto, Colonel Nuñez Masas, the Under-Secretary of Aviation, Lister, "Pasionaria," and a considerable number of army chiefs and officers. They were joined later by Señores Uribe and Moix, the Ministers of Agriculture and Labour, who had been entrusted by their organizations with the task of reassembling their respective members in the event of evacuation.

Dr. Negrín set about drawing up a message for Casado; it was a last appeal for agreement and our final attempt to avert the tragedy which threatened to overwhelm us all. Once again it was General Hidalgo de Cisneros who took it upon himself to telephone Casado, sending him the message over the Teletypewriter. By disclosing our whereabouts we ran the risk that troops might be sent from Valencia to arrest us, but we felt in the first place that the prevention of a break in the anti-Fascist front must necessarily be our first consideration, and secondly that the constant coming and going of people to and from the house, to say nothing of the guerrilla fighters posted at the door, had divested our meeting-place of any secret character it might once have possessed. Dr. Negrín's message to Casado, of which I believe the only copies are the original and the one which I took away with me, ran as follows:

> The Government over which I preside has been painfully surprised by a movement in whose aims of a swift and honorable peace free from persecutions and reprisals, and guaranteeing the country's independence (as announced by the *Junta* in its manifesto to the country), there appear to be certain discrepancies. My Government also considers that the reasons given by the *Junta* in explanation of its actions are unjustifiable. It has consistently laboured to retain that spirit of unity which has always animated its policy, and any mistaken interpretation of its actions can only be due to the impatience of those who are unaware of

the real situation. If they had waited for the explanation of the present position, which was to have been given tonight in the Government's name, it is certain that this unfortunate episode would never have taken place. If contact between the Government and those sectors who appear to be in disagreement could have been established in time, there is no doubt whatever that all differences would have been removed. It is impossible to undo what has been done, but it *is* nevertheless possible to prevent serious consequences to those who have fought as brothers for a common denominator of ideals, and—most particularly—to Spain. If the roots of mischief are pruned in time, they may yet grow a good and useful plant. On the altar of the sacred interests of Spain we must all offer up our weapons, and if we wish for a settlement with our adversaries, we must first avoid all bloody conflict between those who have been brothers in arms. The Government therefore calls upon the *Junta* which has been constituted in Madrid and proposes that it should appoint one or more persons to settle all differences in a friendly and patriotic manner. Inasmuch as it is of interest to Spain, it is of interest to the Government that, whatsoever may happen, any transfer of authority should take place in a normal and constitutional manner. Only in this way can the cause for which we have fought remain unsullied. And only thus can we preserve those advantages in the international sphere which still remain to us through our limited connections. In the certainty that as Spaniards the *Junta* will give heed to our request.

JUAN NEGRÍN

No more could have been asked of a Government which, in the most difficult situation that ever men intent on serving their country have had to face, had been so basely betrayed. It was a document full of concessions. We knew perfectly well that one of the reasons which had decided the new rebels to speed up their plans was the desire to prevent Dr. Negrín from broadcasting his speech that night, as had been announced since the previous Friday. For from this speech the whole population of the central-southern zone would have learned of the pending negotiations and the efforts made to obtain an honourable peace. Casado had heard all this from the lips of the Prime Minister himself. The broadcasting of the speech would have deprived the

Casado movement of its whole *raison d'être*. Hence the determination to stifle the voice of the Government.

But stronger than the indignation aroused in us by the resort to such methods at such a serious time was the need to maintain unity among those who had fought under the same flag. We could foresee the disastrous effect that a breach in the anti-Fascist front would produce in the minds of millions all over the world who, inspired by their nobility and heroism, had supported the cause of the Spanish people. We could foresee the sudden collapse of all resistance, and the disorder and confusion in which evacuation would take place. After the great sacrifices which had been made we could hardly allow ourselves to be swayed by mere considerations of personal pride. We were ready, for we had no other choice, to cede to others a by no means enviable position, if we could do it in such a way as to conceal the fact that a monstrously absurd *coup d'état* had taken place in the course of a struggle originated by a military rebellion. But we were only ready to do this on condition that matters developed normally and that the transfer of powers should not take the contemptible form of a mere *Putsch*.

While this message was being sent I stood on the terrace gazing out over the Levant countryside, clear and lovely on that early spring morning—a countryside made for men to live in contentedly and at peace. Every tree, every stone, every movement of light and shade, held for me a meaning unknown in other and happier days. With a cold feeling at my heart I watched the little children playing in the meadows below. Would their youth be enriched by the gift of freedom, or were they doomed to grow up in a régime foreign to the spirit of the country, from which all true liberty and happiness had been banished? During those last few days we had dreamed of a Spanish stronghold in which, however small it might be, we would make our stand until the hour of reconquest arrived. The memory of those Spanish liberals of the early nineteenth century, who from their island siege-house had for six whole months resisted the assault of reactionary forces,[1] seemed especially inspiring at a time when the whole course of European politics was undergoing a rapid change. While we had never looked upon a general war as an easy means of escape, it was obvious to the sober judgment that if the inevitable conflict between the Western democracies and the totalitarian states broke out

[1] At the siege of Cadiz by Napoleon in 1812.

while there still remained a Republican redoubt in Spain, the tremendous sacrifices of the Spanish people would not have been in vain. The thought that we might lose all merely because our defeat came a few months too soon added to the bitterness of parting; and the green meadows, the trees, the stream winding through the valley until it was lost to sight in the distance, engraved themselves on my mind with an even greater clearness as the time drew near when I must bid them farewell.

Until half past two that afternoon we waited for Casado's reply. From the aerodrome we were warned several times that if the planes were delayed any longer they would fall into the hands of the Casadist forces; it was only by a miracle that this had not happened already. There was not even a cup of coffee for us to drink. Dr. Negrín fell asleep after thirty hours of unbelievable tension, while General Modesto, two other officers, and I sat down to cards to kill time.

Long ago Franco had embarked on a policy of merciless reprisals. There was little doubt that Negrín and all the members of his government and all the officers who had fought for the Republic would be shot, if captured. Sensibly, they fled the country.

Valentín Gonzáles, better known as "El Campesino," here describes how he fled after shaving off his famous beard, which was hidden under the roof of a house in Valencia with the note: "This is the beard of El Campesino. It belongs to the Spanish people. One day we will come back for it."

We got into our powerful car with as many arms as we could handle. Then we roared out of Valencia toward the southwest coast. We had to cross the eastern provinces of Spain and part of the south. Here and there Franco supporters had set up road blocks and control points. But, though the Fascists had won the war, they had not yet managed to establish order. Everything was in wild confusion. The roads were choked with fugitives, civilians and soldiers, some seeking a place where they could hide, others going to surrender themselves.

Without my beard I slipped past at most of the control points. Even so, Falangists recognized me three times and tried to arrest me.

We shot our way out with our automatic weapons. Three times our route was marked by the bodies of those who had tried to stop us.

By a miracle we reached the coast, at the little fishing village of Adra, twenty-five miles from Almería on the road to Málaga. The Franco forces had not yet moved in. Adra was still run by a Socialist administrator called Belmonte. He gave us shelter in his house which also served as the office of the local council of which he was the head.

Night fell. Suddenly the calm was shattered by shots, shouts, the sound of tramping feet, and the clatter of hoofs. The soldiers of Franco had reached Adra.

The Fascist commissioner presented himself at Belmonte's office. We had only just time to hide in another room and lock the door. Through the thin partition wall we could hear the voices of the new administrator, his wife, and his assistants. They had brought a wireless set along, to pick up official messages. Someone turned it on. From our hide-out we listened. It broadcast the message that El Campesino was somewhere in the region. Survivors at the last road block where they had tried to stop us had given the alarm.

The radio ordered, "El Campesino must be taken, dead or alive."

We could hear the Fascists in the next room discussing it. The commissioner gave orders to his assistants to post sentries on all the roads and send scouting parties to look for us. "Let's get out of here," I said to my friends.

We burst into their midst, firing as we entered. The Fascists had no time to act. We killed all who were in the room and rushed out into the streets. The noise of our shooting had roused the sentries outside. As we emerged, they opened fire. We returned it even while we were making for the harbor. The running battle went on all the way from the house to the beach. Belmonte's wife was hit and fell. It looked as if she had been killed on the spot, but there was no time to stop and find out. We ran on.

Several motor launches were moored in the small harbor. We picked out the boat which seemed biggest and most powerful, and pushed off. As we were moving away from the shore, we saw our pursuers putting out after us. We ceased our fire so as not to betray our position, and plowed through the black waves without lights. Thanks either to the darkness or to our choice of a boat, we shook off our enemies.

The engine chugged steadily, our bow cut the water into twin fans of white foam. We set our course for Africa.

Meanwhile Madrid was suffering its last agonies. For more than two and a half years it had withstood the siege of the many armies raised by the insurgents, and now at last it was determined to surrender on whatever terms were possible.

The Madrid Defense Council hoped for a surrender with honor, while the Communists still hoped to fight on. The Communist forces drew back into the city, and for five days there was a civil war within a civil war as the forces under Casado waged a bitter fight against the Communists. The last battle of all was fought when Colonel Cipriano Mera, the Anarchist commander of the Fourth Army Corps, brought his troops from their mountain trenches into the city of Madrid. With hand grenade and bayonet they stormed the last redoubt of the Communists in the Ministry of War. Then the war was over, and in the Casa del Campo and in all the remaining guard posts defending the city the troops threw down their arms. There followed the supreme irony of the war. Without firing a shot the rebels were able to enter the city.

Here an American correspondent, C. D. Gallagher, describes the last moments of the doomed city:

There was no place to sleep, I decided. If the Communists took the hotel in a fight they could not possibly mistake me for a Casado soldier because I had no guns or uniform. What worried me was whether I would have time and enough Spanish to point these things out to rampaging soldiers in the heat of battle.

So I told them good night and good luck and made for Allen's rooftop flat. It was a dreadful walk. There hadn't been any fighting that night. It was coming. And I was walking about that part of Madrid where it was likely to start with machine gunning.

No use trying to sneak unnoticed from the Ritz to the Retiro. That would be exactly the kind of night traveler both Casado men and Communists would be looking for. So what? I swaggered along in the middle of the street. I never felt so lonely. My boots never made such a racket. Every so often I was told to halt by someone I couldn't see.

I stood still as Lot's wife after the miracle while they said: "Mueran!"

When I replied, "Los traidores," they told me to carry on. That was the sign and countersign for the Casado men that night. It changed every day. It means, "Let them die!"—"The traitors."

As we were in Casado territory it was easy to get his passwords. The Communist ones were more difficult. I was given it one night only. It was a pretty one.

The guard: "Are you high society?"

Me: "No, I'm only a semiparasite."

Guard: "Pass, comrade."

Anyway, I eventually made Allen's flat, opened the big iron gates at the main entrance and had a rifle stuck in my belly.

They let me in when they heard my Spanish. "A foreigner," they told the corporal who turned up. A real Spaniard too. He said how sorry they all were to disturb the people living in the building, but as the Communists were in Retiro Park on the other side of the road it had been necessary to make this building a temporary fighting post. The roof was so high they could command the whole of the Retiro. It turned out that this place was hotter than the Ritz.

I sat me down when I got into Allen's flat to have a bowl of soup, and put the lights on. In about two seconds bullets were cracking off the outside walls. I ate my soup noisily in the dark. On the roof there were loud cracks as Casado men sent their bullets into the trees in the park hoping to hit the Communists whose fire had been drawn by my lights.

Allen's flat was a front-line post so long as the domestic fighting lasted in Madrid.

There was a strange happening up the road from here when the Communists began falling back. Casado and Miaja had opened the front lines against Franco in the Estremadura by summoning men from them to come to Madrid to join the fight against the Communists. These reinforcements eventually got the Communists on the hop.

About two hundred of the Communists were in a building up the road from the rooftop flat and were in danger of being surrounded. They broke out one night and retreated across a square in good order and occupied the first big, well-placed building they came to.

It was a hospital. A maternity hospital. I've forgotten the exact figure, but there were somewhere around one hundred nursing and expectant mothers inside. As you can imagine, the fighting stopped pronto. It stayed stopped for some time while baffled Casado men tried to think up a way to dislodge the caballeros in refuge among the mothers.

The Communist rising had cut down Madrid's food supply. They had taken key entrances to the city and Casado carabineros were scared to drive the food trucks through them. They were right about that. What food there was—specially stuff like milk—was carefully distributed to those who needed it most. Who needed good food and milk more than the mothers in the maternity hospital? Casado was forced to continue deliveries of these special rations to the hospital, thereby robbing himself of his surest way of dislodging the Communists—by starvation. Casado gave his rebels the best food he had. For him it was Hobson's choice.

The mothers inside took it in good part when they realized there wasn't going to be any high explosive popping off near their cots. The doctors asked the Communists to make as little noise as possible, and they even took off their heavy, hobnailed boots when walking about in the corridors.

It was all settled in true, gentlemanly Spanish style. Casado offered a short truce to the rebels. Promised not to attack them while they retreated yet again to some other building sufficiently far from the hospital for the battle to be resumed without fear of upsetting the mothers or their babies.

As you know, Casado finally got the upper hand and, though he tried and shot one or two Communist leaders, things were very much the same as they had been before. On the surface, that is. One big change was this: The desire to continue the war proper had left nearly every man in the front-line trenches where they had faced Franco's Moors and Foreign Legion for two and a half years. Both sides had had trouble breaking down fraternization between the opposing front lines. The soldiers were in the habit of shouting at each other over no man's land. Each side calling the others bastards in a friendly way. One thing the Republicans did have was a fair amount of good bread which was lacking on Franco's side. One thing they had none of was tobacco.

So a Republican would shout: "Any Fascist want some good bread?"

"Sí, I do."

"I'll give you a loaf for some cigarettes."

Argument about how much bread was worth how many cigarettes, then two weighted packets would fly through the air over no man's land. Authorities of both sides tried to stop this sort of thing.

I often wondered if this rough banter was ever the cloak for a smart bit of espionage. One of a spy's greatest difficulties is getting his information back to headquarters. What easier way than bawling it out at the top of your lungs over a couple of hundred feet of neutral territory?

After the Communist dustup, the Republican soldiers didn't want to fight any more. There had been too big an upheaval in their own lines for them to know who was who. They couldn't trust their officers. And the tale soon spread about secret comings and goings over no man's land at night. They guessed rightly that a peace was being arranged.

And there was odd chatter on the air at nights. A Republican announcer would break into a program and say: "Ocho—cuatro—dos; tres—siete—cuatro; seis—ocho—nueve . . ." and so on. Just read out a lot of numbers: eight—four—two; three—seven—four; six—eight—nine . . . No explanations. Nothing. The censors would not let us mention it in radio messages back home. We and the rest of Madrid soon sorted it out when we heard similar stuff coming back from Franco stations. They were fixing up the peace again.

It came with a rush and in a queer fashion.

I was in bed about eight o'clock one morning and woke up with one word dinning in my ears. "Blanco—blanco—blanco . . ."

What the hell is that? I asked myself. Blanco—blanco—blanco. I lay on my back, hands behind my head, listening and wondering. The bedside telephone rang. It was Allen.

"For God's sake!" he exclaimed. "Are you still in bed? You'd better get down here as fast as you can. They've arrived!"

He got the tip early and slipped out without calling me. They were still shouting in the streets. They weren't saying blanco—blanco—blanco. I heard them aright by this time. It was Franco—Franco—Franco . . .

While I ducked out of my nightshirt (I prefer them) I wondered if I could make the censorship before the street shooting began. If I didn't get there before it started I would surely miss the story, the fall of Madrid. I put my jacket on as I ran down the eighty stairs. I'll have to make a run for it, I thought, to myself, and went coolish all over. I hate like hell being shot at. It happened to me once or twice before.

And I was in the street . . .

About fourteen kids were playing soldiers on the pavement. There were lots of folk walking about. Smiling. A truck came past. It was filled with young men and girls in blackshirts and waving yellow and red flags. Monarchist flags. They were shouting, "Franco! Franco! Franco!" They gave the outstretched arm salute and everyone on the pavements laughed and did the same to them.

So I walked fast but sedately to the Censura. Madrid had fallen without a fight.

Yellow and red cloths and flags hung from all windows and balconies. And plenty of white cloths too. Sheets and pillowcases. For the first time all Madrid saw the Fifth Column. Its members had lain low for two and a half years. They had gathered blue-black cloth to make blackshirt uniforms and skirts for the girls. Throughout the war they had sabotaged Republican resistance to Franco, but always under the lap. Here they were bawling their heads off in triumphal hysteria in broad daylight. And everybody gave them a hand.

They took Madrid. Not Franco's soldiers. It took the soldiers five hours and more to get in.

In the Censura the five of us were stamping out short messages on our typewriters and young Spanish boys were running them to the radio transmitting station. We kept them short so as to get as much stuff away as quickly as possible. There wasn't any time to write long, balanced pieces of what had happened. All we could do was to take a quick dash around the city, back to the typewriters, write a piece, send it off, and then out again for another look. You see, we didn't know how soon Franco's men would take over the radio station. We knew that as soon as they did, it would be the end of the job for us.

As it happened, Franco's censorship men were the slowest to take over. I had got to that stage when I had to think hard for something else to write. The five of us in what was later described as the "Red Camp" scooped Franco's forty foreign pressmen on his capture of Spain's capital and the end of the Spanish War.

Our Republican censors had vanished; that is, all except one. A woman. She stuck at her desk with her blue pencil and rubber stamp.

She didn't use the blue pencil because she did not know who was in charge at the transmitting station and she didn't want to get in trouble for cutting out any odd sentences that might appear pro-Franco. Even she gave it up eventually and disappeared.

So when we had written a piece we had to put the official stamp on our messages ourselves and initial them.

I knew when I had written my last word on the subject. It was when my runner came back and returned my last telegram. He said: "Italians are in the radio station. They looked at this and said, 'Take it away, we don't want it.'" I packed up my typewriter and began to think of London. My job was finished. I could send no more messages.

There was one good story after that which I couldn't write until I got back to France after being expelled by Franco for the second time.

When Franco's soldiers did arrive it was by Metro, the underground railway that never stopped throughout the war. The only people to hold them up were the ticket girls. After giving the Fascist salute they actually made the conquering heroes buy tickets for the short journey to the occupation.

Only a nut could have guessed that Madrid would finish that way.

Envoi
Of Legendary Time

*W*HEN *the Spanish Civil War was over, many men who had*
been through the Inferno attempted to give meaning to their
experiences, and to discover if possible the ultimate reasons for the
war; and most failed, and all found themselves groping after the
broken pieces of their faith. More than anyone else I know, Ralph
Bates succeeded in describing the undescribable in the following es-
say, which ends with an extraordinary picture of the timeless and
legendary suffering caused by the war.

There were times in Spain, moments only as a rule, when my
vision of the world was suddenly purified. I mean that it seemed
the physical retina itself became more sensitive and that perception,
often a mere result of sensation, really felt like a co-operation of the
willing and loving mind in the work of the senses. In those moments
perception put me in new touch with a world that was lovely, and
itself pure. It is hard to describe this sensation but it is the origin of
much poetry. I think now, as I thought then, of Thomas Traherne
and his "immemorial wheat that never would be reaped." But it was
not the permanence of things which I saw so much as the identity
of things, their real nature, the glowing serenity that Cézanne could
see in the tilt of vineyards and the heavy blue-gray mass of hills
beyond the solid cube of a southern vat house.

There was one morning on the Jarama front, when we were defending the Valencia road that fed Madrid, the noble heart. I have since
written down my memory:

That morning the four poplars were standing up out of the mist like ship masts, and then, as I mounted the hillside, the other poplars came into view and the valley looked like a harbour into which Mediterranean ships had run. . . . How well I remember that morning. The air ran like invisible, cool water over my face. The light, still striking in beams over the Perales hills, was sharp, crystalline. It was a morning when one half believed the open sea lay over the hill. . . .

As I walked up the gully path, past the telephonic dugout, the feeling of the sea's nearness made me say aloud to myself, "The crack of an explosive bullet in a gully is like the smack of water in sea caves." At that moment a covey of little brown partridges whirred up out of the red-brown rubble and the beat of their wings sounded like a spent fragment of shell.

There were many occasions of this renewal of vision; the war and its violence did nothing to hinder their occurrence. On the contrary, they were more frequent than in peacetime. I remember one evening of somber clouds, walking along a still unshattered street in Madrid amidst the wreckage of Cuatro Caminos. There was a gravity about the street that reminded me of the old steel engravings one meets in travel books of the last century, in which solemn houses stand in mathematical perspective, and two stiffly dressed gentlemen always confront one another in polite attitudes. There was peace in that street though beyond the housetops black clouds of smoke ballooned slowly in the acrid breeze. It was a peace faintly touched with nostalgia, like that mood induced by old engravings and the frontispieces of lute books.

Sometimes a part of the landscape would so impress itself upon the imagination that it became a symbol. This was easy in Spain because of the very nature of that landscape. Edmund Blunden somewhere describes the brutal shock he received, when, walking in a rear guard of apple orchards, he came suddenly upon the ugly shapes of big guns. That contrast could barely exist in the austere, harsh landscape of the Castilian steppe. Or it may be that my nature is so different from his that I could not perceive the contrast. I remember an incident in Valencia. At the time of the International Congress of Writers last July I was allotted a hotel room that was already occupied. The city was so full of refugees that in two hours of search I failed to find a room and at last began to inquire in little cafés in back streets. At last, an old waiter offered to share his bed with me and led me off into the darkness, to arrive at the abandoned palace of some ancient and noble family. Next morning I spent some time wandering through the house, walking in stiff and creaking boots through dark, tapestried salons of the eighteenth century, whose walls were hung with solemn portraits, into rooms decorated in the trinket style of the last century. There were fans of mother-of-pearl filigree and cabinets of carved ivory and portraits of ladies painted in what appeared to be egg tempera, and the floors were of waxed parquet. Presently I came to a library, full of ancient classics, modern paper-backed books by Colette, and a fine edition of Mr. Jorrocks in English. Finally, I came to the Mother Hubbard quarters of the departed menials and, looking through a small square window into the courtyard, I saw a gleaming anti-aircraft gun in process of assembly, its bright, efficient steel shining happily. It was a pleasant excitement, this walking through the dead and silent past and coming upon violent but, in this case, merciful modernity.

Yet it cannot have been only a personal idiosyncrasy that I felt no contrast between landscape and the war. The fierce prussian-blue sky, the broken hills of red and ocherous rocks, the deathly gray-green of the gouged valley walls, the monotony or the violence of the earth forms, offered no contrast to the starkness of war. It was a warlike landscape, but noble, as we all of us believed our resistance to be.

In this harmony of act and scene it was perhaps natural that one element of it should have become a symbol of man's resistance. Our Jarama lines of the Fifteenth International Brigade ran through an olive field. Our trenches were a yellow scar upon the hill; over them the gray-green trees leaned. Beyond the sandbays a vineyard lay. In that No-Man's Land throughout earlier spring the vines had been a cemetery of dead men, thrusting up their clenched fists through the soil, but as summer wore on the vine fists put out leaves. Untended, they became luxuriant, so that men crawled upon their bellies among the fluttering green and unloosed a hissing death upon one another.

The olive tree had always been a symbol to me. Its "immobility in the sapless winter had been a reproach to man's embitterment"; its "sobriety of minute blossom had been a rebuke to license." Its harvest at its richest was ever "a reproof to man avid of yield from the meager tillages he gives to life." The olive tree was a symbol of austerity, of frugality. . . . Upon that Tajuña hill slope, defending the Valencian road, the olive field again became a symbol of fortitude, but also of men creating a new thing.

When I first visited the Jarama line the trees were just beginning to put on their fragile net of leaves, though the ungathered fruit, blue-black and wrinkled, still gleamed upon the boughs. And despite the bullet-bleak days of that February battle which had cost the brigade so dearly, our men were still in their springtime freshness. The men's confidence even grew, as the trees shook out their little starry blossoms, yellow-green like lime honey. Then through the long weariness of the Hundred and Twenty Days, through which the brigade held the lines, the trees also were torn and splintered. The never-ending blight of bullets burned up their leaves and splintered the gray boughs, so that yellow wounds stared at the sky. Shells tore their branches away, and the men, seeking fuel, hacked them in pieces. Little by little, as our men became haggard with war, the olive field changed also, until, men and trees keeping pace, they stood shattered and torn, forlorn upon the sad hill. When our men were relieved and dragged themselves down into the valley, the trees suddenly became a symbol of desolation.

But the Jarama men never lost their individuality, despite their utter exhaustion. This was particularly true of the Spaniards. I remember talking to a peasant, and the thrill he gave me. I had been lecturing to the men in the lee of a hill, when one came to me and asked for news of his village. He said, "I have three fields there, good fields; no, I will say that I have one good field—ah, how good it is—and two little fields not so good. But how they please me, my little fields. There is a brook at the bottom of one little field, and two fig trees, and I have a seat there. Ah, you should see that place, so fresh and cool it is." Something of Garcilaso de la Vega sounded in his clear speech, but the factual mind of the Spanish peasant spoke also. When in the second book of Don Quixote, Teresa writes to her husband Sancho, governor of his island realm, she writes so of the things of her village.

Sometimes, lying in my great gilded bed in the commissariat in Madrid, listening to the crackle and boom of the University City or the wabbling thrum of shells running through the flickering night clouds, I would read, taking a book from the cupboards outside my door. A part of the library of the department of philosophy had been stored there by the Fifth Regiment men.

Luis Vives was a Spanish philosopher of the sixteenth century. Living his old age in a poor apartment in Bruges, he wrote free Latin exercises, not to lose his mastery. He did not comment in stiff verse upon old campaigns, or celebrate tedious loves, or sing great causes. He wrote Latin dialogues, of a quarrel between husband and wife because she has put a flower pot on the window sill, and the pot hinders his view of the public clock across the way. Their child cries the while. Or Vives translates the dialogue of two sisters, who have been invited out to eat milk curds and are leaving the house alone. Look at your marmoreal and conceited Góngora. Don Pedro de Valencia, in a letter to Don Luis, says that he viciously imitates the Italians in his burlesque allusions, yet note how your Góngora speaks in that romance, "En la pedregosa orilla." He says that Big Teresa is a nymph who guards undignified animals on the banks of the Vecinguera, which was not the classic stream of the Eclogues, but a kind of sewer in the Córdova of that day. Góngora, the frozen, is full of folk elements, snatches of song, slang, popular ribaldries, and factual allusions wholly Spanish.

The digression must be checked. It serves as a protest against the very force of that olive tree symbol, for so powerful is that symbol that I almost think of our men upon that tiger hill as a company of anonymous men, standing without differentiation, treelike, against the mortal hail that still hisses over the vineyard of death.

Beauty is sensed not only in images and symbols. There are experiences which are lovely in themselves. There are groups of experiences which from the very order and sequence in which they occur have a sharper impact than they would have in isolation. It is a device of writers to place their scenes in evocatory order. One such sequence occurred to me on the Jarama front.   .

It was an evening in June. The weary men had asked for an informal talk and those off watch had gathered a little way behind the trenches on the slope of the hill. These talks, by the way, were something of an innovation, and a strange enough duty, though properly within the work of a commissar. Little by little the men recreated the rôle of bard, or public storyteller, and I was the officeholder. With a bare synopsis jotted down on the back of an envelope I used to improvise novellas and stories as a means of giving instruction on Spanish social life. I recall arriving one evening, spent after the Hundred and Twenty Days, in the village of Albares. We gathered in the square, on one side of which a low wall topped a steep little cliff. There, after dark, I told the men a story of the Mediterranean fishing coast, which was in effect a study of the Catalan family system.

But on one Jarama evening the Seventeenth Battalion (The Abraham Lincoln) proposed that I describe my wanderings in the great mountain chains of Spain. I stood beneath a torn olive tree facing the west, the men sprawled about the rear works of the line. It was a gorgeous evening. Huge cumuli reflected the fire that burned on the horizon, green and violet light mingled in the mid-sky, and away in the east, over the indigo hills of Perales, the red counterglow was deep and intense. It was like a High Mass of the Holy Ghost. It seemed so magical, that solemn splendor, that one half believed that at the pronouncing of a word it might vanish. As if one had pronounced such a word, the light drained out of the sky and the hills became black and encroached upon the imagination. Indeed, they appeared to edge in upon us. I talked quietly, for the enemy must not hear that we were gathered together. Then a hand was raised towards the east and the men sighed "Ah!" and swiftly the huge moon sailed up and grew white.

I was talking about a shepherd whom I had met on the summit of the Cordillera that walls in lovely Liébana, above the village of Aniezo. The shepherd had a piece of string tied to his foot, and this, he explained, was because he had been suffering an extremely painful toothache. He had cured it by tying the string to the tooth and to his ankle, so that the pain had passed into the ground. His speech told me that he was not a hereditary shepherd and as we sat drinking from his wineskin he said that he had been driven from his village by the parish priest for political heterodoxy. He was a Republican.

The moon was now high and the silence unbroken even by a single rifle shot. A little breeze ran about among the vine leaves of No-Man's Land.

I was saying: "He took me to a fountain and as we sat there he pointed around that vast amphitheater of vaporous domes and said, 'Over there, just below that cliff, is a good sweet fountain but it gives little water, and over there is another that is copious, and yonder'—and he pointed to a dome barely visible beyond the violet haze—'is a pleasant and very cold spring, and there are oaks which give a lot of acorns. . . .' "

I was commenting on the Spanish reverence for sweet sources, when suddenly the front line broke into fire. Beginning upon the sector held by the British Battalion, it ran down the front to the Pasionaria's on our left, like a wave that breaks from one end. Rifles and machine guns rattled and banged into the moonlit vines and trees. A Verey light went up and I thought I saw the bullets flashing past like a school of silver fish disturbed by divers blundering into their deep sea grove. Actually, as the dust puffs showed, it was parabolic fire, and horribly intense. Suddenly the cone of fire swept off into the empty hollow of moonlight and impassible stones on our right, and by the most extraordinary luck we were unhurt. The cloak I carried on my arm was shot through in two places.

As we ran back with rifles the firing died down and all became silent. "Some guy must have seen an olive tree move," they said. Tired, overstrained senses frequently report such things. The off-watch men returned to their *chabolas* or "foxholes" and presently a group began to sing, "When Israel was in Egyptland. . . ."

Their voices swelled out upon the shining night and I say before God that music has never moved me so.

"Let my people go." The voices throbbed out of the earth holes and that sad pleading was more significant than any supplication had hitherto been; it was the voice of the noble heart, giving out the meaning of that bitter fight.

A man came out, and as he approached me he took up the words "Let my people go." He said, "The boys invite you to sleep with us," but I answered, "Good night," unable to say more. "Good night," they called as I passed their foxholes. "Good night. Buenas noches. Sleep well." I motored back, crawling without lights through the poplars of Dead Mule Lane, and by zigzag route to legendary Madrid, into which shells were crashing.

The word "legendary" as qualifying Madrid is not intended to have the obvious meaning that the city has become the rallying point, the *castillo famoso* of contemporary freedom. I mean that all that vast landscape that unfolds upon the astonished mind as one tops the escarpment above Alcalá and gazes towards the Seven Peaks, seems to have its existence outside of time. That sense of the legendary about a present experience is hard to describe; it is in a certain manner the sense of the present as past, as well as of the past as present. But the legendary quality is more complex. It must contain a sense of being simple, of that which overhangs a drama, or a tale of embodied good and evil, of love, hate, and treachery, of naïve realism, of this man coveting that man's land or his wife and being slain and the people applauding and swearing new fealty. No doubt "Morte d'Arthur," "Huon of Bordeaux," "The Knight of the Green Girdle," all the chansons de geste of early reading explain how I came by this sense of the legendary. Nevertheless, the landscape itself awakens that feeling, as does all that stupendous faëry of the Pyrenees and the dazzling marches at their feet. From Torla, upon its headland below the vast red curtains of rock that hold up the Perdido, from Bielsa below its exalted pass, from any village that stands up on the edge of its cliff, from Benasque below the Cursed Mountains, from any arrogant castle that stares out over sweeping plains, the knight of Master Pedro's puppet show might any Monday or Thursday come riding down, his palfrey shying from time to time at a German tank, towards walled Zaragoza, where his long-tressed lady awaits the winding of a horn.

I often felt that the Castilian, backbone of our resistance, is exemplary in fortitude because his mind accepts legendary things as natural. Scraps of romance, old ballads, the tales that still linger, the mummers' plays and their proverbs describe things in simple black and white. This tyrant arose and was grievous for the people and they rebelled and slew him; or this disaster afflicted the land and they carried the Virgin around the fields and the famine was at an end. This present struggle is nothing for which they were mentally unprepared, even if they were militarily so. The powers of evil have come again. That they should have marched down the road past our rest camp one day, singing: "The Great Miaja leads us on," is not merely a tribute to the power of a piano-strumming ditty maker. The Castilian, even when he accepts liberalism, does not do so with the outlook of the liberal. He might some day canonize a new prophet and call him San Carlos Marx, but Mr. Mill, whom on the whole he defends in this war, would be to him *Señor Profesor*.

This sense of the legendary, frequently awakened in me during the war, only rarely brought with it that nostalgia which is the tribute most often paid to the past. Nostalgia is awakened most strongly in those who are divided in their loyalties, or who have no dominant loyalty, who are torn between reaction and experiment. They look back at the past with sighs that escape being affirmation, which they also will not give to the present. Again and again an unnostalgic sense of the past was stirred in me. Often, upon the Jarama front, sitting upon a firestep in the midday blaze, or in darkness, there would move into my thought a silent procession of ships, of taut little frigates, or of the galleons of departed monarchies, sailing along the valley of San Martín de la Vega. I would deliberately play host to that imagining, hearing the lazy cries of Portuguese mariners and the creak of spars down there where the Fascist limber wagons rattled. The painted eyes of discolored figureheads would go staring around the Jarama River bends, peering across the unsheaved fields, wondering what uncommon fiesta in Madrid painted the sky with great bonfires. The origin of that imagining lay in a note I had made long ago. The Count-Duke of Los Olivares, pompous and squalid servitor of decadent Hapsburg regalism, had absurdly dreamed of bringing deep-sea ships to the gates of Madrid by canalizing the River Jarama.

There was another intrusion of the past which caused me to marvel. I had been doing some organizing work with the Transport Column, composed principally of American volunteer mechanics and truck drivers. Your American mechanic, trained in Detroit and weathered on four-lane ways, is your Contemporary Man, far tougher than anything conceived by Mr. Cagney, and far more human. His æsthetic senses have perhaps been a little dulled by one hundred thousand miles of roadside hideousness; perhaps he has been made irascible by long hours at the wheel, the burden of his trade. Nevertheless, his brain seeks efficiency, clean driving, a sweet job of "fixing," a masterly overhaul, as naturally as a compass needle swings to the north. I imagine that no man has so little sense of the past as he. 1933 is six models back, in the age of groping, and 1931 stares him into incredulous silence or into derisive uproar.

We were seated beneath an avenue of enormous pepper trees not far from Alcalá. The River Henares ran muddily by, the hot night filled with its sticky, fetid vapour. Gusts of hot wind blew in from the steaming fields. Heaven had collapsed that afternoon and the pools gleamed along the churned-up road. Beneath the trees a party of Frenchmen never ceased to sigh and curse, out of profound French despair, as they splashed around a truck sunk axle-deep in mud. We had eaten and were discussing the question whether tractors could be used upon the surrounding lands. The talk was burly with the Present.

A sheet of paper pitched little somersaults across the circle and I leaned forward and caught it. The glow of my cigarette showed that it was not a contemporary document and I splashed into the road and held it to the light of a truck.

"It's an old letter to a duke," I said to the despairing Frenchman who came round to flash his torch upon the mud.

He sighed and in his voice was the sadness of one who looked back upon Mud and who looked forward to Mud, whose life would be spent in struggling with Mud. He leaned on the radiator and wiped the sweat from his sad and pallid face. He took the letter in his hand, as with futile deliberation of step his squad splashed forward and gathered around the melancholy truck.

"Ces messieurs," he murmured, returning the letter. Cursing softly, with horrible significance, he began to wave the quite immobile truck forward with his hand torch.

It was a letter to a duke whose name I have forgotten, from a high palace official of the latter end of the seventeenth century. The archives of the palace near which we were encamped had been transferred to the National Library, I knew. This letter must have been part of that collection. That the life of courts in that epoch does not engage my emotions is not the consequence of political belief. Or rather, the true aristocrat of Spain is your peasant, your saddle maker, or the tender of olive trees. These preserve their tradition of the old ways, the old techniques and values. But this letter caused me to marvel. Through it I gazed upon a detailed landscape of past time. I had done a few easygoing researches into these fields and the picture was perfectly clear. I never remember a more sharply focused mental picture and one that engaged me less. So keen was that awareness that I walked about for a long time with an impression of double existence.

During the Brunete offensive of July, 1937, my brigade was heavily engaged in what was until then the fiercest battle of the war. One day towards the end of that battle I was approaching Villanueva de la Cañada when a group of soldiers sheltering beneath a white wall, the cemetery wall I believe, waved to me. My chauffeur stopped and we were told that one or two Fascist shells had localized the road. I ordered my driver to continue and he demurred. There was some discussion which naturally ended when I said, "Just drive on." As I spoke, the enemy put up one of the most extraordinary box fires I had yet seen. It covered, I should say, a strip about half a mile long and a quarter of a mile broad, just outside the town and lying across the road. We ran to the cemetery wall and watched it. It was magnificent; gradually it contracted until the shells appeared to plant their red crocuses according to a precisely drawn garden plan. It was splendid and it was German, only it was put down in the wrong place. We ourselves had had occasion to speak ill of the badly drawn Spanish maps. Instead of wiping out the brigades that had just entered the town, the box fire lifted a gigantic brown curtain of dust high into the air above the fields of ploughed stubble. We settled down against the wall, cursing the soft dust which slowly drifted towards us. The box fire ceased, though a few shells plunked into the earth, unpleasantly near.

My thoughts, perhaps because of the dust, began to dwell on the word *cañada,* which means "a sheep track," and then I felt the past as a living thing, the pastness of which I regretted. It was the second such occasion during the war. In the days before the war, in my room at Tossa de Mar, I had kept a sheet of paper pinned to the wall above my worktable. I expect it still hangs there. "Unless a theme is of birth, death, or procreation, unless it is of the passing of time, it is not worth writing." The first part of that maxim had to be taken in a non-literal way, of course.

Looking through the angels that corbeled my window of that fourteenth century house in Tossa, seeing only the battlements of the great walls of the Gothic town and the heaving cork hills beyond, it was sometimes difficult to believe that six centuries had passed since the house was built. I felt then that the sense of the passing of time and of past time was one of the principal sources of poetry. "Où sont les neiges d'antan?" I think of Tossa and of my life there as a legend; it is something I try to recreate. The melancholy of past time gets into every image which occurs to me. In those days, whenever I could stir myself to get a little barrel of wine onto the flat roof, I used to hang out a lantern over the balustrade. My friends down at the shore tavern would catch sight of it and the night would be spent in monstrous yarnings, André Masson outdoing everyone. . . . Why did the Italians bomb my village of fishers?

Crouching against the cemetery wall in the haze of brown dust I thought of the immemorial sheep track that ran along the foothills of the Guadarrama, going down into brown Estremadura and Andalucía. It had been under the jurisdiction of the Mesta, the corporation of sheep owners of wandering flocks, founded in the thirteenth century. Once, the two and a half million sheep of the Mesta had gone every year from the winter pastures on the plains to the summer hills. The Mesta had been the ally of kings—the enemy of people—it had humbled great cities, its wanderings are still told in song. "Ya se van los pastores," they sing in high León, and in the Pyrenees of Aragón. "The shepherds are going away." The Mesta was at last changed into a mere association of stock owners and now its wool factories are still worked during war time by a co-operative in Sabadell. Spanish things endure. The Mesta has gone, though a few of that brotherhood of wandering shepherds still light their bonfires on the black slopes, still tell their tales in old speech of rich and precise vocabulary unknown to the city. Villanueva de la Cañada! What fights between trespassing shepherds and indignant farmers had been fought there, what harshness of Mesta judges had been resented. As I crouched I heard the bleating and the cries. The cloud of dust, like that which old Alonso Quijano or Quixote saw, advanced along the ancient way. But now red crocuses sprang out of the powdered ground, men lay still and mad metal harped and whined.

It was the second time I had felt an ache at the imagination of past time; the first time also had been because of sheep. We were in camp in the Enchanted Range of the Lérida Pyrenees, in a region where villagers still sing on feast days about a twelfth century count. Miguel the cowherd one day clambered up to the bluff above the Lake of St. Maurice where my tents were placed out, and he told me of the war that had begun. The day before I had seen the lake fishermen drag in their nets, which were filled with flashing trout. The fish had prompted me to begin a novel about sponge fishing, and that day, as we marched down the valley to our new enterprise, I imagined myself at the bottom of the sea upon a coral reef, and a cloud of rainbow fishes swimming over it, darting sideways like the shining planes over Madrid. There, above Espot, on the enormous arraslike walls of that valley, I counted six flocks, the tinkling of their bells mingling with the roar of streams. (In this city of New York, every morning between eleven and twelve, I remember Villanueva's screaming cemetery and the flocks upon the steep wall of Espot. A junk merchant goes by my window with a sheep bell slung between two poles on his handcart, calling for old lumber with the sound of far-off enchanted hills.) That morning, I saw the six flocks distributed in windy, glittering space and because I had followed the old tracks with delight I was a little melancholy, sensing that a new life was beginning.

But one's reactions were not only on these levels. There were moments of revelation into the nature of man's heart and mind and there was one chilling experience that so completely transcended anything I had ever known that I seemed to have walked into a vast and deliberately fashioned drama or a religious rite.

I came down off the black hills one gale-swept night during the Brunete battle, into Villanueva. The town was under shellfire and it was burning. At one moment a blazing roof beam would be flung into the sky, describing a yellow scroll, or a huge inverted cone of sparks would soar up and illuminate the billowing smoke, or a column of flame would rush out and burst above the stubbled fields, sending wave after wave of sparks running down the valley. Within the town, stone and metal were tearing up the air. For safety I entered the church. It was an evacuation station and its floor was covered with wounded men, groaning and screaming. (All is not polite moaning; men scream in their agony.) Doctors were going among the men; the church was lit by a few acetylene flares placed in the ground. The long shadows writhed on the walls, like figures in a mobile El Greco. All the church was full of the echoing litany of death. I went up to the dismantled high altar to write my report. Suddenly my imagination, my mind, and my heart were frozen. Bowed over the center of the altar, his head upon his hands, was a wounded man, blood streaming from his head. He was standing as a priest stands when he murmurs: "Hoc est corpus meum." The man was dying, I thought. He seemed to be pleading the sacrifice of Spain. I stood frozen in imagination, hearing that echoed wailing. Far off, the machine guns rattled.

Afterwards I went outside and was sick. I was not sick at the spectacle of pain, but because of the unaccepted sacrifice. That it would not be accepted by the Western democracies, I foresaw, for not one of those governments had the courage even to dispense with hypocrisy. That the Spanish resistance was a sacrifice for more than

Spanish freedom can be seen by anyone now. For had not nobleness gone out of the world and had we not been abandoned, the dictators would not have been encouraged to demand Czechoslovakia and whatever else they next demand. And when we have defeated our enemy in Spain the peoples of the coward democracies may at last take heart. All that I felt in that moment, standing by the altar at Villanueva de la Cañada.

Acknowledgments

The author wishes to thank the following for permission to reprint material in this work:

Mme. Pilar de Ansaldo and Éditions du Rocher, Monaco, for the selection from *Mémoires d'un Monarchiste Espagnol* by Juan Antonio Ansaldo; Ralph Bates and the *Virginia Quarterly Review* for *Of Legendary Time* by Ralph Bates which appeared in the *Virginia Quarterly Review,* Winter 1939; Cassell and Company Ltd. and Curtis Brown Ltd. for the selection from *Mine Were of Trouble* by Peter Kemp; the Chicago *Tribune* for the article by Jay Allen, August 30, 1936; John Dos Passos for the selection from *Journeys Between Wars* by John Dos Passos, copyright by John Dos Passos; Doubleday and Company for the selection from *The Patrol Is Ended* by Oloff de Wet, copyright 1938 by Doubleday and Company, Inc.; Farrar, Straus and Cudahy, Inc. for the selection from *The Owl of Minerva* by Gustav Regler, copyright 1959 by Rupert Hart-Davis; Harcourt, Brace and World, Inc. for the selections from *In Place of Splendor* by Constancia de la Mora, copyright 1939 by Harcourt, Brace and World, Inc., *The Education of a Correspondent* by Herbert L. Matthews, copyright 1946 by Harcourt, Brace and World, Inc., and *Homage to Catalonia* by George Orwell, copyright 1952 by Sonia Brownell Orwell; Hinshaw and Stuhlman for the selections from *The Forging of a Rebel* by Arturo Barea, copyright 1946 by Harcourt, Brace and World, Inc.; Alfred A. Knopf, Inc. for the selections from *Freedom's Battle* by Álvarez del Vayo, copyright 1940 by Julio Álvarez del Vayo, and *Volunteer in Spain* by John Sommerfield, copyright 1937 by John Sommerfield; J. B. Lippincott Company and Herbert L. Matthews for the selection from *Two Wars and More to Come* by Herbert L. Matthews, copyright 1938 by J. B. Lippincott; The Macmillan Company for the selections from *Warriors Without Weapons* by Marcel

The author also wishes to thank Mrs. Ilsa Barea, Mrs. Edwin Rolfe, Jaume Miravitlles and Aristarco Yoldi for their considerable help in the preparation of this volume.

The maps in this book are reproduced by courtesy of *The New York Times.*

Sources

The extracts published in this volume are taken from the following sources:

Page

17. *The General Cause:* Mass Lawsuit brought by the Spanish Nationalist Government, Preliminary Report, Madrid, 1953.
20. *Mémoires d'un Monarchiste Espagnole,* by Antonio Ansaldo. Editions du Rocher, Monaco, 1953.
23. *A.B.C.* (Seville). July 18, 1937.
26. *Memoirs of a Spanish Nationalist,* by Antonio Bahamonde. United Editorial, London, 1939.
32. *In Place of Splendor,* by Constancia de la Mora. Harcourt, Brace, New York, 1939.
36. *The Forging of a Rebel,* by Arturo Barea. Reynal and Hitchcock, New York, 1946.
41. *El Campesino,* by Valentín González and Julian Gorkin. G. P. Putnam's Sons, New York, 1952.
50. Unpublished memoirs, by Jaume Miravitlles.
53. *Nothing But Danger,* edited by F. C. Hanighan. R. M. McBride and Company, New York, 1939.
60. Unpublished memoirs, by Jaume Miravitlles.
67. *The General Cause.*
85. *Chicago Tribune,* August 30, 1936.
91. *The Forging of a Rebel,* by Arturo Barea.
95. *Les Grands Cimetières sous la Lune,* by Georges Bernanos. Plon, Paris, 1938.
100. *The Life and Death of a Spanish Town,* by Elliot Paul. Random House, New York, 1937.
107. *Memoirs of a Spanish Nationalist,* by Antonio Bahamonde.
111. *Unamuno's Last Lecture,* by Luis Portilo. From *Golden Horizon.* Weidenfeld and Nicolson, London, 1953.
120. *Y* (Madrid). November 1938.
124. Unpublished memoirs, by Jaume Miravitlles.
127. *The Forging of a Rebel,* by Arturo Barea.
129. *Ispansky Dnevnik,* by Mikhail Koltzov. Leningrad, 1960.
132. *Martyrdom of Madrid,* by Louis Delaprée. Madrid, 1937.

335

Page

144. *Journeys Between Wars,* by John Dos Passos. Harcourt, Brace, New York, n.d.

147. *The Patrol Is Ended,* by Oloff de Wet. Doubleday and Company, New York, 1938.

154. *Two Wars and More to Come,* by Herbert Matthews. Carrick and Evans, New York, 1938.

160. *Volunteer in Spain,* by John Sommerfield. Alfred A. Knopf, New York, 1937.

162. *Mine Were of Trouble,* by Peter Kemp. Cassell and Co., London, 1957.

169. *Homage to Catalonia,* by George Orwell. Secker and Warburg, London, 1938.

178. *Owl of Minerva,* by Gustav Regler. Farrar, Straus and Cudahy, New York, 1959.

185. *Two Wars and More to Come,* by Herbert Matthews.

195. *Guernika,* by Father Alberto de Onaindía. Bilbao, 1937.

198. Unpublished memoirs, by Aristarco Yoldi.

207. Unpublished memoirs, by Jaume Miravitlles.

211. *Homage to Catalonia,* by George Orwell.

219. Unpublished memoirs, by Jaume Miravitlles.

221. *The Tragic Week in May,* by Augustín Souchy. Barcelona, 1937.

223. Unpublished memoirs, by Jaume Miravitlles.

225. *Sirocco,* by Ralph Bates. Random House, New York, 1939.

233. *Dialogue with Death,* by Arthur Koestler. The Macmillan Company, New York, 1960.

248. *Life and Death of the Spanish Republic,* by Henry Buckley. Hamish Hamilton, London, 1940.

255. *El Campesino,* by Valentín González and Julian Gorkin.

256. Unpublished memoirs of an officer of the Republican Army.

261. *This Is War,* by André Malraux. *Collier's* magazine, May 29, 1937.

273. Unpublished diary, by Edwin Rolfe.

278. Unpublished memoirs, by Robert Payne.

293. *Warrior Without Weapons,* by Marcel Junod. The Macmillan Company, New York, 1951.

299. *The Education of a Correspondent,* by Herbert Matthews. Harcourt, Brace, New York, 1946.

304. *Freedom's Battle,* by Álvarez del Vayo. Alfred A. Knopf, New York, 1940.

312. *Nothing But Danger,* edited by F. C. Hanighan.

319. *Of Legendary Time,* by Ralph Bates. *Virginia Quarterly Review,* Winter, 1939.

Index